YALE STUDIES IN RELIGIOUS EDUCATION

Luther A. Weigle · Editor

Volume XX

THE COLLEGE SEEKS RELIGION

THE COLLEGE
SEEKS RELIGION

BY

MERRIMON CUNINGGIM

Professor of Religion
Pomona College

NEW HAVEN

YALE UNIVERSITY PRESS

LONDON · GEOFFREY CUMBERLEGE · OXFORD UNIVERSITY PRESS

1947

TO

MY MOTHER

PREFACE

THE present study of the ways in which the college seeks religion has been pursued off and on for ten years. Interest in the topic was first aroused in 1936 by the practical problems incident to my first college appointment. I accepted a newly created position of religious leadership with no training for the work and no knowledge of what other institutions were doing in the field. The necessity of the immediate situation, therefore, prompted my first unguided inquiries.

Later on, through the encouragement of Professor Clarence P. Shedd of the Yale Divinity School, to whom this study owes much more than merely the profusion of footnote references his writings have furnished, I undertook a systematic appraisal of the subject. The result was the submission of a large part of the following material, in the form of a Ph.D. dissertation, to the Faculty of the Graduate School at Yale in 1941. I shall always be grateful for the opportunity to work upon a broad topic dealing with immediately pressing problems in religion and education.

In succeeding years the dissertation gathered dust, but the practical aspect of the subject continued to concern me, as I sought on two other campuses to make religion a significant part of the total educational program. Such work offers little leisure, but a tour of duty in the Navy chaplaincy gave me the opportunity for further study and writing. Some of what follows has been written in such odd places as on an ARG in the Philippine Sea and on a battleship in the Indian Ocean.

Certain arbitrary limitations have been imposed upon the treatment. First of all, data are drawn solely from the period since 1900, largely since the first World War. Religion in the colleges in previous years has been dealt with by others, and the distinctive character of present-day programs has developed during this century.

The use of the word "college" in the title suggests another limitation. The field of investigation has been restricted to the familiar four-year span. The college work offered by universities is, of course, included. In order not to imply a concern for graduate and professional schools, "university" is not used even in refer-

ring to universities. Thus both the colleges and the college levels
of the universities make up the subject of study. Junior colleges
are omitted.

But not all types of four-year colleges are dealt with. Teachers'
and Negro colleges present special problems, and one had to draw
the line somewhere. Catholic colleges present no problem at all;
their religious attitudes and practices are fixed and certain. Thus
these three groups are also omitted.

As to bibliographies, the pertinent material for most chapters
is indicated in the footnotes. But since they deal with large topics
on which there exists a wealth of expression, Chapters II, III, and
VII conclude with selected lists of the books which proved most
useful. Thus the reader is spared some of the voluminous footnotes in those three chapters. For Chapters IV, V, and VI, dealing
with the attitudes of college executives toward religion, only a
small portion of the immense body of available reading is referred to.

I am deeply grateful to all who have helped with information
and interpretation. Among the many names I recall with appreciation, it is a pleasure to mention particularly not only Professor
Shedd but also Dean Luther A. Weigle of the Yale Divinity
School, Dean Robert R. Wicks of the Princeton Chapel, and my
father, Dr. Jesse Lee Cuninggim. For tangible help at critical
junctures I am greatly indebted to the Denison University Re-
search Foundation and the Edward W. Hazen Foundation. The
task of proofreading the manuscript in its original form was
generously performed by my sister, Miss Margaret Cuninggim.
As for my wife Whitty, her work is present on every page, and
her name should appear with that of the author.

MERRIMON CUNINGGIM

Granville, Ohio
March 22, 1946

CONTENTS

THE COLLEGE SEEKS
RELIGION

CHAPTER I

THE THESIS

ELIGION has always been present in the colleges of America. Ever since Harvard University was founded to furnish an educated ministry for the colonies, religion and higher education have worked together for common ends. Moreover, that they should do so has continually been upheld as necessary and proper. Both the practice and the conviction have characterized the establishment and early growth not only of denominational and independent institutions but also of some of the state universities.[1]

Prior to the present century the intimacy of this relationship was inevitably subject to ebb as well as flow. At times religion was an aggressive and recognized partner in education; at other times it lacked vitality and was only reluctantly acknowledged. But even when education began to be "secularized" in the later nineteenth century, religion remained a vital part of college life. The institutions of higher education come to the present era with a continuous and keen interest in religion as part of their rightful heritage.

The purpose of this study is to analyze the association of religion and higher education since 1900. The thesis to be maintained is that the secularization of higher education seems to have reached its peak around the time of the first World War, and that since then the colleges have recaptured much of their lost concern for the religious development of their students and have increasingly assumed responsibility for such nurture. The growth of this official interest and sponsorship has been noted by several writers in the field of higher education, particularly by Professor Clarence P. Shedd of the Yale Divinity School. In 1940 he wrote:

1. See Donald G. Tewksbury, *The Founding of American Colleges and Universities before the Civil War* (New York, Teachers College, Columbia University, 1932).

Perhaps the most encouraging factor in the college religious scene is the growing sense of responsibility on the part of college administrators for integrating religion with the whole work of higher education. This is true even of state universities where a good many presidents, who ten years ago felt their hands were tied by legal limitations, now tend to believe that they have more freedom for direct religious leadership than they are using, and who are looking about for some better plan for religion on their campuses. This feeling is buttressed by the conviction that it was the intention of the founders of our universities to free them from sectarian controls but not to divorce them from religion.[2]

Thus far, however, only a passing recognition has been given this "encouraging factor." Many scholars, otherwise well informed in the field of higher education, have failed to recognize it at all. Other leaders in both religion and education who believe that religion *should* have a larger place in the college program have often not realized the place it *does* have at the present time. This study constitutes an attempt to throw light on the trend itself and on the educational and religious factors promoting it.

The treatment of the subject will be largely historical. Attention will be focused first on significant developments in the fields of higher education and religion, in order to indicate the influences leading to the secularization of the colleges and to the subsequent reversal of that tendency. We shall then proceed to an analysis of the various attitudes toward religion that have characterized college administrators throughout the period. A discussion of the leading philosophies of education will then be undertaken in order to show that an interest in religion is entirely consistent with prevailing theories of higher education. Even state universities, as we shall attempt to demonstrate, may desire the integration of religion and education without violating the doctrine of the separation of church and state, when that principle is properly understood.

Interest in religion leads to the development of a sense of re-

2. Clarence P. Shedd, "Religion in the Colleges," *Journal of Bible and Religion*, VIII, 4 (November, 1940), 181. See also his *Two Centuries of Student Christian Movements* (New York, Association Press, 1934), p. 414; *The Church Follows Its Students* (New Haven, Yale University Press, 1938), pp. 135–136, 291–292; and "The Agencies of Religion in Higher Education," *Religious Education*, XXXVIII, 5 (September–October, 1943), 290–294; and Edward W. Blakeman, *The Administration of Religion in Universities and Colleges: Personnel* (Ann Arbor, University of Michigan Press, 1942).

sponsibility manifest in actual programs on the campus. Considerable attention will be given, therefore, to the numerous ways in which colleges have sought to discharge their obligation during the present century. The traditional methods of chapel services and religious instruction will be examined. Particular notice will be paid to more recent developments such as the institution of official positions of leadership. We shall describe in some detail significant programs at certain colleges. In this way the growing scope of the movement toward administrative responsibility will be made clear.

But though the method will involve much description of the past, the aim is a practical one, having reference to the problem of the present. The academic upheaval that followed America's entry into World War II has made it necessary to limit the historical and descriptive material largely to the years before Pearl Harbor. The case for the increased provisions for religion in higher education will rest upon the record of the first forty years of the century. But if today's picture beggars description, today's problem demands some fruitful solution.

Stated simply, that problem is: What shall we do? The question has two foci: What ought we to do? and, What can we do? Colleges everywhere used the war years to examine their total programs thoroughly and to plan extensive revisions. Again and again in this planning recurred the question as to the proper, the desirable, the necessary place which religion should occupy in the coming scheme of things. The practical aim of this discussion is to suggest principles on the basis of which, and ways in which, the colleges should proceed. The rehearsal of the past is undertaken in order to make such suggestions by indirection, for administrators who grapple with the problem today may be benefited by the knowledge that others have already faced the same perplexity and here and there have found answers. Moreover, specific suggestions will be advanced in a concluding section.

The thesis, then, is not merely that secularization is past and that administrative responsibility for religion is increasingly being recognized. It is also that this present trend, with a history of at least twenty-five years, is eminently desirable and should be encouraged. Lest too much be claimed for the discussion, however, it should be pointed out that no attempt is made to cover the whole field of religious activity in the college scene. "Administrative responsibility," "official provisions," and similar expressions are used to indicate that the primary concern of this study is with what the colleges themselves think and do about religion. Except for occasional references we shall omit the extracollegiate agencies and their work. The history, purposes and programs of Christian Associations and church-sponsored religious organizations have been examined by others, particularly by Professor Shedd in his two volumes, *Two Centuries of Student Christian Movements* and *The Church Follows Its Students*.

This deliberate omission, however, is not meant to imply that such unofficial approaches to the general problem of religion on the campus are unimportant. Their work has been and continues to be of tremendous significance. They antedate the recent development of full-fledged administrative programs of religion, and in the long lean years of secularization they stemmed the tide, often unaided and sometimes actively opposed by college administrators. That the historic connection between religion and higher education was kept alive in the early years of this century is primarily their accomplishment. Nor does the awakening of administrative interest herald the end of their work, for they too will enter materially into the postwar picture of what can and what ought to be. The problem of religion in the colleges has many aspects and can be approached profitably from several directions.

The explanation of our thesis is not complete without the statement of one more historic fact. The secularization of higher education was never complete. In the early years of the twentieth century, as well as more recently, a large number of colleges consistently recognized their religious obligations; and it would be erroneous to regard the low point of religious interest and responsibility as common to all institutions. Many colleges have borne their responsibility throughout the whole of their history, and much of the present awakening can be attributed to their faithfulness.

Thus the process with which we are concerned can best be described as growth, not beginning. But just as the phenomenon is not completely new, so is it not merely a revitalizing of the old pattern. The intervening period of secularization could not wipe out the religious need of the colleges, but it could, and did, alter their strategy in meeting it. Today's sense of administrative responsibility is not a repentant return to the past. Though based upon an underlying continuity of concern, it is fully alert to the present problems attending the fields of higher education and religion. To a discussion of these problems and of the development itself we are ready to proceed.

CHAPTER II

COLLEGES IN THE TWENTIETH CENTURY

EVERYTHING the college does has religious significance. Whether it be the treatment of its professors, its fraternities, or its janitors, the institution's manners reflect its morals and its whole scale of religious values. Even when religion is narrowly conceived, and when the college considers its duty discharged solely through its religious activities, nearly every change in the general program and routine influences the program in religion. For an understanding of the place of religion in higher education, therefore, one needs to know something of what the colleges have been doing in the twentieth century.

A brief history of the colleges can best be presented by reference to the major problems which they have faced. Most of the problems of higher education today had their origin in the years around the turn of the century or even earlier. But the period up to and including the first World War differs markedly from the 'twenties, 'thirties, and the years of the second World War; our discussion will be divided accordingly.

A. 1900–1918

1. *The problem of definition*

Around 1900 higher education was enthusiastic about its own possibilities and felt that it had come of age. No part of the country lacked colleges, and they were everywhere looked upon as the capstones of the educational system. Already many thorny problems, such as the higher education of women and coeducation, had apparently been decided. But underneath the surface of optimism and satisfaction, higher education was puzzled about itself. What constitutes a college?

It was a question concerning the correct line of division between the college on the one hand and both higher and lower levels of education on the other. These lines had never been clearly drawn, for America had not sufficiently digested and assimilated into one whole the different parts of its educational system. In the upper reaches, many of the larger colleges were in process of becoming or had lately become universities. Graduate study was being separated from undergraduate work, and the college-versus-university question was debated vigorously. The Association of American Universities, founded in 1900, helped to clarify this part of the picture.

On its lower levels, college education was confused concerning its status with relationship to the high schools. The effectiveness of many small colleges had been diluted by coördinate preparatory schools. The junior college idea, conceived by President Harper of Chicago in 1900, was not yet an actuality, but its mere suggestion boded ill for the struggling semi-colleges that dotted the nation. Drawing lines of demarcation was one of the major interests of the first part of the century.

The question of definition concerned also the kind of education offered within the colleges themselves. The A.B. degree meant almost anything, and therefore nothing. Institutions varied greatly in the thoroughness and extent of the work which they required, and the best of them were none too good. The worst were colleges, sometimes "universities," only in name. Standards were almost nonexistent. The general public, and even the colleges themselves in their relationships one with another, had no clear way of distinguishing good from bad.

To bring some order out of this chaos, there began to be established regional and national accrediting agencies. The first was the Middle States Association, founded in 1888, followed closely by similar groups in other parts of the country. The National Association of State Universities was started in 1895. In 1900 the College Entrance Examination Board was established. All of these groups and others, in their various ways, helped to define the college and to formulate standards by which their relative merits could be judged.

Similarly useful were the philanthropic foundations. Soon after the turn of the century the tremendous new wealth of the nation began to be channeled toward the colleges. The General Education Board was founded in 1903, the Carnegie Foundation for the Advancement of Teaching in 1906, the Carnegie Corporation in 1911, and the Rockefeller Foundation in 1913. The work of these groups, particularly the first two, supplemented that of the accrediting agencies; if their efforts were indirect, they were no less influential. Before colleges received grants, they were forced to meet certain requirements concerning the training of their teachers, admission standards, library, endowment, and denominational affiliations. The Carnegie Foundation's "pension plan" for college teachers was probably its most successful "instrument for resolving the confusion in higher education." [1]

All of these efforts had only indirect implications for religion in the colleges. On its surface no one could object to the desire to make the colleges better institutions, and religious leaders joined in the general demand for higher standards and the approval of efforts in that direction. But frequently the worst offenders against high standards were the small denominational institutions which, by heritage and present government, were most deeply interested in and most closely related to religion. The indirect result, therefore, was that many of the colleges which most sincerely proclaimed a religious aim and sought to fulfill it were, at the same time, the least able or willing to adopt rigorous educational ideals and put them into practice. As the work of accrediting and philanthropic agencies weeded out unworthy colleges, it thereby reduced the total concern for religion which higher education manifested. Partly because of its effort to improve itself academically, higher education became more secular.

The conclusion was sometimes drawn that denominational affiliation was somehow related to educational ineffectiveness. The leaders in higher education were the large, long-established, independent universities which had, for the most part, divested themselves of any direct connection with organized religion, and the rapidly developing state universities, which, with a few early exceptions, had never had any connection with religious groups. Freedom from denominational ties began to be a goal for the smaller colleges which had been established and nurtured by the churches. Around 1910, for example, Brown, Centre, Coe, Drake, Drury, Rochester, Rutgers, Wesleyan, and others became nondenominational. The Carnegie Foundation was charged with aiding this process, and in the light of history the charge seems to be justifiable. In his *Philanthropic Foundations and Higher Education,* E. V. Hollis says:

1. E. V. Hollis, *Philanthropic Foundations and Higher Education* (New York, Columbia University Press, 1938), p. 38.

Finally, in its attempts to hasten the day of real colleges, the Carnegie Foundation sought to weaken the then dominant denominational college control. . . .

The Foundation's remedy was inherent in its conception. Through its undenominational clause an institution could not share in the Carnegie pension fund if it remained in any way under the control of a religious sect. . . . Whether the Foundation intended it or not, its policy did "rob the denominations" of many of their colleges rich enough to have a $200,000 endowment that had come through "the prayers, and the tears, and the sacrifices of the Church." The influence of the Foundation tended also to loosen the sectarian bonds of many church-controlled colleges that did not become affiliated in the system.[2]

To the extent, then, to which the Carnegie Foundation's policy weakened the small denominational colleges or tore the stronger ones away from their denominational moorings, it aided the process of secularization. Other developments of the period, as we shall see, also aided that process, for secularization was a much larger problem than merely the practical question of control of the institution's affairs. One of the academic struggles of the time was between what have been called the "religious" and the "secular" concepts of education. Efforts to define the college and improve its academic work combined with other forces to support the secular concept.

2. *The elective system*

Improvement of the academic work meant tinkering with the curriculum. The old course of study was composed almost altogether of "classical" and "literary" subjects, and nearly the whole of it was required. But man's mind had been wandering into many new fields of the natural and social sciences, and what had been good enough for father seemed woefully incomplete for his son. Greek and Latin, representing the cultural core of the older colleges, found themselves on the defensive in the midst of robust claimants for a place in the course of study. Immediately preceding and following 1900 the curricular offerings of the majority of colleges were greatly enlarged.

Students could no longer take everything which was offered. The enlargement of the curriculum was accompanied by the prin-

2. *Ibid.*, pp. 138–140.

ciple of free election. President Eliot of Harvard had begun his campaign for the "elective system," as it came to be called, in his inaugural address as early as 1869. Adopting the idea Harvard had acted as an example to the vast majority of other colleges. By 1900 they had already instituted, or were soon impelled to institute, some measure of election into their programs. Though a few voices were raised in question, and though Eliot's extreme concept of free choice was not widely adopted, at least the principle of election seemed to have won a decisive victory in higher education by the time of the first World War.[3]

The real significance for religion was not at first evident. It did appear that, whereas many colleges had formerly required the study of "moral philosophy" taught, say, by the preacher-president, now the enlargement of the curriculum and the principle of election meant that fewer students would receive religious instruction or spend a smaller portion of their time in such study. Election, therefore, was part and parcel of secularization.

But this influence was not great because those institutions, largely state and independent universities, which most heartily adopted election and expanded their offerings were the very ones in which religion had never been or ceased to be a discipline represented in the curriculum. Correspondingly, those other colleges, largely church-related, in which religion had always been well represented in the course of study were the ones least affected by the elective principle.

The great harm done to religion by the elective system was of another sort and its significance was recognized later. The system, it is true, brought a breath of freedom into the college program; but for all its good intentions it resulted in the loss of a sense of values. One subject was as good as another; one student was as wise as another in making choices. To the extent to which the principle of election encouraged such conclusions—and the more complete the election adopted the more naturally did such implications arise—to that extent it denied the high values in education and experience which religion represents. In an institution practicing election, religion was bound to be only one among a number of other equal and competing interests, if it appeared at all. Even worse, the whole philosophy of life which conceives of living in

3. See, for example, R. Freeman Butts, *The College Charts Its Course* (New York, McGraw-Hill Book Co., 1939), Pt. III.

terms of high moral and spiritual values was tacitly denied. Religion not merely as a limited subject matter but as the basis of the institution's values was weakened in its influence. The elective system, therefore, did its part in aiding the growth of the secular spirit in higher education.

3. *Bigness and its accompaniments*

Another major problem which the colleges faced in this early period was quantitative. Bigness had begun to descend upon higher education, and the crass fact of ever-increasing numbers came to be the most serious practical concern. Enrollments skyrocketed, and students flooded the institutions of higher learning, particularly those supported by the state. Many new colleges were established; physical plants underwent huge expansion; endowments increased astronomically. In all its aspects, this fact of tremendous physical growth is probably the most important single happening in higher education during this century, for out of the increase have arisen, in one way or another, nearly all the problems which still confront colleges today.

One implication of bigness was that a "democratic" concept of education, as opposed to the older, more aristocratic idea, began to be promulgated. Speaking of this period, William Allen White wrote in 1924:

During the last twenty years, two things have happened: First, the colleges have become tremendously attractive to youth, quite apart from the course of study. Second, the rise in the economic status of the average American family has made it possible for thousands of young people to go to these attractive colleges, who have no cultural background whatever, who are not interested in books and reading, and who regard education as merely an equipment for making a living. . . . They are strangers to the academic life—as isolated and remote as the wild savage in the forest from all that went with the cloistered life of our old American college tradition.[4]

Higher education was no longer for the chosen few alone. All classes of people began demanding a college education for their children, and going to college became increasingly the thing to do.

4. Quoted by J. P. Gavit, *College* (New York, Harcourt, Brace & Co., 1925), p. 251.

Thus education here as well as on its lower levels was no longer merely for leadership, but for citizenship, for followers as well as leaders.

But colleges were not thereby democratized. The doors had been thrown open to the masses, but in the field of administration the element of democracy which tended to characterize the smaller colleges of previous years was necessarily diminished and often lost entirely. Bigness meant complexity of organization, with the addition of many new kinds of administrative officers, vice-presidents, deans of instruction and deans of personnel. Bigness also meant impersonality—the common touch of president and faculty with all the students inevitably disappeared in the larger institutions.

Moreover, this mass of students had to be educated *for* something. A well-rounded cultural training began to seem deficient. Higher education took on a more practical and vocational turn. Students were trained not merely to know and to think, but also to do. Instruction in skills and techniques was added to the course of study. The changes were reflected in the educational philosophy of the time, particularly in the writings of John Dewey, to which reference will be made in a later chapter. For a while these developments received admirable support from the principle of free election of studies and from the enlargement of curricular offerings.

Bigness, with its consequent changes in educational thought and practice, immeasurably complicated the problem which religion faced. For example, chapel services for three hundred students were possible; for three thousand, seemingly out of the question. If the religious growth of the students was to be cared for, many of the colleges began to feel that other agencies through which the mass could be broken down into smaller, more manageable groups should be responsible. The increase in enrollment meant, in numerous instances, the decrease or relinquishment by the college of official responsibility for the religious nurture of its students. It will be noticed in the following chapter how the voluntary religious groups and the churches reacted to this challenge. But no matter how manfully the off-campus organizations filled the gap, bigness often meant that the colleges themselves omitted religion, thus adding to the secularization of higher education.

4. *Secularization*

As the colleges grew and struggled through the first decade and a half of the new century, the difficulties of definition, the elective system and size, together with their attendant problems, were only the most obvious and pressing among a host of others. The first World War brought its own special problem of survival and useful participation in the national effort, and many campuses echoed to the tread of marching feet. Other afflictions of the time developed into their most virulent stage only in the following period. Yet with all the questions of serious import dogging their steps, the colleges prospered, confident of their position as purveyors of learning and culture.

But those who cared deeply about the place of religion in higher education did not enter fully into the optimism of the period. For the direction of the colleges' progress was toward a thorough secularization. As already indicated, the three influences discussed above contributed to this end; but apart from all of them secularization was an unmistakable trend of the times in all education. It is well to note, however, that this secularization manifested itself in two distinct developments which, though not completely separable, affected in different degrees the place of religion in the colleges.

First, secularization meant nonsectarianism. Here higher education took its cue from the public school system, in its earlier successful "battle to eliminate sectarianism." [5] The severance of ties which had bound colleges to their sponsoring churches was often an effort to become free from a denominational brand of religion. If this were all that secularization meant, the proponents of religion would probably view the result with approval. Those who argue for a large place for religion in higher education today are as dissatisfied with sectarianism as any nonreligionist. The trouble was that in higher education, even as in the public schools, religion was often identified in the minds of the uninformed with sectarianism. When one went, the other had to go. Since many institutions, particularly those connected with the state, could not conceive of nonsectarian religion, the only solution was to get rid of religion altogether.

5. See E. P. Cubberley, *Public Education in the United States* (Cambridge, Houghton Mifflin Co., 1919); and S. W. Brown, *The Secularization of American Education* (New York, Teachers College, Columbia University, 1912).

But in that result were seeds for a fruitful change. As soon as it could be shown that religion was broader and more meaningful than any one denomination's interpretation of it, then it could be expected that the part of the process of secularization caused by this misconception would begin to reverse itself. As we shall see, this is what has happened in the last twenty-five years.

Not so easily solved is the second problem presented by secularization, namely, secularism. State institutions, which thought of themselves as necessarily secular, had grown rapidly in the latter part of the nineteenth century, aided greatly by the Morrill Land Grant Act of 1862. Their influence in higher education resulted in dampening the religious ardor of other colleges. By the beginning of World War I religion had become largely peripheral in the leading collegiate centers. Even when institutions gave lip-service to the religious ideals of the past, they tended in practice to ignore the demands which those ideals made upon them in the development of their programs.

Religion was not only peripheral; it was often considered not intellectually respectable. Colleges had become conscious of their role as disseminators of proven, scientific fact. In the minds of many otherwise well-educated persons, a great gulf separated science from religion. Thus many colleges were inclined to soft-pedal or eliminate the "unscientific" concerns of religion.

By becoming secularized the colleges were only succumbing to the spirit of the age, for secularism was characteristic of society as a whole. It was linked to the growing materialism in practical affairs, to naturalism in science and philosophy, to humanism in religion. Thus the struggle between the secular and religious concepts of education was much more a conflict in the realm of thought of the whole society than in the realm of educational practice alone. Secularization as merely the practical business of cutting religion out of the regular college life reached its peak effectiveness sometime during the second decade of this century. But secularization as the reflection of a secular spirit permeating society is still a powerful force; and one hesitates to say even now that its influence is decreasing. In the limited area of educational philosophy, however, secularism has lately been under strong attack; this will be discussed in succeeding chapters.

B. 1919–1946

The colleges soon discovered that the first war had solved none of their problems for them. During the last twenty-five years all the perplexing questions of the previous period continued to plague the colleges, though not always in the same way. Moreover, many new problems began to assume critical proportions. Though obviously the colleges are not the same now as they were at the end of the first World War, the period from 1919 to the present is not conveniently divisible. Events and crises in society as a whole have left their marks upon higher education, for good and for ill. The depression, particularly, disturbed what even tenor there was to the colleges' ways. The nature of the changes to be wrought by World War II defy prediction; one is safe only in saying they will be tremendous. Yet these problems have exerted their influence in such varied fashion and degree that it is difficult to determine the precise moment at which each became significant for our particular concern as to the place of religion in higher education. Thus for our purposes a division into smaller time units is apt to be misleading; the period will be treated as a whole.

1. *The nature of college education*

In the minds of most educators, the college has come to be a fairly well-defined entity. It consists of a four-year course of study between high school and graduate school; its limits are well understood; its result is an A.B. or a B.S. degree. True the junior college, springing to prominence first in California, has developed a terminal education for those who desire to go beyond high school, yet find the four-year pattern more than they want or can take. And recently Chicago, by offering the A.B. degree at the end of approximately two years' study, has caused unrest among more orthodox institutions. These and other developments are forcing a reconsideration of the nature of a college, but for the most part its scope and limits are agreed upon. Unlike the earlier period, therefore, the problem of definition in recent years has not centered in questions of time-span and accreditation, though individual institutions have pursued for themselves ever higher academic recognition.

The problem of definition in this period might be said to be, rather, the effort to define the nature of the education to be offered within the traditional four years of study. What ought a college to be and do? Should it conserve the past, fit into the present, or prepare for the future? Ought its aims to be individual or social, and practical or cultural? Such questions, of course, were asked earlier, but the last twenty-five years have witnessed their most extensive and intensive searching. The air of easy confidence characterizing the earlier period has been dissipated; and this was true even before World War II added its own measure of confusion.

These questions, however, are obviously concerned with educational philosophy even more than with practice, and as such will demand thorough treatment in a succeeding chapter. Suffice it now to indicate two tangible evidences of this increased mental ferment. The first was self-examination. The whole field of higher education was subjected to painstaking scrutiny. Books about the college and its problems were written by the score, and many colleges embarked upon thoughtful analyses of their own programs.

Such introspection often proceeded to the point of stern criticism, even condemnation. Here administrators were aided in their thinking by those who did not possess administrative responsibility and who, therefore, saw with less obscured vision and spoke with less reticence. Through the "flood of good, bad, indifferent, and even contradictory criticism" the "general dissatisfaction with today's American college" became abundantly clear.[6] The notes on which the critics played most often were "superficial," "chaotic," "no adequate philosophy," "no appreciation for values," "non-intellectual," "too much control," "too little control," and on and on. If the colleges were sick, doctors were not lacking, and the patients were not allowed seclusion.

The result of such examination was bound to be experimentation on a wide scale. This is the second significant evidence of the stern philosophizing of the time. Heroic efforts were instituted to solve the problems that had been recognized. Some movements were almost nation-wide; others concerned only individual institutions. Some attacked the total pattern of the college's work; others seized upon particular problems for experiment. The discussion in the following paragraphs will identify many of these

6. P. A. Schilpp, ed., *Higher Education Faces the Future* (New York, Horace Liveright, 1930), Introduction.

national and local improvisations. In the 'twenties and 'thirties the whole collegiate world showed itself willing to clean house, to break with the past, to take tremendous gambles with its future, if need be, in order to answer more satisfactorily its own questionings concerning the proper nature of higher education.

The two phenomena of self-examination and experimentation, taken together, had indirect, though significant, influence for the place of religion in higher education. While the college was engaging in honest confession, it was often led to the point where such confession was good for its soul; thus in recognizing its faults the college often noted its omission of religion as high on the list. Moreover, when it overcame its institutional inertia sufficiently to experiment in better teaching or better housing, it often proceeded to have a try at better preaching and better praying. The many recent innovations in the field of religion owe at least something to the general spirit of introspection and experiment which characterized the times. Religion could lose nothing by such maneuvers, for after the wreckage wrought by the process of secularization it had nothing to lose. It could and did gain much.

The influence was not merely that colleges were led to experiment by bringing religion back into their programs; it was also that religious leaders themselves were impelled to try new methods. The old chapel service and the old course in moral philosophy were gone forever; new wine demanded new wineskins. Descriptions of college religious programs in succeeding chapters will illustrate to what a great extent both self-examination and experimentation were utilized.

2. *The course of study*

The area in which the increased philosophizing of the time showed most tangible results was, of course, in the curriculum. The course of study has received an extensive overhauling in the last twenty-five years. Other new subjects have been added to the offerings and the number of "departments" has increased. But the career of the elective system since the first World War has not been as triumphant as it gave promise of being. Even at the time of its greatest adoption and even in Harvard, its original home, questions were raised as to its soundness.[7] Educators saw the old "cultural" and "liberal arts" courses slipping out of the colleges,

7. See Butts, *op. cit.*, Pt. IV.

and sprang to their defense. With greatly increased student bodies and enlarged courses of study, the elective system, it became clear, offered no guide-lines to the young. Students were unprepared for free election; and more, the growing complexity of the curriculum was too much even for adequately prepared students. The situation has been summed up by Chancellor Hutchins of Chicago:

. . . with education . . . the great criminal was Mr. Eliot, who as President of Harvard applied his genius, skill, and longevity to the task of robbing American youth of their cultural heritage. Since he held that there were no such things as good or bad subjects of study, his laudable effort to open the curriculum to good ones naturally led him to open it to bad ones and finally to destroy it altogether. Today, though it is possible to get an education in an American university, a man would have to be so bright and know so much to get it that he wouldn't really need it.[8]

The result has been, therefore, that in recent years a measure of prescription has been winning its way back into the curriculum. The benefits of the elective system, consisting of its influence in opening the doors for the inclusion of valuable new disciplines and its placing reliance upon the students to make at least some of their own choices, have been preserved. At the same time, the extravagant dangers of the system have been eliminated. Colleges have discovered or rediscovered certain subjects here and there, and consequently certain values, which they dare not allow their students to ignore.

But there has been no unanimity as to what these subjects and these values are. The experimentation has varied widely. Only English composition and physical education are well-nigh universally required. Then, depending upon the individual institution's aims, other courses are added to the prescribed list: philosophy here, history there, "introductory science" yonder. Many colleges such as Chicago, Colgate, and Columbia have inaugurated "survey" courses in whole fields of study, cutting across departmental lines. The effort has been to develop a broad understanding of various areas of human knowledge and human activity and their interrelationships rather than a narrow "mastery" of individual segments.

Such an effort has led some institutions to change the nature

8. Robert M. Hutchins, *Education for Freedom* (Baton Rouge, Louisiana State University Press, 1943), p. 25.

and direction of their entire programs. Soon after World War I Swarthmore began to develop its pattern of honors work, the better to care for the exceptional student who, in the rush toward "democracy," had been rather generally neglected. Honors courses are now a feature of many colleges in various sections of the country. To find out whether there is such a thing as a liberal understanding, by attention both to content and to method, the Experimental College at Wisconsin existed from 1927 to 1932. Minnesota set up its General College to provide a more suitable and less stringent type of higher education for those of lesser ability. "Problem-centered" or "functional" curricula, an outgrowth of the progressive education movement which in turn had sprung largely from John Dewey, became fashionable. Adopted in various degrees by many colleges, they received their most thorough trial in two new experimental institutions, Sarah Lawrence, founded in 1926, and Bennington, established in 1932. A closer coördination of college with the workaday world was developed at Antioch. Rollins in Florida embarked upon "creative education"; Reed in Oregon emphasized "originality, social understanding, and character." Over on the other wing, owing its ideology to Hutchins of Chicago rather than to Dewey, was St. John's, encouraging an understanding and appreciation of the past through its "hundred best books." And Chicago itself underwent a profound reorganization of its whole program. All these and many other colleges came to be known as centers of experimentation concerning the content of the curriculum.

Interest was focused not alone on what was taught but how. Colleges began to rediscover the old-time importance of the teacher and his personality—Mark Hopkins on one end of the familiar log. Consequently the training of teachers received careful investigation, and teachers' colleges grew in importance and adequacy. Different methods of teaching supplemented or even displaced the traditional classroom, lecture approach: tutorials, seminars, laboratory experience, work projects, reading periods, and directed use of vacations for academic credit. Many of the colleges mentioned above combined experiments in method with their changes in content and organization. Swarthmore, together with others such as Harvard and Yale, began to use the tutorial system, instituted first in this country by Princeton with its "preceptors" as long ago as 1905. Antioch's contribution was by way of staggering periods of study in residence at the college with periods of work in industry or other nonacademic pursuits. All the colleges which adopted "problem-centered" curricula encouraged their students to learn by doing as well as by listening. Long before the present war forced colleges to speed up their programs, Hiram experimented with a form of concentration in which students took fewer subjects and completed them in shorter periods of time. Such efforts as these, combined with direct attacks upon content, were evidence of a desire to enrich the course of study.

Whatever the educational philosophies back of such wholesale changes, the increased interest in the course of study had great significance for religion. Even as the elective system endangered the colleges' sense of values, even so its gradual decline was propitious for their reassertion. The shift toward partial prescription of courses evidenced a renewed concern for the permanently good and true things of the mind. Religion, broadly conceived, was bound to benefit.

Religion benefited in tangible ways. The enlargement of curricular offerings applied to this field, so that, as we shall see more fully later, departments of religion or religious education were added in large numbers in all types of colleges, including state universities. The offerings of most of these departments were elective, but the establishment of guide-lines for the students worked in many colleges toward the requirement of courses in religion.

Even colleges which still omitted religion as a subject in the course of study were not loath to recognize its importance, justifying their omission on the ground that religion as a system of value-judgments and as a way of life was taught throughout the curriculum, in all departments. Whether or not this self-justification was sound, the very fact of its being advanced indicated a new concern for religion. The phenomenon of omission of direct instruction unaccompanied by any such self-justification was limited largely to a few of the most militantly experimental colleges of the "progressive" school of thought and to technological schools. For the large majority of colleges their willingness to make curricular changes and adopt new methods of teaching worked to emphasize the importance of religion as a mental discipline or a fruitful activity. The attention paid to the curriculum, therefore, played its part in reversing the tide of secularization.

3. *Security*

Bigness as a practical interest has continued to hound the colleges. With the close of the first World War the number of students again increased, and during the 'twenties colleges prospered materially in new buildings and larger endowments. Till approximately 1930 the problem was the happy one of continual growth and expansion.

But with the coming of the depression things went into reverse. If the question of numbers was somewhat alleviated, the question of finances rose to sharp attention. Retrenchment became the motto. Colleges were forced to learn how to reduce as well as to expand. Even with the partial return of economic prosperity in the late 'thirties the problem was far from solved. Though once again numbers of students increased, no comparable increases in endowment took place and colleges received smaller returns on the endowment they already possessed. If an institution, by virtue of its state connection, was free from worry about endowment, it was often no more confident of its financial security, since legislatures were notoriously unpredictable. The question of the material condition of the college, therefore, was no longer one of bigness; it was the more critical one of balance between increase here and decrease there, the problem of soundness. The earlier concern about size became the problem of security; in many instances it was a desperate fight for survival.

The matters incident to physical growth before World War I became more critical in the later period. "Democracy" in higher education came to mean, often, mass education on a low level. Colleges were not as independent as formerly, and benefactors sought to exercise control in the same way in which businessmen controlled their corporations. Academic freedom began to be increasingly a trouble-spot for an institution which, no longer cloistered, felt many pressures from society at large. Thus growth and its consequent complexity meant, on the one hand, more democracy of a sort, in that everybody and his ill-equipped brother was going to college now, and, on the other hand, less real democracy, in that institutions became academic factories, corporations, hierarchies, but not republics.

Moreover, it was more fully recognized in the 'twenties and 'thirties than in former years that numerical increase of students indicated the necessity of the rapid expansion of opportunities for a practical education. Vocationalism became characteristic particularly of the large state universities, but even some of the more "exclusive" colleges did not escape. It was possible for students to take for academic credit courses in such things as cosmetics, shorthand, and salesmanship. These extreme departures from the older classical core of studies prompted wails of agony from many educational philosophers; the terms "chain-store" and "filling-station" were hurled at the offending institutions. But when World War II put a premium on the possession of immediate skills rather than of mature understanding, vocationalism seemed to have found for itself a permanent place in the undergraduate curriculum.

All of this happened, however, not without systematic efforts to solve the problems both of size and security, and to stem the tide of pseudo-democracy and vocationalism. Concern for the horde of new students and their welfare came to be an all-consuming occupation; this development will be discussed in a separate section below. Financial stringencies provoked efforts to effect large savings and to raise money in new ways and from new sources, not altogether successful. One of the experiments, widely adopted, was an annual call upon the alumni to act as a "living endowment."

Since bigness and complexity had proved themselves inimical to the intellectual life, many institutions which could afford it began to limit their enrollments rigidly, and some of the larger ones experimented in dividing themselves into smaller units to try to recapture the virtues of intimacy and simplicity of the small college. The most thoroughgoing maneuvers of this sort were those of Harvard, with its division into "houses," and Yale, with its "college plan." Vocationalism was roundly attacked both in the realm of educational philosophy and in practice; many of the experiments noted in the preceding section were directed to the correction of this abuse. Thus the 'twenties and 'thirties witnessed steady efforts to conquer the problem of bigness and its attendant evils; but the problem of security, made more critical by the coming of the war, was still unsolved.

Religion was affected, both for good and for ill. Great size, false democracy, organizational complexity, all made religion's task harder. Vocationalism held its special danger, for whenever emphasis is placed solely on know-how, without knowing why, religion suffers. Those colleges most heartily espousing a practical education were, almost without exception, the ones with least provisions for religion: state universities, teachers' colleges, independent institutions pursuing "progressive education," and schools of technology. The financial problem, too, had its unfortunate repercussions: a college faced with an unbalanced budget or a large debt was inclined to hesitate about the extension of its religious program.

But the efforts to solve these perplexities were often indirectly beneficial. Whenever a college, faced with a threat to its security or even survival, examines more frankly its reasons for being and its ultimate objectives, religion stands to gain, for it is inevitably connected with values in learning and in growth of personality. Similarly, to the extent to which vocationalism is diluted by a consideration of purposes as well as skills, to that extent religion profits. And in actual practice the provisions for religion showed a surprising ability to survive the necessary cuts in collegiate budgets.

4. *Secularism*

Enough has already been said to indicate that the tide of secularization in higher education has definitely turned and that many of the college's problems of the past twenty-five years have led toward an increase in the attention paid to religion. Except in isolated strongholds, sectarianism has lost its struggle; and its demise has aided, rather than hindered, the inclusion of a liberal religion in the colleges' programs. Further on we shall notice in detail how the attitudes of college administrators, the trends in educational philosophy, and the developments in religious programs, all attest to the reversal of the process of secularization.

But the spirit of secularism has continued to be characteristic of the collegiate scene. All that was said before concerning secularism has persisted: that it looked upon religion as peripheral, or worse, as useless, and not intellectually respectable; that it took its cue from the general secular spirit infecting society, the materialism in practical affairs, the naturalism in science and philosophy, the humanism in religion. College professors by the hundreds, particularly many in the natural sciences, thought of religion as an opiate, or at least a sign of weakness. Dedicating themselves to the scientific method, they ignored the possibility that truth could be arrived at in any other way. Science became, in fact, a sort of religion. Many were willing to preserve the adjective "religious," but the noun "religion," if it indicated a belief in an Ultimate Good which went beyond, even though it did not contradict, the dictates of reason, was discarded.

When it came to the world of practical affairs, this whole point of view used much the same language which religion used. Both talked about the worth and dignity of the individual, both believed in democracy as that form of government and of society in which man would rise to his highest development, both followed a moral code based vaguely on the Golden Rule.

In the confusion caused by the identity of many of their concepts, the sharp difference between secularism and religion was often lost upon both parties. The difference was that religion related such concepts to the spiritual world and its nature, a world which its opponents denied. To religion, man was an animal, but more than an animal—man was a son of God. To the nonreligionist, man was also an animal-plus; in fact, man himself was God. By the use of his intelligence alone, said the secularists, man could bring in the kingdom.

Even this simplified picture of a complicated battleground goes further than the great majority of secularists carried their thinking. They were content to rest their case on the supremacy of the scientific method, and the false assumption that religion was afraid of it or would not use it as far as possible. In practice they simply omitted religion, especially participation in organized religion, from their lives.

The college students of the time, impressionable and immature, observed the conclusions of their elders without understanding or appropriating even those limited value-judgments which went into their making. Moreover, they had come to adolescence in an age characterized by the steady diminution of religious sanctions in private living. They thought the practice of religion was an unnecessary and stupid embellishment and, often, a deterrent to a "good time." Thus the secularism of the student world was even greater than that of their agnostic professors. More than any other one characteristic of the colleges in the last twenty-five years, this problem of the secularism of their faculties and students has represented a stumbling block to religion. Augmented by crass materialism in various aspects of the colleges' programs, the secular spirit has infected all features of the campus life.

But there are many signs of hope. Numbers of college executives have been restive under the trend, and their recent renewed interest in religion has been caused in large measure by their recognition of the dangers of secularism in its various manifestations. Secularism is dangerous because it offers no firm foundation for the resting of man's spirit in a complex and mysterious universe. Secularism is weakening in its hold upon the colleges because this danger is being combated, with some only partially and hesitantly, with others clearly and forthrightly. This much is, of course, only the bare beginning of an analysis; a full discussion of its dangers and their recognition, its inadequacies and their antidotes, will be postponed to Chapters XVI and XVII. As a comment now upon an actual development, it is enough to say that the spread of the secular spirit in higher education has, at the least, been arrested. In this fact lies promise for a growing emphasis on the place of religion in the colleges.

5. *The students*

In all that has been said for both periods, the students have been directly implicated. Their nurture has, of course, been the colleges' primary problem throughout the history of higher education. Since the first World War, however, adequate care for the personal needs of students has constituted a specialized concern, surpassing in intensity any such efforts expended upon them in the past.

These needs were beginning to be recognized in the earlier period. The students of the century's early years, it is true, were still a chosen lot, but because of the havoc being wrought by the elective system they were not distinguished for their intellectual interest. President Thwing of Western Reserve concluded a survey in 1914: ". . . these investigations indicate that the American college student studies, studies *somewhat;* but I believe they do not indicate that he is a *hard* worker." [9] Students had begun to discover the lure of the extracurriculum. Woodrow Wilson's famous remark about the collegiate sideshows was made as early as 1909: "The sideshows are so numerous, so diverting—so important if you will—that they have swallowed up the circus, and

9. C. F. Thwing, *The American College: What It Is and What It May Become* (New York, Platt & Peck Co., 1914), p. 79. Italics are his.

those who perform in the main tent must often whistle for their audience, discouraged and humiliated." [10]

But the problem did not unfold in all its seriousness until after World War I. The trend toward superficiality and lack of purpose was confirmed. Great impetus was given to the growth of extra-curricular activities at the expense of study. The pictures of student life of the 'twenties are full of gaiety and cynicism, of wild parties and tragic wanderings of spirit. Their favorite interests were fraternities, athletics, and the other sex. It was the age of the coonskin coat and the pocket-flask,

> . . . for we all came to college,
> but we didn't come for knowledge,
> so we'll raise hell while we're here.

With the coming of the depression, a new note of seriousness was discernible. Intellectual pursuits became more respectable. Parties were not so wild, nor outside activities quite so important. But the problem remained, for the host of students was still so large that many were continually getting lost in the blind alleys of the collegiate maze.

The colleges reacted nobly to the challenge. One result was the effort to select students more intelligently. Thus increasing emphasis through the years has been placed upon admission requirements not limited merely to the previous academic records of the applicants.

But by far the larger amount of energy has been expended in taking care of them once they were admitted. Led by the University of Maine in 1923, colleges provided for periods of orientation, often called "Freshman Week," and for orientation procedures lasting the first full academic year. The whole field of organized guidance and personnel work has been developed largely since the first World War. Educators attacked excesses in the fraternity system, in intercollegiate athletics, in the social life of their students. From having been concerned with the intellect alone, higher education began to take upon itself a responsibility for the development of the whole person, his health, his housing conditions, his total pattern of living. In many institutions students themselves were given a share in the process; the movement of "student government" is of fairly recent origin.

10. Woodrow Wilson, "What Is a College For?" *Scribner's*, XLVI, 5 (November, 1909), 576.

And even as the colleges saw their problem and went to work on it, they recognized its relationship to the broader problem of society at large; once again, it was shown, the college was no longer cloistered. Dean Gauss of Princeton wrote in 1930: "If the undergraduate suffers from anything, he is suffering only from those things from which our country itself is suffering." [11]

Religion had much to gain from this increased interest in the welfare of the students. The philosophy of the education of the whole man, which lay back of all the developments in this area, pointed up as never before the omission of religion. If a college paid attention to everything about the student but his religious life, then the implication was bound to grow that religion was unimportant. Often such a result did take place. But the converse began to be even more characteristic of the collegiate scene: for fear of leaving this very implication in the minds of their students, colleges began to take at least some measure of responsibility for their religious development. Thus the new philosophy had a direct influence on bringing religion into the educational picture.

Religion also received indirect benefit. Even when the religious programs themselves were not augmented, the larger concern for the individual brought religious values into consideration and into active functioning. For religion has always stood for the fullest development of the individual personality. When the colleges began to care for their students outside as well as in the classroom, then they assumed for themselves, whether or not they consciously recognized it, a religious task.

6. *World War II*

Thus the colleges came to the second World War, beset by problems and striving valiantly to solve them. We have discussed them under several main headings, yet such division is essentially misleading. All were inextricably interrelated one with another; no college could attempt a solution for one without becoming involved in the others. The nature of college education meant a consideration of the curriculum; the kind of course of study was dependent upon the size and relative security of the institution; all revolved around the students and their welfare; and the mood in which the colleges labored was predominantly one of secularism.

11. Christian Gauss, *Life in College* (New York, Charles Scribner's Sons, 1930), p. 107.

Religion was involved in all these concerns and in their totality. For approximately the first two decades of the century, the practical ways in which these affairs were determined were, in most instances, prejudicial to the inclusion of religion in any large and meaningful way in the life of the colleges. The next two decades, however, saw a reversal of this influence. Almost without exception the efforts to solve the perplexities of the times resulted either in a reaffirmation of religious values or in increased provisions for religion in the colleges' programs, or both. The future held great promise.

But the second war once more threw into confusion and uncertainty the schemes and activities of higher education. The Army and Navy invaded the campuses. If nothing quite as dismal as the SATC of the first war was sponsored, the numbers of trainees, the length of the war, and the immediate purposes of training programs combined to change the whole character of the colleges. Whatever the college's stand on vocationalism before the war, it was forced to emphasize the practical skills and techniques incident to fitting men to fight. Traditional courses in the liberal arts necessarily suffered. Regimentation in a variety of ways was adopted: in studies and outside activities as well as in military drill. Men marched in formation in more places than merely on the improvised drill field.

Speed became paramount. Colleges experimented with all sorts of schedules, but concentration and acceleration were characteristic of them all. The joke about the lad who, because of a visit to the washroom, missed his whole sophomore year, wasn't as funny to students or faculty as to laymen. A tiredness encompassed the college scene, and the caliber of academic work was lowered thereby. The amount of time spent in extracurricular activities was sharply decreased. Higher education as a whole moved to the tempo set by the training units; civilians in all colleges and even in institutions for women alone succumbed to the pressures for practical training and for speed.

Colleges freely forsook their former courses of study and their more leisurely pace not alone for lofty motives of patriotism, to aid in the war effort, but also out of enlightened self-interest, in order to survive. The population of men students declined rapidly after America's entrance into the war. Thus coeducational and men's colleges plunged into a terrific competitive scramble to get units of the Army or Navy on their campuses. Those who failed entirely faced serious financial crisis, and some had to close their doors. Even those who succeeded were not automatically secure, as the ones which housed some short-lived Army unit discovered. Nobody was on easy street, for all that Army or Navy help meant was an escape from disaster, not affluence. As welcome as such aid was, however, it brought another awkward problem, for with government funds there came, inevitably, a measure of governmental control. The phrase "education by contract" summed up the situation.

Yet there were compensations. The war gave a healthy spur to the experimentation which already characterized the college scene. New ways of doing things were discovered which would probably prove useful for days of peace as well as for war—ways of teaching, of arranging an academic schedule, of making financial savings. The Army and Navy units resulted in the attendance at college of countless men who would otherwise not have had the opportunity. As never before, native intelligence and ability rather than the size of father's pocketbook determined whether or not a boy would receive a higher education. And the students themselves came primarily to study and to learn—that in itself was an improvement on the past.

But the greatest benefits derived from the experience were the evaluation of the present and the preparation for the future which the colleges began to make. Faced with terrific upheaval, they were led to inquire what was permanently good and what expendable in their traditional programs. Thus the war gave extra impetus to the self-examination and experimentation characteristic of the 'twenties and 'thirties. Higher education no longer possesses the undiluted optimism of the turn of the century; rather, it has a chastened confidence that, though many difficult problems remain and new ones will certainly arise, the answers will somehow be found.

Religion is moving once more into a central place in higher education. Religious programs have been subject to all the uncertainties and disasters which have affected other aspects of college life during the war years. But their relative strength seems to have grown rather than lessened.[12] The serious evaluation of higher education, provoked by the war, will enhance rather than diminish

12. See Clarence P. Shedd and Granville T. Walker, "War-Time Adjustments in the Teaching of Religion," *Journal of Bible and Religion*, XII (May, 1944).

religion's significance. Dependable estimates as to the final effect of the war upon religion in the colleges must be postponed. Yet this much is already clear: religion occupies a larger place in the colleges' thinking and practice than at any time in the twentieth century. To furnish documentation for this judgment is the purpose of the succeeding chapters.

SELECTED BIBLIOGRAPHY FOR CHAPTER II

Among the host of books and other writings in the field, the following proved most useful for this study:

A. For the period 1900–1918:

The American College. New York, Henry Holt and Co., 1915. 194 pp.

BUTLER, NICHOLAS M., *The Meaning of Education.* New York, The Macmillan Co., 1907. 230 pp.

FLEXNER, ABRAHAM, *The American College; A Criticism.* New York, The Century Co., 1908. 237 pp.

HARPER, WILLIAM RAINEY, *The Trend in Higher Education.* Chicago, University of Chicago Press, 1905. 390 pp.

HOLLIS, ERNEST V., *Philanthropic Foundations and Higher Education.* New York, Columbia University Press, 1938. 365 pp.

KEPPEL, FREDERICK P., *The Undergraduate and His College.* Cambridge, Houghton Mifflin Co., 1917. 374 pp.

MILLAR, ALEXANDER C., *Twentieth Century Educational Problems.* New York, Hinds and Noble, 1901. 231 pp.

SHARPLESS, ISAAC, *The American College.* New York, Doubleday, Page and Co., 1915. 221 pp.

THWING, CHARLES F., *The American College: What It Is and What It May Become.* New York, The Platt and Peck Co., 1914. 294 pp.

———— *A History of Higher Education in America.* New York, D. Appleton and Co., 1906. 501 pp.

VEBLEN, THORSTEIN, *The Higher Learning in America.* New York, B. W. Huebsch, 1918. 286 pp.

WEST, ANDREW F., *Short Papers on American Liberal Education.* New York, Charles Scribner's Sons, 1907. 135 pp.

and: Many of the items listed under Section B.

B. For the period 1919–1941:

ANGELL, ROBERT C., *The Campus.* New York, D. Appleton and Co., 1928. 239 pp.

BUTTS, R. FREEMAN, *The College Charts Its Course.* New York, McGraw-Hill Book Co., Inc., 1939. 464 pp.

COLE, LUELLA, *The Background for College Teaching.* New York, Farrar and Rinehart, Inc., 1940. 616 pp.

EDWARDS, RICHARD H., ARTMAN, J. M., and FISHER, GALEN M., *Undergraduates.* New York, Doubleday, Doran and Co., Inc., 1928. 369 pp.

GAVIT, JOHN P., *College.* New York, Harcourt, Brace and Co., 1925. 342 pp.

GRAY, WILLIAM S., ed., *Current Issues in Higher Education.* Chicago, University of Chicago Press, 1937. 153 pp.

—— ed., *General Education; Its Nature, Scope, and Essential Elements.* Chicago, University of Chicago Press, 1934. 188 pp.

—— ed., *Recent Trends in American College Education.* Chicago, University of Chicago Press, 1931. 253 pp.

JOHNSTON, JOHN B., *Education for Democracy.* Minneapolis, University of Minnesota Press, 1934. 280 pp.

—— *The Liberal College in Changing Society.* New York, The Century Co., 1930. 326 pp.

KELLY, FREDERICK J., *The American Arts College.* New York, The Macmillan Co., 1925. 198 pp.

KELLY, ROBERT L., ed., *The Effective College.* New York, Association of American Colleges, 1928. 302 pp.

SCHILPP, PAUL A., ed., *Higher Education Faces the Future.* New York, Horace Liveright, 1930. 408 pp.

Swarthmore College Faculty, The, *An Adventure in Education: Swarthmore College under Frank Aydelotte.* New York, The Macmillan Co., 1941. 236 pp.

WILLS, ELBERT V., *The Growth of American Higher Education; Liberal, Professional and Technical.* Philadelphia, Dorrance and Co., 1936. 225 pp.

and: Many of the items listed in the Selected Bibliography for Chapter VII.

C. For World War II and the future:

Alumni Committee on Postwar Amherst College, A Report of the, "Amherst Tomorrow," *Amherst Alumni Council News,* XVIII, 3, February, 1945.

Committee on the Re-Statement of the Nature and Aims of Liberal Education, Report of the, "The Post-War Responsibilities of Liberal Education," *Association of American Colleges Bulletin*, XXIX, 2, May, 1943.

Faculty Committee on Long Range Policy, Report of the, *Amherst College* [Amherst, Mass.], "January, 1945." 157 pp.

Harvard Committee, Report of the, *General Education in a Free Society*. Cambridge, Harvard University Press, 1945. 267 pp.

Higher Education and the War, The Report of a National Conference of College and University Presidents, . . . January 3–4, 1942. American Council on Education Studies, Series I, No. 16, Vol. VI, February, 1942.

MILLER, J. HILLIS, and BROOKS, DOROTHY V. N., *The Role of Higher Education in War and After*. New York, Harper and Brothers, 1944. 222 pp.

NASON, JOHN W., "What Have We Learned?" *Journal of Higher Education*, XV, 6, June, 1944.

CHAPTER III

RELIGION IN THE TWENTIETH CENTURY

MOVEMENTS in the field of religion in the twentieth century have had large influence in determining what part religion was able or allowed to play in higher education. For an intelligent comprehension of the place of religion in the colleges, one needs to know not only what was happening generally in those institutions, but also what changes and developments were taking place in the churches and in the thinking of religionists. Our discussion of such matters will of necessity be brief and incomplete, but an effort will be made to identify the major areas of thought and action.

A. RELIGION VERSUS SCIENCE

At the turn of the century it appeared that religion was involved in a death struggle with science. The world of scientific knowledge had been tremendously expanded in preceding decades. Nearly every advance seemed to cut across and call into question some cherished item of faith or dogma. The latter half of the nineteenth century had furnished what looked to be the crushing blow to religion in the large acceptance in various fields of Darwin's theory of evolution. Along with increased discovery of "facts" there developed the notion that the only valid way of arriving at truth was through a dispassionate analysis of observable phenomena, the "scientific method." With its dependence upon revelation, religion was looked upon by many scientists as "unscientific" and therefore both unnecessary and false.

It is not the part of this essay to discuss the contentions of the scientists or to analyze the philosophical strains which were supporting their positions: rationalism, naturalism, empiricism, positivism, determinism and crass materialism. The "isms" were hard at work, together producing the all-encompassing secularism of the times, the influence of which upon the college scene has already been noted. But relevant to this discussion is the strategy which religion adopted toward these concerted attacks upon its position. The answers can be reduced to two. Some religious leaders condemned science, called the conflict irreconcilable, and refused to face the demand for a new interpretation of religion. Others sought to make their peace with scientific discoveries, denied that any conflict existed or needed to exist, and tried to rephrase their religious beliefs in the light of the new knowledge. The first represented the abdication of the field to science; the second consisted of a more orderly retreat from long-established positions. In either case, religion was on the defensive in the early years of the century before the new champion, science.

In recent times the controversy has diminished greatly in its fury. The causes were several. First of all, the second of the two approaches suggested above triumphed among religious leaders; the "conflict," religion decided, was no real struggle of diametrically opposed forces after all. Moreover, in making its adjustment to new theories and facts, religion substituted an affirmative for a defensive stand, both about itself and about science, conceived now as its ally. Science in the meantime had begun to find some of its more enthusiastic assumptions inadequate and to recognize the limitations of the scientific method as the sole avenue for arrival at truth. And as the Western world girded itself to oppose the monstrous doctrines of fascism and nazism, science and religion discovered that they held certain values in common. The idea of a "master race," for example, was both irreligious and unscientific. Critical differences of opinion between the two continue to exist, but the gulf of separation has been bridged.

The trend of this controversy has had its reflections in the colleges. In the early years of the century, the larger institutions tended to discount religion because of its alleged opposition to science. The attacks of some religious leaders upon such theories as that of evolution confirmed these institutions in their decision to eliminate all pursuits which militated against a free search for truth. At the same time the multitude of small church-related colleges gathered their religious loyalties around them ever tighter, thereby sometimes gaining a reputation in educational circles of not being academically sound. Religion's reaction to the progress of science was, up to approximately World War I, a contributing factor in the secularization of much of higher education.

In the last twenty-five years, however, the trend has been in the opposite direction. When it was discovered that religion and science could work together in harmony, the colleges which had dispensed with religion began to take it back into the academic fold. When, later, it was realized that the two needed each other's support against the attack of mutual enemies, then religion's place in the colleges became more secure. And when, in recent years, science has confessed, both by public statement of its high priests and by public example in the latest war, to its inability to save the world, the role of religion has become of crucial importance in such citadels of man's searching as the colleges. The diminution of the old controversy and the substitution of a new partnership have had a profound effect in giving religion a large place in higher education.

B. FUNDAMENTALISM VERSUS MODERNISM

The two approaches which religion made to the pretensions of science in the early years of the century constituted two warring camps within religion itself. On the one hand were the "fundamentalists" who opposed scientific findings in as well as outside of religion, who fought Darwin as the incarnation of the devil, and who guarded with fervor the dogmas and religious mores of the past. On the other were the "modernists" who professed a respect for science and the scientific method, who used that method in the examination of religious knowledge, and who reinterpreted the faith of our fathers in the light of a new day. The struggle between these two general positions, with their varied ramifications, has loomed large in the religious picture of the twentieth century.

The battle has been most fiercely joined on the question of the proper interpretation of the Bible. The fundamentalists have held strictly to an idea of "verbal inspiration" that postulated absolute accuracy in every word, dictated by God. Their sins have been catalogued as "literalism, legalism, bibliolatry, and archaism." [1] The modernists, on the other hand, have followed the leadings of "higher criticism." They have looked upon the Bible as the record of man's longing and search for God and for meaning in human life, composed by numerous hands in various stages of man's spir-

1. Amos N. Wilder, "The Christian Tradition in Modern Culture," in George F. Thomas, ed., *The Vitality of the Christian Tradition* (New York, Harper & Brothers, 1944), p. 211.

itual development and consequently reflecting different levels in the attainment of spiritual insight.

At the beginning of our period the modernist position was already accepted by leading scholars but had not yet seeped into the thought of the churches in any large measure. Judging by the volume and intensity of comment, the innocent bystander would have thought that most churchmen were "defending" the Bible and the Christian religion against the iconoclastic scholars. In the intervening years, however, a gradual change has been wrought until now it is difficult to find any leading churchman who would espouse the fundamentalist point of view. Yet that is not to say that fundamentalism is dead, for in many individual churches and in a few colleges of various denominations the fundamentalist position is still advocated. As wartime always inclines people to seek an easily identifiable authority, today fundamentalist "truth" has once again proved attractive to many ill informed on religion. But in thinking circles the real battle is long since done, and modernism has emerged triumphant.

The conflict has played a part in keeping religion out of higher education. For fear that the only religion which could or would be taught and preached would be fundamentalist in tone, many colleges in early years preferred not having any at all. Thus while the controversy was at its height, it hindered the efforts of those who sought to incorporate religion in institutions of higher learning. Then as it became clear that modernism, with its respect for scholarly endeavor and its liberal spirit, would triumph, the inclusion of religion was made easier.

But the effects of the controversy were still evident in latter days in the college scene. Teachers of religion and even college presidents have been exposed sometimes to snipers' fire from fundamentalists outside the college walls, and occasionally heresy hunts have been instituted. These, however, have not been widespread or critical in their influence. The real danger growing out of the old fight has been within the college itself, in the religious misconceptions of many faculty members and students. Though modernism has won its victory, the churches have done a poor job in telling their laymen about it. Thus hosts of scholars, well informed in their own particular fields, have continued to labor under the fundamentalist notions of their early youth and of their former local churches, and are in reality religious ignoramuses. Either they accept ideas in the field of religion which they would long since have discarded in some other field, or they ignore religion because they think that those are the only ideas religion has. The same false alternative obtains in greater degree in student bodies. In either case, religion suffers, and the vestiges of an obsolete fundamentalism render more difficult the task of making religion a vital force on a college campus.

C. RELIGIOUS EDUCATION

The emergence of such issues as the two thus far discussed indicate the importance of possessing religious knowledge as well as faith. The ignorance of religious people about their religion, not to mention those who professed no faith, was truly appalling. Around 1900, therefore, religious leaders began to argue that religion not only could be but had to be "taught as well as caught." Horace Bushnell had laid the groundwork in his *Christian Nurture,* originally published in 1860, but "religious education" as a conscious movement within the churches dates from the turn of the century. Impetus was furnished by such volumes as the symposium, *Principles of Religious Education,* of 1900, and George A. Coe's *Education in Religion and Morals,* of 1904.[2] Direction to the movement was given by the Religious Education Association, founded in 1903, and later by other coöperative and denominational agencies.

The purpose was to encourage the teaching of the subject matter of religion in Sunday schools and secular institutions. The movement has grown phenomenally throughout the century until not merely the Sunday schools but all parts of the churches' life have been affected. The changes marking the differences between today's churches and those of fifty years ago have been caused, it is safe to say, more by their wholesale assumption of an educational responsibility than by any other one factor. Nor has the field of secular education been neglected; numerous efforts have been instituted to incorporate religion into the public schools of the land. The churches have taken seriously their duty to teach.

All this, of course, has had direct influence upon the colleges. The moving spirit in the founding of the Religious Education As-

2. Horace Bushnell, *Christian Nurture* (New York, Charles Scribner's Sons, 1916) ; *Principles of Religious Education* (New York, Longmans, Green & Co., 1900) ; and George A. Coe, *Education in Religion and Morals* (New York, Fleming H. Revell Co., 1904).

sociation was a university president, William Rainey Harper of Chicago, and among its early leaders were other chief executives such as W. H. P. Faunce of Brown, H. C. King of Oberlin, J. H. Kirkland of Vanderbilt, Rush Rhees of Rochester and C. F. Thwing of Western Reserve. Such men as these were interested in religious education because, among other reasons, the institutions of higher learning were beginning to acquire a reputation for "godlessness," and they were seeking to stem the tide in their own colleges. Throughout the years leaders in the movement have always paid large attention to the campus, and theirs have often proved the decisive efforts in persuading colleges to allow religion a place in their courses of study. It is no accident that the revival of religion in higher education has followed closely the growth of the religious education movement.

Religious education advanced a more basic argument for its recognition than mere ignorance of the field. Religious leaders began to be interested in the "whole man," not just his "soul," at about the same time that education proclaimed its concern for a similar unity, not just the mind. As long as man was easily divisible into "mind," "body," and "soul," then religion could take salvation of the soul as its special sphere, education could center attention upon the discipline of the mind, and they could go their separate ways in peace. But, religious educators began to argue, the theory of the "whole man" brings religion and education together and demands that colleges give religion its rightful place. Thus the influence of religious education, through its development of a theory of education similar to that of the colleges, has resulted in the inclusion of religion not merely in the curriculum but in the total program.

But in spite of the growth of the movement, the churches often performed their newly conceived educational functions in shoddy fashion. The actual task of teaching in the Sunday schools was necessarily left largely in the hands of amateurs, who themselves were often grossly ill informed. Thus even students from churchgoing families continued to arrive at college abysmally ignorant of their faith. Moreover, the huge increase in the number attending college meant also an increase of students from homes without any church connection. Of late years, therefore, some colleges have been persuaded to include religion because of this yawning omission in knowledge which the students bring. In this regard, it may be said that the failure of the religious education movement, as well as its growth, has resulted in an increased provision for religion in the college scene.

D. THE SOCIAL GOSPEL

Religion's developing concern for the "whole man" meant, also, an awakening interest in the whole life of man. The Hebrew-Christian tradition has always made place for prophetic souls who sought to apply their religion to the betterment of society, and the nineteenth century, particularly in Great Britain, witnessed an astounding growth in social consciousness among the churches. Around 1900 religious leaders in America, led by such pioneers as Washington Gladden and Walter Rauschenbusch, were beginning to preach a "social gospel." Gradually their efforts produced a profound change in the message of the churches so that, as the century grew older, every part of man's activity was subjected to searching scrutiny in the light of the Christian ethic. Churchmen plunged into the forum, the market place, and the arena to build the kingdom of God on earth. In the last decade or so, the earlier optimism and utopian pretensions of the movement have given way to a more realistic estimate of society's problems and of the tremendous obstacles in the way of bringing in the kingdom. But the efforts themselves have not slackened. That Christianity must concern itself with society's diseases is a conviction that is here to stay.

The areas in which the new social conscience has been applied are multitudinous. Temperance, child labor, woman's suffrage, prison reform, the labor movement, race relations, business ethics, the abolition of war, the maintenance of peace—these are only some of the more prominent problems to which Christians have addressed themselves. At first the movement expressed itself largely in efforts of amelioration for underprivileged individuals and groups. In later years it has deepened and broadened by an examination of and attacks upon the causes for injustice, inequality, and misery. The various parts and the whole structure of society have been subjected to analysis and improvement in the light of Christian demands.

Colleges and their religious programs have taken note of the development. It would be difficult to maintain that the rise of the social gospel, in itself, had any large influence in bringing religion back into higher education. But the kind of religion that was brought back, as the result of other factors, was determined in large measure by this movement. College religious programs have followed its emphases with enthusiasm. Moreover, institutions committed to an interest in the whole life of man were more inclined to incorporate religion if it possessed a similar breadth of vision and liberality of spirit. To this extent, therefore, the social gospel rendered easier the task of making a place for religion in higher education.

E. ECUMENICITY

The nineteenth has been called the "Great Century" in the expansion of Christianity. The tremendous growth of the missionary movement in all churches brought every part of the world within the Christian orbit of influence. In the twentieth century missionary activity has continued to receive a large amount of the churches' interest, owing to the impetus given to it by the preceding years. The strategy of the movement, however, has undergone change. The former philosophy of taking the gospel to the heathen has become one of sharing religious insights with those of other lands and of building autonomous churches in the non-Christian nations. Doubts concerning the importance of the missionary enterprise have sometimes been expressed by consecrated churchmen as well as by outsiders, and for a time the old fire perceptibly cooled. Of late, however, the churches once again are emphasizing without apology their world-wide mission, this time stressing the virtues of closer association among Christians of all lands and of coördination of efforts in the missionary fields.

The recognition by various groups of Christians that the new day calls for larger coöperation is a significant development not limited solely to the area of missionary activity. Though there is nothing in our period comparable to the nineteenth-century extension of missions, yet one of the distinctive marks of the present era has been the demand for unity of effort and unification of organization in all parts of religion's domain. The universality and oneness of Christian endeavor have been expressed in a variety of ways under the general rubric of "ecumenicity." Increasing coöperation has been fostered by the Federal Council of Churches of Christ in America, founded in 1908, by numerous other interdenominational bodies for performing particular functions established in succeeding years, and by American participation in world-wide religious agencies, culminating in the recent formation of the World Council of Churches. A sense of community has been built by the large numbers of conferences of church leaders, locally, nationally and internationally, drawn from all denominations but Rome. Actual unification has been attempted among scores of church bodies and effected in a growing number of instances, the largest being the Methodist union of 1939 of three separate groups totaling almost eight million members. The efforts of religion to discard its outmoded sectarianism and to speak with a united voice constitute one of the most notable developments of the twentieth century.

Since sectarian emphases had worked against the presence of religion in the colleges, the trend of recent years in the opposite direction has had its expected effect in making religion more acceptable to higher education. The breadth of understanding and activity implicit in both the missionary movement and the various expressions of ecumenicity commended itself to an institution of large horizons such as the college. Moreover, once religion was included, this growth of coöperation influenced the nature of collegiate religious programs, for such programs almost without exception, even among colleges sponsored by individual denominations, have been interdenominational or nondenominational both in spirit and in practice.

F. THEOLOGICAL THOUGHT: LIBERALISM AND NEO-ORTHODOXY

As would be expected, such developments as religious education, the social gospel and ecumenicity were accompanied by a widespread searching of mind and heart and a thorough effort to undergird the activity with a dependable philosophy. This ferment of thought was especially notable in the field of theological inquiry. Amid all the cross-currents of opinion, two distinctive contributions can be identified as the products largely of the twentieth century.

The first has been called, for lack of a better word, "liberalism." Rooted in the previous century, it sprang to fullest flame in the first three decades of the present period and its glow still suffuses all of religion. Liberalism in theology denoted both a certain attitude of mind and a certain content. As attitude, it was closely kin to the general liberalism of the times, with its devotion to truth, its respect for a dispassionate search for knowledge, and its tolerance and open-mindedness. As content, it emphasized the centrality of Christ, which resulted in assertions concerning the adequacy of Jesus' gospel for the present day, the validity of the Christian experience, and the perfectibility of man and society.[3]

But because of liberalism's own weaknesses and the catastrophes of society, a reaction was bound to set in. The last ten or fifteen years have witnessed the second major theological movement, commonly referred to as "neo-orthodoxy." Such a term covers a variety of positions but a general area of agreement is discernible. Criticism has been leveled at the unrealistic optimism and subjectivity of the liberal theology, although such gains as the objective study of the Bible, the developing social consciousness, and the growth of ecumenicity have been cherished. The positive contributions of the new movement consist of forceful reinterpretations of past thinking—Calvin, Luther, Augustine, and Paul— and of a more realistic appraisal of the present scene, based upon a less sanguine estimate of man's nature.

Both liberalism and, in recent years, neo-orthodoxy have been related to the general winds of opinion blowing over Western culture in the twentieth century. Both, therefore, have found points of contact with the philosophies of education which the colleges were promulgating. While the colleges, at least until the depression, were expanding and confident, utilitarian and secular, the spirit of liberal theology during the same period was to a large extent sympathetic. When, however, higher education came to examine its own basic purposes more thoroughly and to rediscover values from its neglected past, it found the neo-orthodoxy of the time advocating similar points of view. Thus the temper of theological thinking has to a large extent paralleled that of educational thinking. This fact has been significant for the problem of the inclusion of religion in the colleges: institutions were more inclined to welcome religion when they knew its analysis of the present and its prevailing mood were similar to their own.

G. RELIGION'S INTEREST IN STUDENTS

As we have seen, therefore, the major developments in the field of religion have had large significance for the colleges' religious

3. See Henry P. Van Dusen, "The Nineteenth Century and Today," in George F. Thomas, ed., *op. cit.*, pp. 168–174.

life. The influence, in the main, has been a happy one. It is true that the struggles in the early years of the century—religion versus science and fundamentalism versus modernism—worked toward the secularization of higher education. But the way in which those controversies were settled, together with the effect of the growing movements of religious education, the social gospel, and ecumenicity, and the trend of theological thought, all combined to help reverse the process of secularization and to indicate both the propriety and the necessity of the inclusion of religion.

Before the colleges acted in any large measure, however, religion itself attacked the campus. Its approach was twofold. First in point of time was the voluntary, non-denominational method represented by the Young Men's Christian Association, the Young Women's Christian Association, and the Student Volunteer Movement. Spreading rapidly in the closing years of the nineteenth century, these agencies were generally accepted for at least the first two decades of our period as the major channels through which the religious interest of the students was to find expression. In recent years they have continued to perform tremendously useful functions and, in spite of some criticism, their programs are probably more effective today than ever before.

But it remains true that these voluntary agencies bulk less large in the total collegiate picture than they did thirty or forty years ago. As the colleges grew in size and complexity, the Associations found it increasingly difficult to serve alone large bodies of students or to wield an influence upon administrations with which they had only unofficial connections. Moreover, the growth of church-sponsored student religious programs inevitably decreased the scope and therefore the significance of the Christian Associations. That they have continued to make progress is eloquent testimony not merely to their firm rootage in the past but also to their keen insight into the spiritual needs of students and to their success in fulfilling them.

The church-sponsored programs represent the second approach made by religion to the campus. As the numbers of students increased in the early part of the century, particularly in tax-supported institutions, different denominations began to feel that sufficient provision was not being made for the religious life of their adherents. Accordingly in the first decade many of them instituted student work on the state university campuses. From 1910 to 1920 such work was put on an organized, national basis, and came to rank in scope and importance with the programs of the Christian Associations. The 'twenties and 'thirties witnessed a steady growth of the movement in its various expressions—"the college pastorate," the denominational "foundation," "club," "association," and "student movement." Of late years the movement has spread into the independent and church-related colleges, until now it covers the whole collegiate world. The efforts of the churches to follow their students constitute one of the most substantial developments in the life of organized religious groups in the twentieth century.

On the face of it this movement would seem to be a divisive force, separating the campus religious life into numerous independent parts, all bearing denominational labels; and as a matter of fact a few of the church-sponsored programs have been characterized by a narrow sectarianism. But for the most part a sincerely coöperative spirit has grown among the various denominational efforts and between them and the nondenominational Christian Associations. On most campuses some sort of over-all religious council has been established to coördinate the various programs, and many religious activities have been sponsored in concert. Another local expression of coöperation has been the establishment of a number of "Schools of Religion" or "Bible Colleges" at the side of tax-supported institutions, to furnish instruction in religious subjects.

On a national scale the professional leaders in the field have been organized in various groups, beginning with the Association of Church Workers in State Universities, formed in 1910, now called the Conference of Church Workers in Universities and Colleges of the United States. In 1912 the Council of Church Boards of Education was organized; this became the parent group of the Association of American Colleges, founded in 1915. The Y.M.C.A. and the Y.W.C.A. have learned to coöperate with each other through the National Intercollegiate Christian Council, and interdenominational action has been fostered by the National Commission on University Work of the Council of Church Boards of Education. Christian Associations and church groups pooled their activities during the war in the highly successful War Emergency Council for Student Christian Work, set up in 1942. This organization encouraged the formation in 1944 of the broadest coöperative venture yet undertaken, the United Student Christian Council. Nearly all student groups support or take part in the World Student Christian Federation, the World Student Service Fund, the Student Volunteer Movement, and the University Christian Missions. Coöperative organizations, therefore, are not lacking. Though the interest of organized religion in students has not been expressed in a permanent united program, the will to coöperate has largely saved the total movement from sectarian and divisive emphases.[4]

These various efforts have had large influence for both the inclusion and the exclusion of religion from colleges' official programs. On the one hand, higher education has often been led to sponsor a program of its own because of the alleged inadequacy or competition of the unofficial movements or because such movements seemed to need official supervision. On the other, their presence on or at the side of the campus has persuaded some institutions that the religious life of their students was already well cared for and thus that no official program was needed. The general trend, however, has been toward a larger concern for religion on the part of the college, for whether the voluntary agencies did a good or a poor job, their presence and activity served to underline the importance of religion for the students.

H. STUDENT RELIGIOUS ATTITUDES

One further development in the field of religion, of an entirely different sort from the "movements" thus far discussed, has significance for the college scene. The attitudes toward religion on the part of young people, particularly of students, have influenced both the nature and the extent of the college religious programs. For the early years of the century it is difficult to get an accurate picture of students' points of view. Since waves of religious fervor would beat upon the campuses at various times and then recede, a survey at any one date would show large concern at one place, neglect at a second, and cynicism at a third. So far as is known, no thorough analysis of attitudes was attempted in the early years of the century, but President Thwing of Western Reserve, an

4. See Clarence P. Shedd, "The Movements of Religion in American Higher Education," *Journal of the American Association of Collegiate Registrars*, October, 1945, pp. 13–20.

acute observer of the academic life, summed up the situation in 1914:

The grandfather, who was in college sixty years ago, asked in dread and fear, "Is my soul saved?" . . . The father, who was in college thirty years ago, . . . asked, "Is your soul saved?" The son does not ask either question. He is content to live the life of the Christian. Salvation is taken for granted in a world of, by, and full of, goodness.[5]

But times have once again changed, and the student of 1914 who took salvation for granted, yet was still worried about studying on Sunday,[6] is father to the student of the present day who hardly knows the meaning of the word "salvation" and is both ignorant and contemptuous of religious customs and institutions.

Since the early 'twenties numerous studies have been made of the religious attitudes of undergraduates. The results have shown marked, though not overwhelming, interest in questions of a religious nature, coupled with a general distrust of organized religion. What interest existed, however, was pitifully uninformed, usually conservative, and often not recognized as such. In recent years the trend toward a more serious attitude in all subjects on the part of students has had its counterpart in a heightened interest in religion. The war has given an impetus to this modest "return to religion," though it remains to be seen whether a comparable return to the church will take place. And it is tragically true that, in spite of all the good work done by religious agencies and by colleges themselves, the majority of student bodies is still composed of happy pagans who are blissfully ignorant in the field.[7]

The influence of the religious attitudes of students upon the problem of the place of religion in higher education has been pronounced throughout the twentieth century. In the early years most students came from church-going families and possessed,

5. C. F. Thwing, *The American College: What It Is and What It May Become*, p. 154.

6. *Ibid.*, pp. 157–163.

7. See Lincoln B. Hale *et al.*, *From School to College; A Study of the Transition Experience* (New Haven, Yale University Press, 1939), chap. viii; Daniel Katz and F. H. Allport, *Students' Attitudes* (Syracuse, Craftsman Press, 1931); chaps. xv, xvi, xvii; R. C. Angell, *The Campus* (New York, D. Appleton & Co., 1928) chap. ix; and Charles W. Gilkey, "The Place of Religion in Higher Education," in the University of Pennsylvania Bicentennial Conference symposium, *Religion in the Modern World* (Philadelphia, University of Pennsylvania Press, 1941).

therefore, a smattering both of religious knowledge and of faith. Thus, though student interest was not uniformly keen, the colleges felt they could safely leave the task of encouraging religious growth to other agencies. But since the first World War the students' increasing religious poverty of information and of personal conviction have forced the colleges to reëxamine their purposes and programs. State institutions, independent universities, even church-related colleges, were turning out graduates by the thousands who were religiously illiterate and insecure. Church-related colleges, independent universities, even state institutions, could not rest easy under such abysmal results of their educational procedures. The outcome has been that numbers of them have proceeded to rectify the tragedy by making increased provisions for religion in their curricula and in their extracurricular life. Probably more than any other single factor, this realization of the religious shallowness of students has been responsible for the growing place which religion is occupying in higher education.

SELECTED BIBLIOGRAPHY FOR CHAPTER III

Among countless books in the field, the following were illuminating for one or more of the sections above:

ANDERSON, WILLIAM K., ed., *Protestantism: A Symposium*. Nashville, Commission on Courses of Study, The Methodist Church, 1944. 290 pp.

COE, GEORGE A., *What Is Christian Education?* New York, Charles Scribner's Sons, 1929. 300 pp.

ELLIOTT, HARRISON S., *Can Religious Education Be Christian?* New York, The Macmillan Co., 1940. 338 pp.

Hazen Books on Religion. New York, Association Press, 1936–40. 12 vols.

HOPKINS, HOWARD, *The Rise of the Social Gospel in American Protestantism, 1865–1915*. New Haven, Yale University Press, 1940. 352 pp.

KATZ, DANIEL, and ALLPORT, FLOYD H., *Students' Attitudes, A Report of the Syracuse University Reaction Study*. Syracuse, The Craftsman Press, Inc., 1931. 408 pp.

MARITAIN, JACQUES, and fourteen others, *Religion and the Modern World: University of Pennsylvania Bicentennial Conference*. Philadelphia, University of Pennsylvania Press, 1941. 192 pp.

SHEDD, CLARENCE P., *The Church Follows Its Students*. New Haven, Yale University Press, 1938. 327 pp.

――――, *Two Centuries of Student Christian Movements*. New York, Association Press, 1934. 466 pp.

SHIPLEY, MAYNARD, *The War on Modern Science*. New York, Alfred A. Knopf, 1927. 415 pp.

SMITH, H. SHELTON, *Faith and Nurture*. New York, Charles Scribner's Sons, 1941. 208 pp.

SPERRY, WILLARD L., ed., *Religion in the Post-War World*. Cambridge, Harvard University Press, 1945. 4 vols.

THOMAS, GEORGE F., ed., *The Vitality of the Christian Tradition*. New York, Harper and Brothers, 1944. 358 pp.

WEIGLE, LUTHER A., *American Idealism*. New Haven, Yale University Press, 1928. 356 pp.

WILLIAMS, J. PAUL, *The New Education and Religion: A Challenge to Secularism in Education*. New York, Association Press, 1945. 198 pp.

CHAPTER IV

ATTITUDES TOWARD RELIGION:
THE CHURCH-RELATED COLLEGE

RECENTLY a responsible position in the administration of one of America's foremost universities became vacant. A certain faculty member who had a large interest in the religious life of the students was suggested for the job. But the remark with which the president dismissed his name was, "Oh, he's just a 'Christer.'"

That bit of institutional gossip indicates something of the president's attitude toward religion. The knowledge of this attitude gives a clearer understanding of the reason for the small part which religion plays in the life of that campus. Of course such a story dare not be given documentation. It is included only to illustrate the importance of considering, and trying to discover in more legitimate ways, the attitudes of colleges toward the religious growth of the students. Obviously, what a college says about religion has an unmistakable bearing on what the college actually does for the undergraduate.

Nevertheless, the difficulty of discovering such attitudes is apparent. What are we to take as expressing the college's genuine stand on religion? The place which religion holds in college histories may give us a clue, but they are notoriously rose-colored and often oppressively subjective. A long and careful firsthand examination of individual institutions may furnish us with decided opinions as to the present situation, but for the past we are dependent upon hearsay. And even for the present we find our opinions are too easily shaped by such unverifiable stories as the one reported above. Statements in college catalogues, when they bear the stamp of careful composition, are indicative of institutional points of view, but often they fail to meet this basic requirement.

Probably the most accurate basis for determining college attitudes to religion is an examination of the statements of administrators, particularly college presidents. Yet even this method has been assailed. Cynics ask, Can one put any reliance upon what college presidents say? Percy Marks wrote: "One would think from reading their speeches that they were a hopelessly commonplace tribe, as devoid of ideas and as incapable of honest thinking as a hack writer of sensational editorials." [1] It has been suggested that the type of institution which they represent, church-controlled, independent, or state-supported, commits them to a certain attitude. [2] And even if they do not represent a denominational college, any support of religion which they affirm may be motivated at least partially by the belief that their constituency wants to hear such pious utterances.

But though such doubts can sometimes be substantiated, the conviction still remains that what college presidents say is important. With all their faults, as recognized by President Harper of Chicago many years ago, the typical member of their group "is not usually a 'liar' or a 'boss.' " [3] Even Marks admitted: "The wonder is not that they seek refuge in platitudes but that they manage to offer those platitudes with sufficient seriousness to hold the public respect, and the greatest wonder is that they dare to speak at all." [4] Recently a volume on higher education which has received wide reading has been composed completely of *What College Presidents Say*. [5] The following discussion will be based, therefore, primarily upon the statements of college presidents, with corroborative material from other sources. If such material often seems inadequate, it is still the best available.

The treatment will be historical, and will be divided into three chapters corresponding to the three major types of institutions, church-controlled, independent, and tax-supported. Often the line of demarcation is far from clear. An institution may claim to be independent while still preserving some form of denominational connection, or vice versa. In a few cases, such as Cornell University, Syracuse, and Alfred, some departments or schools are state-supported while others are free from public control. Moreover, a host of institutions have changed type during this century. The

1. Percy Marks, *Which Way Parnassus?* (New York, Harcourt, Brace & Co., 1926), p. 51.

2. Edgar W. Knight, *What College Presidents Say* (Chapel Hill, University of North Carolina Press, 1940), p. 350.

3. W. R. Harper, "The College President," in R. N. Montgomery, ed., *The William Rainey Harper Memorial Conference* (Chicago, University of Chicago Press, 1938), p. 34.

4. Marks, *op. cit.*, p. 52.

5. Knight, *op. cit.*

categorizing of such doubtful colleges in the following discussion will largely follow their present rather than their original type. For all institutions the determination of type will rely in the main upon the "Lovejoy College-Rating Guide" and the guidebook of the American Council on Education, *American Universities and Colleges*.[6] We shall begin with the church-related colleges.

A. CONTINUITY OF INTEREST

The most prominent fact about the attitude of the denominational colleges to religion is the consistency with which they have professed a religious aim. Owing their foundation to men whose paramount interest was religion, they have not betrayed the faith of their fathers. Thus, throughout the twentieth century, the presidents of the church colleges have eagerly given their testimony concerning the place of religion in higher education. Only a few quotations are necessary to illustrate this widely acknowledged attitude.[7]

President John H. Harris of Bucknell, who held office from 1889 to 1919, may be taken as typical of the early years of the century. Although he himself was not a minister, he preached thirty-one baccalaureate sermons between 1890 and 1924, all full of evangelical fire and Christian conviction. His attitude to religion was stated in his inaugural address:

The institution which devotes her energies to the training alone of the intellect fails in her most important function. Character is the man, and the strength of character is moral goodness. Morals must find their root in religion and draw their strength from it, and the only religion of force to transform the life of man is the religion of Jesus the Christ.[8]

In the middle years of our period the emphasis was continued. At a conference at Ohio State University in 1920, President John W. Hoffman of Ohio Wesleyan said:

6. See C. E. Lovejoy, *So You're Going to College* (New York, Simon & Schuster, 1940), pp. 267–340; and C. S. Marsh, ed., *American Universities and Colleges* (4th ed. Washington, American Council on Education, 1940).

7. See, for example, Floyd W. Reeves *et al.*, *The Liberal Arts College* (Chicago, University of Chicago Press, 1932), chap. ii; and Leslie K. Patton, *The Purposes of Church-Related Colleges* (New York, Teachers College, Columbia University, 1940).

8. John H. Harris, *Thirty Years as President of Bucknell* . . . (Bucknell University, 1926), p. 103.

A complete education must therefore provide for the proper development of the spiritual life as well as the most effective training of reason and imagination. . . . Religion should pervade the entire educational process. . . . While no school can preserve the great variety of forms of faith our students bring to the classroom, every school is under the most sacred obligation to preserve the reality of religious faith in the student.[9]

Recently other voices have pursued the same theme. The President of Muhlenberg, Levering Tyson, reminded his audience at his inauguration in 1937 that the college's

. . . chief purpose was not only to make it possible for young men . . . to be trained as ministers, or as laymen . . . , but also to be a witness, to bear vital testimony, that a living religion must be an active force in the life of an educated man. From the start this purpose steadfastly has been maintained. . . . Times have changed. . . . Nevertheless, Muhlenberg has stood firm in support of its original purpose. I would be recreant to my trust if I did not state here and now, unequivocally, that I will continue this fundamental purpose. All my predecessors have been ministers of the gospel. As the first layman you have chosen to be president of your College, I want particularly to express my determination to uphold this policy, my belief in its soundness, and my pride and confidence in making this public declaration.[10]

The catalogues of denominational colleges offer further evidence of their interest in religion.

The religious tradition bequeathed by the Quaker founders has been carefully cherished. . . . The aims of Haverford have been gradually developing and its function is becoming more and more clear—"to encourage the growth . . . of vigorous bodies, scholarly minds, strong character, and a real religious experience." [11]

The College [Illinois College] is convinced that appreciation of spiritual values and growth in moral qualities are fundamental purposes of a college of liberal arts.[12]

9. John W. Hoffman, "The Religious Ideal in Education," in T. C. Mendenhall, ed., *History of the Ohio State University*, Vol. III, *Addresses and Proceedings of the Semicentennial Celebration, October 13–16, 1920* (Columbus, Ohio State University Press, 1922), pp. 106–107.

10. *Induction to the Presidency of Levering Tyson, October 2, 1937* (pamphlet. Allentown, Muhlenberg College, 1938), pp. 29–30.

11. *Haverford College Bulletin*, XXXIX, 2 (November, 1940), 7–8.

12. *Illinois College Bulletin*, XXVIII, 3, Series I (March, 1940), 81.

The College [Westminster College, Pennsylvania] recognizes its distinctively Christian traditions and character; its aim is consciously to inculcate the basic truths of the Christian religion and to inspire its students to lives of Christian service.[13]

The aim and purpose of the University are clearly set forth in the following statement formulated by the University Senate:

". . . Furthermore, inasmuch as religious faith is the essential basis of right conduct and as that faith is best cultivated through the aid of Divine Revelation, the University of the South regards as indispensable to the realization of its ideals of cultured and useful manhood, systematic courses of instruction in the Bible. Finally, as there is no true progress without a goal, the University of the South states this to be the end and objective of its effort in any and all of its departments: the realization of the Kingdom of God, which is the kingdom of love, as interpreted in the life and teaching of Jesus Christ." [14]

The pattern of continuity can be traced not only in denominational colleges as a group, but in the records of many individual institutions. For this purpose college histories prove useful. Though a few pay little heed to the religious life of the institution, the great majority show conclusively the presence of the religious aim and interest in all periods of the college's existence. Notable among those whose chronicles have been published are Colby, Emory, Gettysburg, Hanover, Haverford, Lafayette, Maryville, Wooster, and Yankton. Their judgments are sometimes exaggerated, but there is no disputing the intensity of interest which characterized the colleges' attitudes toward religion.

Particularly interesting is the history of Otterbein College, since it was written not by a faculty member or alumnus, but by a graduate student at Ohio State University. His unprejudiced testimony confirms the enduring religious emphasis of the college:

Christian idealism is not another department of instruction. It does not consist of certain classes in Religious Education, in Bible, a daily chapel service, and a few religious meetings. Christian idealism is rather a spirit which may underlie and motivate the entire life of an institution, including all student activity, all departments of teaching, and all phases of the administration.

13. *Westminster College Bulletin* [Pennsylvania], Catalogue Issue, January–March, 1940, 16.

14. *Bulletin of the University of the South*, XXXIV, 4 (February, 1940), 20–21.

. . . Otterbein College, from the very first, has been largely
characterized by such a spirit.[15]

Again, in summary, he noted that Otterbein's

. . . religious history has differed from that of many colleges
in that she was largely free from over-emphasis on doctrinal
matters. . . . Otherwise her religious thought and practices
have followed general trends, passing from the emotionalism of
the earlier days, through a stage in which the attitude was more
calm and earnest, to the post war period which has been characterized by a tendency toward indifference. But throughout all the
changes of the years, the thing which has remained uppermost
in the life of the college has been her Christian idealism.[16]

Such an estimate coincides with the attitude of President W. G.
Clippinger, who said in 1927:

Self-realization is accomplished and education is complete only
when the student transcends the bounds of sense and time and
comes into the world of spiritual realities. . . . Any education
which falls short of religion, and of spirit, and of ideals in its program, is faulty.[17]

B. FROM DEFENSE TO AFFIRMATION

But while there has been consistent interest in religion throughout the century, marked changes have occurred within this pattern. First of all there may be noted a gradual shift from a defensive to a more positive attitude.

In the early years the secularizing tendencies in education were
felt sharply by the church colleges. As President W. L. Poteat of
Wake Forest said, "The complete secularization of education
means in the end national disorder, disintegration, and decay." [18]
The denominational institutions were thought to be "the only
bulwarks against the growing evil of secularism in modern life." [19]
The newly elected President of Gettysburg College, W. A. Gran-

15. W. W. Bartlett, *Education for Humanity: The Story of Otterbein College* (Westerville, Ohio, Otterbein College, 1934), p. 236.

16. *Ibid.*, pp. 255–256.

17. W. G. Clippinger, *Student Relationships* (New York, Thomas Nelson
& Sons, 1927), pp. 128–129.

18. Quoted in Frederick Eby, *Christianity and Education* (Dallas, Executive Board of Baptist General Convention of Texas, 1915), p. 194.

19. *Ibid.*, p. 190.

ville, said in 1910: "We cannot remain a Christian nation without Christian leaders, and where do our Christian leaders come from if not from denominational colleges?" [20]

Such an attitude went hand in hand with the usual notion that the state universities could do nothing in the field of religion. The church-related colleges were on the defensive against the increasing secularism of the larger institutions. Writing at a time when the situation had already begun to improve, W. S. Athearn, President of Butler University, accused the church colleges "of the neglect of the specific service [religious education] for which they have been founded and of unwarranted imitation of the standards, ideals, and content of secular education." [21] Thus he blamed them "for their feeble Christian testimony on the college campus. The atmosphere is apologetic." [22]

But with the passage of years a new note of confidence crept into the statements of church college presidents. The denominational institution no longer apologized for its interest in religion, no longer defended its continued existence merely as a deterrent to the secularization of education. Administrators boldly talked of the dominant part which religion ought to play in their educational programs. W. A. Harper, President of Elon College, wrote in 1928:

The church colleges must undertake to do all that any other type of institution of higher learning may legally undertake, and at the same time must go beyond and make religion and the teaching of religion the primary, the permeative, the integrating, the unifying force of all their life and program.[23]

The year before, the new President of Denison, A. A. Shaw, had said in his inaugural:

We cannot be satisfied to consider the Christian Religion as a department in the curriculum. It must become the enlivening and integrating spirit of the whole institution.[24]

20. Quoted in S. G. Hefelbower, *The History of Gettysburg College, 1832–1932* (Gettysburg College, Gettysburg, 1932) p. 290.

21. W. S. Athearn, *The Minister and the Teacher* (New York, The Century Co., 1932), p. 202.

22. *Ibid.*, p. 206.

23. W. A. Harper, *Character Building in Colleges* (Cincinnati, Abingdon Press, 1928), p. 178.

24. *Inauguration of President Albert A. Shaw, Denison University, October 21, 1927* (pamphlet. Granville, Ohio, 1927), pp. 36–37.

The central place which religion should hold has in recent years been the theme of numerous administrators. At his inauguration as President of Marietta College in 1937, Harry K. Eversull expressed the desire that his institution provide "a God-centered education":

Here then is the basic point about which the higher learning in the small endowed colleges must revolve—namely, the idea of God. Here is the heart and soul of higher education, for here is the one form of education capable of lifting society from the depths of hedonism, creating in the minds of men the ability to think fearlessly and clearly, and to appreciate values which are essential to a morally ordered corporate life.[25]

C. F. Wishart, President of the College of Wooster, referred in 1938 to the "Babel of discord" in the college scene, and added:

Prominent educators are not blind to this deplorable situation. Men like President Hutchins, of the University of Chicago, are boldly asserting that some integrating factor must be found to remedy this hopeless confusion. . . . Why not organize your thinking around religion? It is the one common denominator of all intellectual life. . . . This powerful universal, indestructible instinct which impels men to worship and to pray is the one factor which binds men together and whose constructive influence reintegrates the soul and the social order. . . . Surely if there was ever a time when moral and ethical and religious training should be at the center of every college campus, that time is now.[26]

Related to this more confident attitude is the disappearance of the older notion that a college's denominational affiliation provided sufficient testimony to its religious character. Mere organic connection with a church was recognized as proving nothing. Thus the Dean of Brothers College of Drew University, Frank G. Lankard, recently pointed out:

We must not take our religious tradition for granted. There is a fallacy in the assumption made all too often that in a denomina-

25. *The Inauguration of Harry K. Eversull as Ninth President of Marietta College, October 20, 1937* (pamphlet. Marietta, Ohio, Marietta College Press, 1937), p. 38.

26. C. F. Wishart, "Religion," in symposium, *On Going to College* (New York, Oxford University Press, 1938), p. 230.

tional college no special attention needs to be given to the task of character building and of religious faith, feeling that this phase of the work will go on by itself.[27]

The consequence is that in Brothers College, as in other denominational institutions, the problem of religion is being given particularly serious consideration at the present time:

We regard religion as being so vital and creative in democracy and culture that we want our entire educational program to be carried forward in an atmosphere which is friendly to and surcharged by vital and creative religious ideals. We conceive of our entire program as a reverent search after truth in a setting where a vital religious faith is recognized as being the greatest motivation to the highest and noblest living.[28]

C. THE PASSING OF SECTARIANISM

A second change in the church colleges' interest in religion has been the progress from a sectarian to a nonsectarian emphasis or spirit. This is not synonymous with, though it is related to, the shift of a college from denominational affiliation to independent government. Whereas a small percentage of colleges broke away from their church connections in the first decades of the century, nearly all colleges have been characterized by a decreasing emphasis on sectarianism.

In the early days many denominational colleges were still obviously Lutheran, or Methodist, or Baptist, or whatever. A "vital connection with a particular denomination" was felt to be necessary.[29] All the paraphernalia of the conservative point of view often accompanied this sectarianism: a suspicion of science, a fundamentalist approach to the Bible, a revivalistic methodology. Traces of such attitudes are still evident here and there. For example, in 1935 the faculty of Oklahoma Baptist University published a symposium entitled *Why Christian Education,* the preface of which stated: "The university is frankly conservative. It re-

27. F. G. Lankard, "Brothers College Today and Tomorrow," in C. F. Sitterly, *The Building of Drew University* (Cincinnati, Methodist Book Concern, 1938), p. 239.

28. *Ibid.,* p. 234.

29. Eby, *op. cit.,* pp. 195–197.

flects and represents the Baptist churches of Oklahoma, in atmosphere and attitude. Its objective is, therefore, CHRISTIAN CULTURE." [30]

Chapter III, written by the "Dean of Faculties," was significantly entitled: "The 'B.' in O.B.U., a Baptist Obligation and Opportunity."

Such manifestations of a sectarian spirit are happily uncommon in the college picture today. Its frequent companion, fundamentalism, is still a problem in many of the churches across the land, and thus a factor which has to be taken into account in college programs of instruction in religion. But the colleges themselves have passed beyond such battles. The changes in religion through the years have been eagerly accepted by higher education. For sectarianism particularly, the trend has been strongly toward a more ecumenical and liberal point of view. In 1917 the President of Haverford College, Isaac Sharpless, wrote: "Haverford makes no claims to being undenominational." [31] He continued, however, with a prophecy which is being fulfilled: "But sectarianism . . . is something for which men care less each year and its strength sooner or later will be undermined." [32]

Lafayette College illustrates the shift in emphasis. John Henry MacCracken, its president during and immediately after World War I, had a large interest in the inclusion of religion in higher education:

Some way, some how, some where, as we take stock for the future of America, we must make provision for that ideal college, where knowledge shall be exact and complete, character robust and gracious, and Christianity not only a welcome guest, but the ruling spirit within its walls.[33]

But for Lafayette it seems to have been the Presbyterian form of Christianity with which he was most concerned. In his inaugural address in 1915 he contended that the college

30. Faculty of Oklahoma Baptist University, *Why Christian Education* (Shawnee, Okla., Oklahoma Baptist University Press, 1935), Preface.

31. Isaac Sharpless, *The Story of a Small College* (Philadelphia, John C. Winston Co., 1918), p. 227.

32. *Ibid.*, p. 224.

33. John H. MacCracken, *College and Commonwealth* (New York, The Century Co., 1920), p. 395.

. . . may seek to train leaders, prophets, seers. She may even be religious, Presbyterian if you please, and make religious exercises a part of her compulsory curriculum.[34]

His successor, William Mather Lewis, had no less pronounced an interest in religion, but the element of sectarianism was absent from his thought. His sentiments are outstanding for their conviction, their lack of denominational tinge, and their clarity in stating the abiding religious purposes of the church college. At his induction into office in 1927 he said:

Lafayette has always been known for the positive religious influence which is here exerted. Empty formalism finds no place; but a vital expression of the belief that education which fails to stress spiritual values is inadequate to the needs of a workaday world. Here we shall maintain religious activity which does not end with stimulating lofty desires and exalted emotions but which carries over into the everyday life of the campus, finding its expression in loyalty and good sportsmanship, in kindliness and clean living. Here we shall strive for those ends which release spiritual verities from watertight compartments and with them flood and purify the most routine and commonplace activities of life.[35]

And again in 1932, at the New York University centennial conference, he said:

Above and beyond all there stands the element of religion, without which the abundant life is impossible, the religion which, surmounting creeds and doubts and the cynicisms of little men, carries the soul into the central presence. This religion is not to be found so much by youth through preachments as through those opportunities for meditation which in the overcrowded program of university life we so often deny them.[36]

A simple statement in the college catalogue sums up the matter: "Lafayette College is affiliated with the Presbyterian Church. The College is however, Christian rather than denominational." [37]

34. *Ibid.*, p. 19. This Presbyterian emphasis runs throughout the volume, particularly in chaps. xxvii, xxviii, xxix, and xxx.

35. W. M. Lewis, *From a College Platform* (New York, Dial Press, 1932), pp. 98–99.

36. *The Obligation of Universities to the Social Order* (New York, New York University Press, 1933), p. 403.

37. *Bulletin of Lafayette College*, XXXIV, 7 (March, 1940), 6.

Lafayette is not alone. With both the past struggles against secularization and the overemphasis on denominationalism in mind, the church colleges today join in an overwhelming chorus to affirm their nonsectarian religious purposes. Impartial investigations have borne out their protests. In 1932 a study of the aims of thirty-five Methodist institutions led to the conclusion:

Statements culled from recent issues of their bulletins and literature emphasize the fact that they are Christian in spirit and aims, although not sectarian in any narrow sense, whether in curriculum or in the general atmosphere of the college.[38]

And Robert L. Kelly, former Executive Director of the Association of American Colleges, wrote in 1940:

While most colleges related to the Protestant churches now have Departments of Religion or of Biblical Literature and extensive programs for assisting their own youth, very few undertake to offer even elective courses which interpret the peculiar doctrines of the denominations to which the colleges are related. They do not teach the creeds. The sectarian spirit has largely been eliminated.[39]

D. THE ADVENT OF RESPONSIBILITY

A third development in the thinking of church colleges is concerned with the distinction between mere interest in, and self-assumed responsibility for, the religious life of the students. In the early years many administrators considered that encouragement of such voluntary groups as the Young Men's Christian Association was adequate evidence of their zeal for religion. The historian of Birmingham-Southern wrote:

There has always been in the minds of those who have been at the head of the College a realization of the fact that the religious welfare of the students is one of the chief concerns of the administration. . . .[40]

But, to illustrate this concern, he mentioned three agencies: the Methodist Church built at the side of the campus, the pastor of

38. Reeves, *et al., op. cit.,* p. 406.

39. Robert L. Kelly, *The American Colleges and the Social Order* (New York, Macmillan Co., 1940), p. 267.

40. W. D. Perry, *A History of Birmingham-Southern College, 1856–1931* (Nashville, Methodist Publishing House, 1931), pp. 75–76.

which served as chaplain of the College; the Young Men's Christian Association; and "a religious life conference" held for a week each year in the college chapel.[41]

Similarly President H. P. Houghton of Waynesburg College, in his inaugural address in 1916, declared his interest:

I come now to the religious or spiritual side of our four-sided college. Denominational control of an institution does not necessarily make an institution Christian. . . . Every college . . . under denominational control or not, should and must stand for the highest Christian principles and beliefs.[42]

But what makes the college Christian? He looked primarily to two agencies: the character of the professors, and:

Strong factors in the building up of fine Christian characters in the college are the Young Men's and Young Women's Christian Associations.[43]

Noticing such attitudes on the part of both denominational and independent colleges in the early years of the century, President Harper of Chicago wrote:

. . . it is probably true that those institutions founded avowedly as Christian colleges all through the states have done too little in the way of making provision for a sound religious education of the students committed to their care; while in the larger institutions or universities on private foundation—partly because of ignorance or uncertainty as to the definite thing which should be done, partly also from indifference, and partly because of that cowardly spirit which too frequently in these days characterizes even good men and good institutions in connection with anything that is religious—the entire matter has been allowed to drift on and on with nothing tangible to show in the form of result.[44]

Here a word of explanation should be inserted lest any disparagement seem intended for the work of the Christian Associations. The point is not that any program sponsored officially by the college is better than any voluntary activity. No one at all

41. *Ibid.*, pp. 76–77.
42. *The Business of the College, Inaugural Address by H. P. Houghton,* June 14, 1916 (pamphlet. Waynesburg, Pa., Waynesburg College, 1916), pp. 13–14.
43. *Ibid.*, p. 14.
44. William R. Harper, *The Trend in Higher Education* (Chicago, University of Chicago Press, 1905), pp. 55–56.

acquainted with the history of religious work on college campuses could think so. The contention is simply that unless protestations of interest lead to a certain measure of responsibility, their sincerity is suspect. In 1929 Laird T. Hites condemned roundly the situation in which the church college

. . . declares publicly . . . that the principal reason for its existence is to develop religious values in students—and then places the entire matter of student guidance in religious affairs on a purely voluntary basis, without leadership, and without financial support.[45]

In more recent years the church colleges have not ceased to foster voluntary groups, but many of them have begun to recognize that such agencies cannot carry all, or perhaps even the major part, of the responsibility. In 1923 President Harris of Bucknell wrote:

The Christian Associations are very helpful in promoting the religious life of the College. At the same time the President and Faculty must not shift the whole responsibility upon them.[46]

Recognizing the beneficial "efforts of the churches" and of "voluntary associations of students," President Harper of Elon, writing in 1928, placed particular emphasis upon

. . . the agencies provided by the institution itself in its administrative attempts to supply a religious atmosphere and opportunity for self-expression spiritually for its students.[47]

He felt that in the last analysis the college must be responsible:

The coordination, correlation, and integration of these provisions and agencies of the religious life of our college campuses is a problem of major concern for college administrators and one that they cannot decline to face or fail to undertake measures to remedy.[48]

And so, during recent years, the interest of the church-related colleges in religion has proceeded to the recognition of their own obligation to function. A fitting conclusion for this section is furnished by the statement made in 1933 by Homer P. Rainey, then

45. Laird T. Hites, *The Effective Christian College* (New York, Macmillan Co., 1929), p. 206.

46. Harris, *op. cit.*, p. 75.

47. W. A. Harper, *op. cit.*, p. 97.

48. *Ibid.*, p. 110.

President of Bucknell, later of the University of Texas, and now of Stephens:

A college must plan for the religious development of students in the same way that it provides for their growth in all other fields. Religion and morality are an area of human experience on the same basis as chemistry or music. Religion is also a matter of "experience-getting"—of living creatively. The liberal college, therefore, must offer opportunities for the full development of one's religious life. It must provide the facilities for acquiring religious experiences, and, furthermore, it must stimulate and encourage students in the acquisition of these experiences.[49]

49. Homer P. Rainey, "The New Educational Program at Bucknell University," chap. vi in W. S. Gray, ed., *Needed Readjustments in Higher Education* (Chicago, University of Chicago Press, 1933), p. 86.

CHAPTER V

ATTITUDES TOWARD RELIGION: THE INDEPENDENT COLLEGE

INDEPENDENT colleges are an ill-defined group. "Church-related" and "state-supported" are delimiting, and "independent" means everything not thus designated. Lacking definition, they also lack corporateness, for though there is a National Association of State Universities and a National Conference of Church-Related Colleges, there is no federation of the independent institutions. Thus the independents range from those founded originally with religious purposes, such as Harvard and Dartmouth, to those founded with frankly secular purposes, such as Clark and Johns Hopkins. They may have passed out of the control of churches gradually, as with Amherst and Williams, or broken away suddenly, as with Vanderbilt. They may still preserve some tenuous connections with denominations, such as Duke and Northwestern, or may on the other hand be partially state-supported, such as Cornell University and Rutgers. Whatever they are, they represent all varieties of educational philosophy and program, from St. Johns of Maryland to Sarah Lawrence, from Reed to Rollins, and from Mills to Massachusetts Institute of Technology. It is not surprising, then, that every shade of attitude toward religion is represented among the independent colleges.

A. INDIFFERENCE AND HESITANCY

First of all, the indifferent or negative attitude is well represented. Now a tactful college executive would hardly go out of his way to proclaim his lack of interest in the religious life of the students. This attitude is discernible, therefore, not in outright disavowal but in the omission of religion where the subject could properly and profitably be introduced. Histories of colleges in which the factor of religion plays no part may reflect nothing more than the inadequacy of the author's survey. But even the most prejudiced author could ignore the subject entirely only when the religious interest of the college under consideration was so slight that its omission would cause no serious distortion of the actual conditions. Similarly, the statements of college presidents which omit the subject might signify merely the incompleteness of their treatment. But one would hardly suppose that such obviously important statements as inaugural addresses would be intentionally incomplete.

When, too, a college, in some special celebration or conference, presents nearly every aspect of human life but religion, the exclusion would seem to be based upon something other than accident. One recalls, for example, the negligible role of religion in the program of the Harvard Tercentenary in 1936, and the fact that among the sixty-two honorary degrees awarded to distinguished guests on that occasion, only two could be thought of as being related to their religious work.[1] President C. F. Wishart of Wooster felt the implication from the Harvard celebration to be that "after three centuries of higher education, the scholars of the world had to confess that they had made no real impact on human character and conduct."[2] Or perhaps it was merely that Harvard did not care. As one of its own family admitted: "Harvard University has often been reproached for indifference or infidelity concerning religion."[3] A perusal of the important speeches and writings of Presidents Eliot, Lowell, and Conant fails to reveal any adequate grounds for questioning such a reproach.

Yet Harvard has not been alone. It is singled out for special mention because of the institution's great influence in higher education. When Siwash ignores religion, harm is done to Siwash and, in a limited area, to religion. But when Harvard adopts a negative attitude, it is likely to have repercussions throughout the college scene and upon religion generally. Actually the situation is not as discouraging as the attitudes of its chief executives would indicate, for Harvard sponsors a not insignificant religious program. It is deplorable that Harvard's lack of bark is worse than its bite.

No useful purpose would be served by listing other omissions of this sort, whether motivated by lack of interest or by positive opposition. Suffice it to say that throughout the century a number

1. *The Tercentenary of Harvard College* (Cambridge, Harvard University Press, 1937), pp. 217–221.

2. *On Going to College*, p. 230.

3. F. G. Peabody, "Voluntary Chapel," in S. E. Morison, ed., *The Development of Harvard University Since the Inauguration of President Eliot, 1869–1929* (Cambridge, Mass., Harvard University Press, 1930), p. lvii.

of independent colleges and their administrators have disregarded the subject of religion on occasions in which its consideration was strongly indicated.

Equally as elusive as the indifferent or negative attitude is that characterized by varying degrees of tentativeness. For these institutions interest in religion seems to be present but is qualified by a certain reservation or hesitancy. This qualification may be recognized in such circumlocutions as the identification of religion with "truth" or "reverence" or "the higher and better things" or "rich, purposeful, rounded, effectual character." It may be noted in the skillful use of passages of Scripture unaccompanied by any forthright original statement: " 'Except the Lord doth build the house, they labor in vain that build it.' " It may consist in references to the religious purposes of those connected with the college in the past, unsupported by any commitment on the part of the speaker for the present. All these types of hesitancy and reservation can be given documentation from among the speeches and writings of administrators of independent institutions.

A qualification of a different nature is one which has already been mentioned in connection with the church-related colleges— an interest in religion coupled with a willingness to allow the voluntary religious organizations to undertake the major part or all of the task of caring for the religious life of the students. When this relinquishing of responsibility is prompted by a conviction, justified by the facts, that the voluntary groups can do a better job for the college than the college can do through its official action, then there should be no question as to the sincerity of the institution's interest in religion. But when this conviction and the facts to bear it out are lacking, the college faces the charge of insincerity in its protests of concern. In any one instance it is difficult to judge which of these alternative explanations is trustworthy. Whatever the proper interpretation of their action, a number of independent institutions through the years have adopted this strategy. It has been especially characteristic of urban universities in which the religious resources of the community are rich and varied. Putting the very best face on the practice, however, one is still inclined to catalogue as only hesitant interest that expression of concern which owns to little or no consequent obligation of its own. Note the weakening effect of the final phrase in the following statement of President Dixon Ryan Fox of Union College (New York), made in 1937:

Few of us, at least in the private colleges, want to encourage students to accept mere doubt as a creed. We have been talking of philosophy, but we have come to the door of religion. Certainly many of us feel that the student should be encouraged to step through that door and look about, to contemplate what religion has done and is doing for man and not to reject it until he has given it a fair experimental trial, whether under college auspices or not.[4]

B. INTEREST AND RESPONSIBILITY

Present all along with the indifferent and tentative attitudes toward religion have been examples of independent colleges and of their administrators showing a strong, positive interest. In the early days of the century many of these executives took the lead in the new religious education movement, their particular concern being the field of higher education and its growing secularization. All the men mentioned before in the discussion of that movement —Harper of Chicago, Faunce of Brown, King of Oberlin, Kirkland of Vanderbilt, Rhees of Rochester, and Thwing of Western Reserve—spoke on the subject at various times with vigor and clarity. Henry Churchill King concluded one of his discussions of the relationship between religion and education:

It is not possible for us to stand strongly for education in its full modern sense and not find ourselves driven to the recognition of essential religion.[5]

Charles F. Thwing played on this general theme throughout his long career at Western Reserve. In 1929 he republished his inaugural address of 1891 to show his continuing allegiance to the ideas expressed there:

The denominational college is loyal to a denominational interpretation of Christianity—all honor to it. The Christian college is loyal to Christianity itself. . . . The great college and university are to be as free from denominational control as they are to be pervaded with the spirit of Christianity. . . . In aim the college

4. D. R. Fox, "The Liberal Arts and the College," in "Sesqui-Centennial Celebration Addresses," *Franklin and Marshall Paper*, I, 12 (December, 1937), 11.
5. Henry C. King, *Personal and Ideal Elements in Education* (New York, Macmillan Co., 1915), p. 83.

is to be Christian. . . . In method and agency the college is to
be Christian. . . . In motive the college is to be Christian.[6]

At his induction into the presidency of Amherst in 1912, Alexander Meiklejohn declared that

. . . a student should become acquainted with the fundamental
motives and purposes and beliefs which, clearly or unclearly
recognized, underlie all human experience and bind it together.
He must perceive the moral strivings, the intellectual endeavors,
the esthetic experiences of his race, and closely linked with these,
determining and determined by them, the beliefs about the world
which have appeared in our systems of relgion.[7]

In recent days mention of religion has occurred with increasing
frequency, and has consisted of more than mere interest. Accompanying nearly every statement of concern is an implied or, more
often, a direct recognition of responsibility for making that concern tangible and operative. The later the quotation, the more
likely it is that the sense of obligation as a necessary concomitant
of interest will be unequivocal and enthusiastic.

One further characteristic of the following selection of remarks
calls for mention. Divorced from organic relationship with any
church, the independent institutions feel less compulsion to speak
out on the subject of religion than church-related colleges. The
statements of their executives are less automatic and consequently
more significant. An examination of their wording indicates that
they tend also to be less platitudinous than the opinions of church
college presidents. Their significance is enhanced when one remembers that the independent colleges in larger degree than either
of the other two groups serve as the pace-makers for higher education. The impact of such institutions as Yale, Princeton, Swarthmore, and Oberlin upon the educational scene is still the major
source of fruitful ferment. When these speak for religion the rest
of the collegiate world takes notice.

In the former section the majority of available illustrations came
from the earlier years of the century; for this section the preponderance of example is furnished by the last two decades. Among

6. C. F. Thwing, *Education and Religion* (New York, Macmillan Co.,
1929), pp. 240–241.

7. A. Meiklejohn, *Freedom and the College* (New York, The Century Co.,
1923), p. 184.

the host of statements to which reference might be made, the following are representative:

President James L. McConaughy of Wesleyan (Connecticut) said at his inaugural in 1925:

A college that is not Christian is not a college at all. . . .
Christianity is the only religion that is concerned with each individual. . . . Inevitably, then, a college deeply concerned with the individuality of each of its students must be truly Christian. This is Wesleyan's opportunity and task. To accomplish it, we rededicate all the idealism and power of this Christian college.[8]

Hamilton Holt, President of Rollins, recognized his institution's responsibility in 1930:

Then I also believe that religion or one's philosophy of life should play a large part in education. . . . For if you limit the educational process to sharpening the mind, without at the same time developing the will power to keep it sharpened, and the moral sense to use it for a worthwhile project, you may be educating a menace to society, rather than an ally.[9]

In 1932 President Ernest H. Wilkins of Oberlin argued that other things may have to wait until the student has been graduated:

But for the field of religion the college student is already of age, and into that field, if provision be well made, he may, within college, enter with rightful and fruitful immediacy.[10]

. . . the college can hardly desire not to provide under its own auspices the opportunity for general religious worship, conceived not as a means of education, but as an end in itself—as an occasion when students may, for a time, come together out of strenuousness into quietness, out of multiplicity into unity, under circumstances such that communal religious consciousness may in good measure be attained. I therefore believe that the college should, with such frequency as it may deem wise, provide voluntary services of worship in its own chapel.[11]

8. *The Installation of President James L. McConaughy as Tenth President of Wesleyan University, June 5, 1925* (pamphlet. Middletown, Conn., 1925), pp. 44, 47.
9. Hamilton Holt, "Creative Education," chap. xv in P. A. Schilpp, ed., *Higher Education Faces the Future*, pp. 313–314.
10. E. H. Wilkins, *The College and Society* (New York, The Century Co., 1932), p. 20.
11. *Ibid.*, p. 95.

His estimate of the importance of making opportunity for worship was shared by President Robert C. Clothier of Rutgers, at his inauguration in 1932:

And finally, it is my sincere belief that the university chapel, on whatever campus it is located, can and should be a vibrant influence in the spiritual life of the campus and should make its contribution to the development of the individual. Whatever his creed or doctrine, which is a matter of individual conscience, it is impossible to think of a man or woman as truly educated who lacks an understanding and grasp of spiritual values, who has not acquired a reverent sense of his relationship to this incredible universe in which he lives. I believe in a university chapel as the center from which this attitude of life spreads to classroom and dormitory, to fraternity house and athletic field. I think of it as the theatre for the expression of religious thought where the student may acquire, in an atmosphere of reverence, a knowledge of spiritual truths. I believe in it, too, for the reason that the student who attends may, if he wishes, bow down and worship his Father who is in Heaven.[12]

Henry M. Wriston, then President of Lawrence and now President of Brown, wrote the following in 1937:

Has not the moment come when education may dare to base its program upon the integrity of life? We know that while we learn with the mind, the drives which impel us to learn are emotional. Therefore to insist upon intellectuality as the only aim is to deny the whole process of education itself.[13]

Thus religion must have a place in the college's program:

Religion will make its uniquely rich contribution to the life of the students if it is part of their environment—a natural, inevitable part, rather than an "activity" which gyrates in its own orbit, separate from other activities. To fail to make religious experience part of the student's life is to destroy utterly the foundation upon which alone the college may justify its existence. To impoverish that experience by sectarian or other irrelevancies is tragic, but to neglect it is fatal.[14]

12. *The Inaugural Address of President Robert C. Clothier, June 11, 1932* (pamphlet. New Brunswick, Rutgers University, 1932), pp. 13–14.

13. H. M. Wriston, *The Nature of a Liberal College* (Appleton, Wis., Lawrence College Press, 1937), p. 116.

14. *Ibid.*, p. 120.

Many independent colleges reflect through their catalogue statements this positive interest in religion. If "nonsectarian" or "interdenominational," this interest is all the more vital and compelling, and is indicative of the assumption of responsibility for the religious life of the students which many have undertaken. The following statements are representative:

In accordance with this ideal [of the founders] the College [Lake Erie College] has continued to be interdenominational in its management but distinctly Christian in spirit, welcoming students of every faith.[15]

In practice as well as by charter, Syracuse University is nonsectarian, but it upholds the Christian traditions which are its background, and with liberality of viewpoint tries to provide an unmistakable Christian influence.[16]

The purpose of the founders of this College [Milwaukee-Downer College] was to establish an institution for the liberal education of women, at once distinctly Christian and distinctly non-sectarian. In full sympathy with this purpose, recognizing the essential value of religion to character, the administration of the College encourages the religious life.[17]

C. EBB AND FLOW

Thus in the independent colleges there have always existed attitudes toward religion ranging all the way from indifference through various degrees and types of tentativeness to that positive interest which expresses itself in self-assumed responsibility to care for the students' religious life. The fact that indifference and hesitancy were more characteristic of the century's early years whereas interest and responsibility were more evident in recent times indicates the presence of an ebb and, particularly, flow in these attitudes. This ebb and flow is discernible in the life of individual institutions as well as in the independent group as a whole. For some colleges, the interest seems to lessen and become tentative as the century grows older; for others, there is a con-

15. *Bulletin of Lake Erie College*, Series 35, No. 5 (January, 1940), 93.

16. *Syracuse University Bulletin*, LXIX, 1 (July 1, 1939), 29.

17. *Bulletin of Milwaukee-Downer College*, Series 22, No. 3 (February, 1940), 21.

tinuity of positive interest; for a third group, a steady growth in concern throughout the period is clear.

Of the first of these Dartmouth is a good example. Judged on the basis of its presidents' attitudes, Dartmouth cares less about religion now than it did at the turn of the century. Under the leadership of President W. J. Tucker, who served from 1893 to 1909, the College assumed a pronounced responsibility for religion. The historian of the College noted that "Dr. Tucker's appeal was for the recognition of religion as the central element of life." [18] At his inauguration Tucker said:

The college performs an office which, I take it, no man will question as it translates the original and constant religious impulse into terms of current thought and action, making itself a center of spiritual light, of generous activities, and, above all, of a noble and intellectual religious charity. [19]

His successor, Ernest Fox Nichols, continued this emphasis:

Religion is a side of the student which the present formal curriculum does not touch directly. To fill out and complete our system, therefore, some broad and effective religious teaching should be provided. . . . It is in a comparative study of religious teachings that I firmly believe Christianity will soonest achieve its rightful and vital supremacy in the minds of college men. [20]

Ernest M. Hopkins followed Nichols in 1916. With his coming the former clear enunciation of religious interest and responsibility became tentative and vague. In his inaugural there was no mention of religion; the closest he came was in the sentence:

Scholarship as a product of the college is incomplete except as it be established on the foundation of character which is not only passively good, but which is of moral fibre definite enough to influence those with whom it is brought into contact. [21]

In 1919, discussing the purpose of Dartmouth, he seemed to identify religion with idealism, and the religious purpose of the early college was translated into one of service:

18. Leon B. Richardson, *History of Dartmouth College* ([Hanover, N.H.], Dartmouth College Publications, 1932), pp. 745–746.

19. Quoted in *ibid.*, p. 669.

20. *The Inauguration of E. F. Nichols as President of Dartmouth College, October 14, 1909* (pamphlet. Hanover, N.H., Rumford Press, 1909), pp. 60–61.

21. *The Inauguration of E. M. Hopkins, Eleventh President of Dartmouth College, October 6, 1916* (pamphlet. [Hanover, N.H.], Rumford Press, 1916), p. 66.

The founders' altruistic purpose of converting the heathen savage to the glory of God becomes in modern parlance a desire to convert society to the welfare of man. Either purpose requires the highest idealism, and the highest idealism is the purest religion, the symbol of which is God and the manifestation of which is the spirit of Christ. May this ever be the spirit of Dartmouth College! [22]

Again in 1930 he made oblique references to religion, but no definite statement of interest:

. . . the college has responsibility to cultivate the feelings as well as the minds of its membership. . . . If the only options available to the American college were to graduate men of the highest brilliancy intellectually, without interest in the welfare of man-kind at large, or to graduate men of less mental competence, possessed of aspirations which we call spiritual and motives which we call good, I would choose for any specific college the latter alternative. [23]

It is not to be disregarded that the words "holiness" and "health-fulness" and "wholeness," with the implication that if wholeness were attained, somehow or other holiness also would be present; but still no mention was made of religion:

It is not to be disregarded that the words "holiness" and "health-fulness" and "wholeness" derivatively go back to the same root. . . . The influence of our colleges and universities, today as in former times, should be in behalf of that wholeness of man which is healthfulness and which is holiness . . . the initial obligation rests upon us to make the college influential in the development of those traits vital to well-proportioned goodness. [24]

From the firmness of Tucker and Nichols, therefore, Dartmouth has proceeded to the hesitancy of Hopkins. Those who covet Dartmouth's former leadership in religion are hoping that the trend will be reversed under the new President, John Sloan Dickey.

Throughout the period a second and much larger group of independent colleges have attested to their keen interest in religion. For fruitful illustration one could refer to the executives' state-

22. E. M. Hopkins, *Dartmouth College: An Interpretation of Purpose*, Dartmouth College Reprints, Series I, No. 3 (Hanover, N.H., December, 1919), p. 11.

23. E. M. Hopkins, "Attributes of the College of Liberal Arts," chap. vii in P. A. Schilpp, ed., *op. cit.*, p. 167.

24. *College Responsibilities in Modern Life* (pamphlet. [Hanover, N.H.], Dartmouth College, 1938), p. 6.

ments, institutional histories, and other publications of Columbia, Goucher, Mount Holyoke, Oberlin, Pomona, Wellesley, Wesleyan and Yale, to mention only a few for which documents are readily available. The remarks of the presidents of some of them have already been given; others will be treated later in a description of administrative programs of religion. For the present the University of Chicago can serve as a provocative example.

Chicago's first President, William Rainey Harper, who wielded large and beneficent influence over the educational scene, set the tone for his institution in the century's early years. Writing in 1905, he argued strongly for the place of religion in colleges and universities.

If the higher institutions of learning in recent years have, with a remarkable degree of unanimity, felt the demand made upon them to undertake physical education as a necessary part of the college and university work, it will hardly be possible to draw a line that will shut out religious education.[25]

His attitude was that religion, as religious education, ". . . is a part of the whole education of a man, lacking which the man lacks completeness, and unity, and, consequently, strength." [26] President Ernest DeWitt Burton, who was influential in the University's affairs long before he became its chief executive in 1923, spoke for the middle years of our period. Discussing the "Ideals of a University," he said:

Finally, the University stands for religion . . . religion is something more than morality, and . . . the University stands for both. . . . It stands for it because we believe that the whole history of the race shows, and never more clearly than now, that learning and religion can never be safely divorced. Each needs the other. Religion needs the free atmosphere of the university to keep it from becoming superstition or bigotry. Learning needs religion to keep it from becoming selfish and pedantic.[27]

Just before his death he said:

In the last two weeks I have seen more clearly than ever before in thirty years what this university ought to be and may become.

25. W. R. Harper, *The Trend in Higher Education*, pp. 57–58. See his full discussion in chap. iii, "The University and Religious Education."

26. *Ibid.*, p. 77.

27. E. D. Burton, *Education in a Democratic World* (Chicago, University of Chicago Press, 1927), pp. 52–53.

. . . In that future and for its realization, the moral and religious life of the university is more central and important than I have ever before realized it to be.[28]

President Robert M. Hutchins gave the subject silent treatment during his first years at Chicago. But the administrative policy had been so firmly set that the University's sponsorship of religion, to be described in detail in a later chapter, was not disturbed. Moreover Hutchins himself, without doing violence to his general educational philosophy, which will also be discussed later, came to welcome the study of theology on the campus:

Theology and the theological school are at the apex of the university and its studies because they seek to supply the answers to the ultimate questions about the most fundamental matters with which the university is concerned. Metaphysics and natural theology deal with these questions, too. But intellectual history reveals nothing so clearly as their inadequacy for the task. The existence and nature of God, the character and destiny of the human soul, and the salvation of man are problems which remain obscure in the light of natural reason. Theology, which adds faith to reason, illuminates them.[29]

This is not far from religion. In fact, "religion," rather than merely "theology," is the word he used in a recent attack upon the position of John Dewey. Hutchins argued that the student must seek the "integration in his own life" of the three factors, "philosophy, science and religion," and that only the kind of education which provides for all three can "help us meet the most urgent necessity of our time." [30]

The recent administrative changes at Chicago give Hutchins the title of Chancellor and bring Ernest C. Colwell to the presidency. Since Colwell was formerly Dean of the Divinity School, the confident expectation is that in him the University will find another strong champion for the ideal of a vital religion in higher education.

While some colleges were allowing their interest in religion to grow perfunctory and dim, and others were evidencing a continu-

28. Quoted in R. H. Edwards, J. M. Artman, and Galen M. Fisher, *Undergraduates* (New York, Doubleday, Doran & Co., 1928), p. 251.

29. Quoted in an editorial, *Christian Century*, LX, 46 (November 17, 1943), 1327.

30. Robert M. Hutchins, "Education for Freedom," *Christian Century*, LXI, 46 (November 15, 1944), 1316.

ous and hearty concern, still another group were passing step by step from various shades of indifference to real responsibility for the religious growth of their students. Once again, several institutions could be chosen as examples. Because its progress has been well documented Princeton will be used as the illustration.

It would be untrue to the facts to say that Princeton had ever been without an interest in religion. But in the early years of the century the attitude seemed to be that of encouraging the work of voluntary groups while continuing as well as possible what had been done in the past. In 1915 the Philadelphian Society, which was Princeton's unit of the Young Men's Christian Association, held a series of religious meetings, and President John Grier Hibben signified the approval of the administration in the following words:

In a place devoted to the pursuit of learning, where our students are brought face to face with the great world problems of the past and of the present, and are ever encouraged to think their way into and through these problems, it would be strange indeed were their thoughts never particularly directed to the serious consideration of the place of religion in their lives.[31]

Princeton's appeal for endowment funds in 1919 was made, with respect to religion, in order to "maintain" existing provisions:

The authorities of the University recognize the importance and significance of making an especial effort at this time to maintain all of the Christian activities of the University in a manner befitting our religious tradition, and in recognition of the faith and hope of those who were the original founders. . . .[32]

But times changed, and maintenance and encouragement were not enough. Though this benevolent hands-off policy was characteristic up to the 'twenties, that is not to say that Princeton's religious life was not well cared for. It so happened that the Philadelphian Society was strong and extremely active; and possibly mere encouragement from the administration was sufficient during the first two decades of the century. But in the early 'twenties

31. John G. Hibben, Introduction, in Albert P. Fitch, *Religion and the Undergraduate* (pamphlet. [Princeton, N.J.], published under auspices of *Daily Princetonian*, 1915), p. 3.

32. The Endowment Committee of Princeton University, *Princeton* (pamphlet. Princeton, N.J., 1919), p. 45.

the Society was captured by the Buchman group, and this eventually led to its demise.

Princeton then began to examine its problem more thoroughly. Another large influence in prompting this increased concern was the conference of administrators in 1928 on "Religion in the Colleges," to which Princeton played host.[33] Also instrumental was the gift of a chapel, completed in the same year, which, perforce, inaugurated the University's increased provisions for religion. The development of Princeton's official program of religion in its various aspects will be described later; the significant fact for the moment is that the concern of the administration kept pace through the succeeding years with the growth in responsibility. When in 1935 the University contemplated the institution of religious instruction in the regular curriculum, President Harold W. Dodds spoke of the increased interest in religion as the recognition of administrative obligation:

By the terms of our charter we are non-sectarian and it is not our desire to encourage any particular sectarian form of religion. Yet we recognize that to develop a fuller understanding of religion and its significance is an integral part of the University's educational responsibility. We believe that religion should have a place at Princeton, both as the way of life fostered on the campus and in the curriculum offered by the University.[34]

In 1940 a full-time Professor of Religious Thought, George F. Thomas, was added to the faculty, and the action was explained by President Dodds:

Princeton's historic position and present conviction and the acute needs of the time place on this University a heavy responsibility of developing in our students a fuller understanding of religion and its significance.[35]

The following statement made in 1941 by the "Trustees' Committee on Princeton's Religious Program," inviting alumni to join

33. See Galen M. Fisher, ed., *Religion in the Colleges* (New York, Association Press, 1928).

34. *A Statement by the President Regarding the Place of Religion in the Curriculum and on the Campus* (pamphlet. [Princeton, N.J.], 1935), p. 1.

35. H. W. Dodds, Introduction, in George F. Thomas, *Religion in an Age of Secularism* (pamphlet. [Princeton, N.J.], Princeton University, 1940), p. 5.

in its support, might as truthfully have begun, "In Princeton . . .":

In America at large the need for men who can lead the nation back to the deeper springs of its democratic way of life and foster knowledge of the history and genius of our religion is being recognized more clearly than at any time during the present century. At this critical hour Princeton has embarked upon a program which will enable her to reclaim her historic role in religion and make a major contribution in education.[36]

36. *Princeton's Program of Religious Instruction* (pamphlet. [Princeton, N.J., Princeton University], 1941), pp. 6–7.

CHAPTER VI

ATTITUDES TOWARD RELIGION: THE TAX-SUPPORTED INSTITUTION

STATE and municipal institutions pose a special problem. They are usually thought of as being almost wholly secular, and of necessity so, by reason of their tax-supported nature. It is often considered that the principle of the separation of church and state prevents their manifesting any strong religious interest and assuming any real responsibility for the religious life of their students. Whether or not, and to what extent, this is true will be given separate treatment in a later chapter. Suffice it to say now that the necessity for their neutrality on the subject of religion is at least debatable.

The fact of their neutrality is also open to question. They have been called secular because it is thought they ignore religion and fail to provide religious activities; yet, as we shall also see in detail in a succeeding section, many state institutions do officially undertake a not inconsiderable religious program. These, together with many more of those which do not have an official program, give considerable encouragement to the voluntary programs of Christian Associations and church-sponsored agencies active on their campuses. It has been suggested earlier that, for some church-related and independent colleges, an encouragement of the unofficial organizations unaccompanied by any assumption of responsibility may sometimes indicate a hesitant or even insincere interest in religion. But encouragement of voluntary programs on the part of tax-supported institutions may, and often does, mean just the opposite: an intense interest, expressed in the only, or at least the best, way which those institutions deem possible.

When one examines the history of such institutions prior to the twentieth century, their secular nature is even more questionable. In their founding and early years religious interests were often prominent, a few times actually in control.[1] Both secularization

1. See Donald G. Tewksbury, *The Founding of American Colleges and Universities before the Civil War*, pp. 174–207.

and secularism have had their unfortunate influences upon the state and municipal colleges in this century, but the presence of such influences has not been fully determinative of what these institutions thought and did in the realm of religion. There has still been sufficient latitude to permit a variety of attitudes toward religion.

A. NEGLECT

One must not grant too much, however, for it remains true that neglect and indifference have been a common story. By the beginning of this century the state colleges were largely divorced from any connection, except of an indirect sort, with religious groups or activities. Moreover, the subject of religion was and continued to be generally ignored by administrators of tax-supported institutions. Throughout the period under consideration scores of their inaugural addresses and other significant utterances have remained silent on the question, and histories of many state and municipal institutions have left religion almost completely untouched.

Related to this widespread neglect were certain defensive attitudes. In the first two decades of the century the state institutions were widely attacked for their alleged godlessness.[2] Even of the University of Michigan, whose record of continuing interest in religion has been clear, its historian wrote in 1920:

The religious life of the students has never been neglected, though the careful non-sectarianism of the University led it at first to be regarded with suspicion by the various religious bodies of the State, and their opposition, sometimes veiled, and sometimes open, proved embarrassing.[3]

What mention many administrators made of religion, therefore, was often merely an effort to refute charges of their institutions' pagan character. In his inaugural address in 1908 President Albert R. Hill of the University of Missouri said:

2. See Paul M. Limbert, *Denominational Policies in the Support and Supervision of Higher Education* (New York, Teachers College, Columbia University, 1929), p. 61; and E. V. Wills, *The Growth of American Higher Education; Liberal, Professional and Technical* (Philadelphia, Dorrance & Co., 1936), p. 70.

3. Wilfred Shaw, *The University of Michigan* (New York, Harcourt, Brace & Howe, 1920), p. 192.

But there are those who profess to see in this emphasis upon the scientific spirit some danger to the moral life. Now, the moral danger from it is certainly inappreciable. Thinking leads to faith, or to that kind of doubt which is as humble as faith.[4]

The usual defense, however, was not such as to condone the doubt-producing atmosphere. It consisted rather of the argument that state institutions could not rightfully be called irreligious because they pursued truth disinterestedly and because on their campuses voluntary and church-sponsored groups were influential. For the second of these arguments the testimony of the historian of the University of Illinois is illuminating. Writing in 1917, he noticed that the "Christian Associations were most prominent, for the faculty heartily encouraged them as evidences that Illinois was not irreligious."[5]

In 1900 both arguments were used by Elmer Ellsworth Brown, then Professor of Education at the University of California, later to be United States Commissioner of Education, and still later Chancellor of New York University. Discussing "Religious Forces in Higher Education" he said:

Now if you will permit me to speak in this large sense of all the forces which make for righteousness as Christian forces, I think a strong case might be made out for our state institutions of higher education.[6]

He emphasized as "one element of the higher life" for which the state universities stood,

. . . the hungering and thirsting after truth. . . . This disinterested love of truth is . . . a very Christian thing. . . . I verily believe that some of the noblest Christian influences in our colleges or anywhere are to be found in such form or formlessness as this. . . . Yet I am sure that to many of you this sort of thing must seem at best very vague and wholly unsatisfying. And I would not be understood as taking an attitude of indifference to those Christian forces which stand in some tangible relation with organized Christianity. . . . So it is fair to ask what Christian

4. *Exercises at the Inauguration of Albert R. Hill as President of the University, December 10–11, 1908* (pamphlet. Columbia, Mo., 1909), pp. 75–76.

5. Allan Nevins, *Illinois* (New York, Oxford University Press, 1917), p. 205.

6. E. E. Brown, "Religious Forces in Higher Education," *Pacific Theological Seminary Publications*, No. 3, p. 4.

forces are to be found in our higher state institutions of learning, which have some direct connection with distinctively Christian institutions.[7]

The forces he found operating were two: the proportionately larger church membership of faculty and students of the University of California than of the citizenry of the state as a whole; and the work of the voluntary religious groups. Of the latter he said:

The Young Men's and the Young Women's Christian Associations are by the form of their organization peculiarly well fitted to carry on a wholesome religious work in our state universities . . . And the very difficulties under which they work tend to make them an excellent school in the direction of Christian zeal away from objectionable courses into which youthful enthusiasm is sometimes led, and into channels of the greatest usefulness.[8]

From his argument, therefore, it is obvious that when he concluded, "No university can be complete in its equipment unless it makes some sort of provision for the study of this deepest thing in life," [9] he had reference not to something which the university itself should do, but rather to what it should encourage other agencies to perform.

This too resolves itself basically into a counsel for neglect of religion, but neglect of an entirely different sort from that which simply ignores the subject. This is solely disinclination to assume any official responsibility for the religious program, though accompanied by a real desire that religion be well provided for by voluntary agencies. It is only a relative neglect, therefore, for it still leaves open the possibility that the main object—namely, the adequate religious nurture of the students—will be attained.

On this very point defenders of the state universities were found among others than their chief executives. President Harper of the University of Chicago discussed the question before the National Education Association in 1900:

A great outcry has always been made against the state university that its tendencies were anti-Christian, and that its students were under influences many of which were evil and powerful; but

7. *Ibid.,* pp. 5–7.
8. *Ibid.,* p. 10.
9. *Ibid.,* p. 16. See the strikingly similar argument of President George E. MacLean of the State University of Iowa in *Bulletin of the State University of Iowa,* New Series, No. 32 (May, 1901).

a careful study of these institutions shows that the facts do not support these charges. In many, if not in all, of the state universities there is cultivated a deep religious spirit, and the Christian activity and interest in Bible study are greater by far in proportion than in some of the smaller colleges which are under denominational control.[10]

"The Christian activity and interest in Bible study" were, of course, the work of the Y.M.C.A.'s rather than that of the institutions. Giving all due credit to their activities, one may fairly hold that the "deep religious spirit" which the Christian Associations often successfully cultivated was not necessarily the possession of the colleges and universities themselves. We have already allowed for the possibility that the relinquishment of official responsibility did not always mean lack of interest on the part of administrators, and certainly did not mean absence of some sort of fruitful religious program. We must also allow for the alternative possibility that total dependence upon voluntary religious organizations indicated the institution's indifference or neglect. At any rate, it will later be made clear that during this century the religious life of the tax-supported institutions has largely been expressed through the work of voluntary organizations, and much of the interest which administrators have expressed has consisted solely of moral support for the work of these unofficial agencies.

B. THE FEAR OF SECTARIANISM

The explanation for both the absolute and the relative neglect of religion lies largely in the fear of sectarianism. The bogey of the separation of church and state plagued the college officials, and the common assumption was that the tax-supported institution could not recognize religion in any official way. That this reasoning, as we shall see in a later chapter, was incorrect is beside the point; what mattered was that it was widely followed. Even the undenominational Christian Association was not always welcomed on the state university campus; at the University of Oregon during the closing years of the nineteenth century "formal religious exercises of any sort were frowned on, and even a college Y.M.C.A. was regarded with suspicion." [11]

10. W. R. Harper, *The Trend in Higher Education*, p. 373.
11. H. O. Sheldon, *History of the University of Oregon* (Portland, Binfords & Mort, 1940), p. 63.

The situation was such that a man like William Oxley Thompson, President of Ohio State University from 1899 to 1925, who had a profound personal interest in religion, felt that as chief executive his hands were tied and the best that could be hoped for was that the institution "permit" other agencies to do the job:

. . . the duty would seem to be incumbent upon the State University to permit the best possible opportunity for the study and development of the religious ideals among students.[12]

The following statement for Ohio State is typical of the attitude of most tax-supported institutions throughout at least the first three decades of the century:

The state of Ohio has been most generous in its attitude toward religion, while standing unalterably for a separation of church and state. . . . There could be no disposition on the part of the State University to coerce a man's religious beliefs any more than to suppress them. The attitude of the University, therefore, upon all questions of religion, is at once open, candid and sympathetic, while liberally tolerant of all differences of opinion and belief.[13]

Moreover, the supposed inability of state colleges to function officially in the field of religion has often been used by administrators of church-related colleges to illustrate their superiority over the "secular" institutions.

But the facile employment of the phrase, "the separation of church and state," did not decide the matter permanently. As early as 1905 President Harper, giving due recognition to the situation of the moment, nevertheless made one of his amazing prophecies:

A university, founded and conducted by the state, it is generally conceded, may not under any circumstances devote its energy to subjects relating to religion or theology. . . . [But] sooner or later the state will be forced to consider more definitely and scientifically than it has yet done what shall be its policy . . . in respect to that large and vital group of subjects which, in theory as well as in practice, is indissolubly associated with life itself, whatever aspect of life may be considered.[14]

12. T. C. Mendenhall, ed., *History of the Ohio State University*, II (1926), p. 142, from the President's report for 1910.

13. *Ibid.*, p. 142.

14. W. R. Harper, *op. cit.*, p. 55.

During the 'twenties a few educators began to question the apparent solution to the problem. In 1927 Dean Hawkes of Columbia wrote:

What do parents and students have a right to expect of colleges in religion? I am . . . speaking . . . of the state or privately endowed colleges that call themselves non-sectarian. If such institutions propose to offer a well-rounded education, the subject of religion cannot be neglected.[15]

And in the same year Herbert L. Searles made an investigation, sponsored by the State University of Iowa, into the status of religion in the state universities. His attitude was:

No university which seeks to understand and interpret the best in the culture of the past and present, which seeks to be a spiritual as well as intellectual leader, and which has at heart the greatest service to the church and state, can fail to make a place for the study of religion in its curriculum.

The principle of the separation of church and state is recognized throughout this work, but no such issue is raised by the introduction of the non-sectarian study of religion into state universities.[16]

He saw four reasons for the inclusion of religion in education:

. . . because of the obligation resting upon the university for making available to its students the means of a complete education in various fields of the world's thought; because the aims of education and religion conceived of in personal and social terms are similar; because of the demand for trained leadership in general and religious leadership specifically; and because of the need of the interpretation of religion in terms of modern thought.[17]

But he did not blind himself to the many problems connected with such a possible development. As he examined the situation of that day, he noted the neglect and the marking time, but he saw as well signs of a change in attitude among the state institutions:

In the first place it is clear that there is a trend in favor of the gradual development of the study of religion in state universities.

15. Herbert E. Hawkes, *College—What's the Use?* (New York, Doubleday, Page & Co., 1927), p. 94.

16. Herbert L. Searles, *The Study of Religion in State Universities*, University of Iowa Studies, Studies in Character, I, 3 (October 15, 1927), 10.

17. *Ibid.*, p. 62.

On the other hand the question as to method is so complicated and the difficulties are so obvious that there is another trend in the direction of remaining at a standstill. Still another group is of the opinion that this is not a field which the state university should enter and that all differences may be avoided by adherence to this position.[18]

C. CONCERN

That the first of the trends Searles identified is today the most powerful, and that the fear of sectarianism seems to have been at least partially dissipated, are convictions born out of the changes which have taken place in the last ten or fifteen years. Since about 1930 there has occurred a tremendous increase of interest in religion on the part of tax-supported colleges and universities. Prior to that time the majority of administrators' references to religion were, as we have noted, either concerned with the work of voluntary groups or hesitantly accepting the obligation of training for something called "character" or "the spiritual life." At the centennial celebration of Indiana University in 1920, President Edward A. Birge of the University of Wisconsin said:

In the university the modern state has resumed one, and that the chief, of its older and higher functions. It recognizes no longer as a matter of theory but in practical form the truth that the state as well as the individual has a spiritual life which must find full expression.[19]

Then he discussed all the usual problems of the college, such as curriculum, cost, and selection of students, as part of that recognition, but failed to mention religion. Similarly, at the inauguration of Lotus D. Coffman as President of the University of Minnesota in 1921, President Henry Suzzallo of the University of Washington spoke concerning extracurricular activity: "We shall need to take it over as a great opportunity for developing character and culture in men and women." [20] But though his topic was "The University in the Development of Character and Culture," he

18. *Ibid.*, pp. 48–49.
19. *Indiana University, 1820–1920, Centennial Memorial Volume* ([Bloomington, Ind., Indiana University], 1921), p. 206.
20. *The University and the Commonwealth; Addresses at the Inauguration of Lotus D. Coffman . . . May 13, 1921* (Minneapolis, University of Minnesota, 1921), p. 70.

nowhere defined character or told what the college could do or mentioned religion.

Such references as these may be generously interpreted as the beginnings of interest in religion, or at least in religion's functions and values. For approximately the first three decades of the century few state college executives, when speaking of their institutions' own obligations, went any further. But this tentativeness did not prove satisfying for long. As sectarianism diminished and as the conception of the separation of church and state grew less rigid, many state universities sought to discover exactly how far they could go in caring for the religious life of their students, and as a result began to realize that, legally, they could do more than they had done in the past. In 1933 Philip A. Parsons made a survey of religious influences on the campuses of twelve state institutions in the Far West. Among other purposes he wanted "to determine if possible the extent to which religion is a problem in the consciousness of . . . administrative officers and faculty." [21] His findings were:

In five of the institutions studied the administrative officer is keenly alive to the seriousness of the problem and anxious to do something constructive about it. At two universities the president is in a receptive mood and cooperating with a committee of his faculty and religious leaders from the town. In five institutions the administrative officers appear not to be greatly concerned over the situation but are apparently willing to hear proposals from interested groups looking toward the establishment of more definite spiritual and religious influences in the campus situation.[22]

President G. W. Rightmire of Ohio State University evidenced his own interest and discovered the keen interest of other state-college administrators, by means of a letter of inquiry which he sent out on April 15, 1938. His questions were:

I. To what extent have courses in religion been given a place in the regular University curriculum?
II. Are religious activities made the specific responsibility of a member of the University staff?

21. Philip A. Parsons, *Report on the Survey of Religious and Character Influences on State University and College Campuses in the Area West of the Rocky Mountains*, MS, 1933, p. 1.
22. *Ibid.*, p. 4.

III. Is University credit given for off-campus work in the field of religion?

IV. Are special or regular convocations of a religious character held?

V. What is the nature of the cooperation between the University and the denominational religious groups?

VI. In what ways not previously mentioned does the University endeavor to make a contribution to the religious life of the students?

VII. What has been the public reaction to your program? [23]

The facts relating to the problems he raised will be given in succeeding chapters; what is of interest now is the keen concern which his letter showed. This concern has continued to grow. As a result of numerous visits to state university campuses, Professor Clarence P. Shedd wrote in 1941:

State universities are more concerned today about religion than they have been at any other time during the present century. Conversations during this past year with presidents, deans, faculty, and undergraduate groups in thirty state colleges and universities in every part of the United States make this abundantly clear.[24]

The most heartening evidences of the increasing interest are the public statements of numerous chief executives. For the last fifteen years voices have been crying in the wilderness of indifference and neglect, and in their profound concern for religion they have spoken as firmly and as convincingly as the officials of church-related and independent colleges. In an address to his faculty in 1930 President Raymond H. Hughes of Iowa State College said:

Our duty to Iowa and our duty to God demand that we use every means to develop noble character—in the hearts of the students. We must look to the churches of Ames and to the organized religious work on the campus to carry part of this responsibility, but they can carry only a part. The tone and influence of the College is fixed by the faculty as they individually stand before their classes. . . . If we could so mobilize the members of this

23. Harvey Walker, ed., *Religion in Institutions of Higher Education*, a summary of replies from twenty-three institutions to President Rightmire's letter; mimeographed MS.

24. Clarence P. Shedd, "Religion in State Universities," *Journal of Higher Education*, XII, 8 (November, 1941), 408. See also references to his writings in Chapter I of this volume.

staff from the president to the youngest stenographer, from the business manager to the most recently employed laborer on the farm, that each of us would stand like a rock for righteousness, it would have a profound influence on the students. . . . I pledge you my own endeavor to do my best to stand openly for righteousness, and I invite you to give this greatest service to the College. Let each of us endeavor to make the spirit of Jesus Christ felt on this campus.[25]

Then in 1932, at the New York University centennial conference, President Robert G. Sproul of the University of California pointed out:

The university is doing well its task of helping to make life extensive. . . . It needs to do much better its job of developing man's power to grasp and to interpret the spiritual values and nuances of living.[26]

He developed his meaning in his now famous testament of faith:

Is religion itself a legitimate field of learning in the university? Is it a specific experience of the race, a necessity for each growing citizen, and a way of cultural growth for the future, or is it only a vestigial activity, an antiquated pre-scientific anachronism? For my part, I believe that religion (not the sects) is basic to morals, central in our American culture, unique as a dynamic within the individual, able to save us from ourselves and lead us out into nobility. I believe that without religion we are forced to substitute weak conventions for permanent values and abiding standards; that, without religion, civilization, with no adequate reinforcement for the great strains that come upon it, must yield inevitably to disintegration and decay. Believing these things, I believe also that the university which makes no effort to stimulate in its sons and daughters a sensitiveness to the issues of religion is likely to be a danger rather than a benefit to the state. Certainly it cannot serve its people as fully as it should unless it finds some way, as it has always done, to blend with knowledge and culture the rugged force of character and the spiritual power that give to these life and value. So only may knowledge become wisdom.[27]

Similarly President Eugene A. Gilmore expressed his conviction for the State University of Iowa at the Opening University Vesper Service in 1935:

25. Quoted in Milton C. Towner, ed., *Religion in Higher Education* (Chicago, University of Chicago Press, 1931), p. 133–134.

26. *The Obligation of Universities to the Social Order*, pp. 379–380.

27. *Ibid.*, pp. 382–383.

In these Vesper Services, held periodically throughout the year, the University endeavors to show its belief that religion occupies a vital place in education. These services evidence our firm conviction that a deep abiding and livable religion is an essential part of the entire University program and necessary for the achievement of true education. . . . And why this concern about religion? Simply this: Life cannot go on without spiritual meaning. If it is to have aim, direction and purpose, if it is to have essential and abiding meaning, it must have the inspiration and support of religion.[28]

Such opinions as those of Hughes, Sproul and Gilmore are now common among administrators of tax-supported institutions. They indicate that streams of interest in religion have begun to flow in the desert of secularization. And state college bulletins support them:

Though the College [Woman's College of the University of North Carolina] is non-sectarian in its management, the students are surrounded by religious influences. . . . The College employs a full-time, trained Director of Religious Activities. It is her duty to coordinate all these religious activities and organizations and advise students about their own personal religious problems.[29]

The Citadel is non-sectarian, but its high objectives cannot be achieved unless its educational program is founded on a solid religious life. Divorced from the spiritual aspirations of the individual and of the group, education is likely to destroy greater values than it creates. The basic purpose of education is to integrate its curricula with character-building activities and a normal religious life to the end that young people may be not only more efficient but better motivated by a sense of duty and obligation.[30]

An effort to generalize concerning the attitudes of colleges and educators to religion is even more precarious than the attempt to determine what those attitudes have been and are. But from the wealth of contradictory and indefinable information certain patterns seem to be discernible. First of all, *throughout the century there has been a strong undercurrent of interest in religion,* an interest which the colleges have inherited from the early days

28. *Religion in a State University*, Address by President E. A. Gilmore, September 22, 1935, State University of Iowa (pamphlet).

29. *The Woman's College of the University of North Carolina Bulletin*, XXIX, 3 (April, 1940), 37.

30. *Bulletin of the Citadel*, IV, 2 (May, 1940), 47.

of their history and in which they have continued to the present time. This consistency is most clearly recognizable in the church-related colleges but has also been characteristic of many of the independent institutions and of at least a few of the tax-supported schools.

Accompanying this continuous interest in religion have been certain changes in emphasis. These may be represented by reference to attitudes prevalent toward the beginning of the century, and corresponding points of view more generally held today. From the discussion in the last three chapters it seems clear that:

In the early years,

1. Even though the colleges were never completely secularized, *a secular concept of higher education was dominant.* The church-related colleges which renounced it were on the defensive, and the majority of the independent and state institutions accepted it with little question.

2. *Religion was often thought of in terms of denominational creeds and practices.* Many of the church-related colleges which sponsored religion were consciously sectarian, and the independent and state-supported schools ignored religion because of their fear of sectarianism.

3. *An interest in religion was seldom accompanied by an assumption of official responsibility for caring for the religious life of the students.* The only widespread administrative practice of the time, as we shall see later, was the chapel service, and this was limited almost wholly to the church-related and independent colleges. All types of institutions looked largely to voluntary groups for their religious provisions.

4. *Differences in attitudes to religion followed rather closely the differences in the types of colleges.* Church and state colleges promulgated, respectively, a religious and a secular aim, and the independent institutions wavered in between.

Correspondingly, it has been pointed out that:

Within recent years:

1. *A much larger interest in religion is noticeable.* The attitude of the church-related colleges has become more positive and confident. Both independent and state-supported institutions are giving the matter more thorough concern.

2. *Religion is thought of almost wholly in nonsectarian terms.* This is true for all types of colleges, including those sponsored by the various denominations.

3. *Interest in religion is increasingly accompanied by the recognition of the college's responsibility for the students' religious life.* As later chapters will make clear, this recognition has very often proceeded to the actual assumption of such responsibility among all types of colleges, even among tax-supported institutions. Such a development among state schools is an indication that the older and more rigid conception of the separation of church and state has been weakened and in some places discarded.

4. *Attitudes toward religion no longer seem to differ according to the types of colleges.* Such differences as exist at the present time depend for their explanation more largely upon local conditions and the personal prejudices of individual administrators than upon whether or not the colleges are church-related, independent, or state-supported.

From an observation of these changes in the attitudes of colleges and educators, it is possible to draw a second general conclusion: *The trend during the period has been in the direction of a greatly increased interest in religion.* The flow has been especially rapid in the last decade and a half. It is fruitless to try to set a precise date for the beginning of such a trend. Prophets of the more positive attitudes were crying in the early years. But the preceding discussion seems to justify the conclusion that the greatest changes have occurred since the end of the first World War.

So far as the author is aware there has been no other extensive study of the changes in the attitudes of colleges and administrators to religion. But the movement, if "movement" it can rightly be called, has been obvious enough to provoke at least passing comment from many educators. In 1925 President Burton of the University of Chicago detected it,[31] and in 1927 President J. H. T. Main of Grinnell felt that "a new spiritual renaissance is beginning to gather momentum." [32] It was in the same year that Herbert L. Searles, as mentioned above, noticed such a trend in the state universities, while at the same time admitting the presence of forces working in the opposite direction.[33] And three years later President T. C. Knoles of the College of the Pacific

31. E. D. Burton, *Education in a Democratic World*, p. 106.

32. *Proceedings and Addresses on the Occasion of the Inauguration of E. J. Jaqua as First President of Scripps College* (pamphlet. Claremont, Calif., Scripps College, 1928), p. 170.

33. Searles, *op. cit.*, pp. 48–49.

was of the opinion that "in the field of higher education secularization seems to be halted." [34]

During the 'thirties increased recognition was given to this
development of interest in religion. In 1933 Professor Hugh
Hartshorne and his associates mentioned

. . . the great number of pronouncements and testimonials of
university executives. These statements disclose varying conceptions of the way religion should be treated, but they evince the fact
that all share the deepening conviction that something positive
must be done to permeate our secularized institutions with a new
spirit and to coordinate the thinking of students upon life's essential problems.[35]

Several times in recent years, as we have already noticed, Professor Clarence P. Shedd of Yale University has referred discern-
ingly to the movement. In 1940, after his investigation of *What
College Presidents Say,* Edgar W. Knight came to the conclusion:

It appears, however, that college presidents are nowadays, more
than in the past, raising searching questions about their students,
are more concerned than formerly for their . . . spiritual welfare.[36]

Thus, if there has previously been no systematic examination of
the attitudes of colleges to religion, at least certain writers in
the field have begun to detect the way in which the wind is blowing.

Another good barometer of the increased concern has been the
recently manifest "great readiness" of administrators "to disrupt
busy schedules in the interest of conferences on religion." [37] In
1928 the Princeton meeting on "Religion in the Colleges," mentioned above, was attended by over two hundred delegates from
institutions of all sorts, of whom over fifty were college presidents.[38] Then in 1930 a National Student-Faculty Conference on

34. T. C. Knoles, "American Education—Whence and Whither?" chap. ii
in P. A. Schilpp, ed., *Higher Education Faces the Future,* p. 60.

35. Hugh Hartshorne, Helen R. Stearns, and Willard E. Uphaus, *Standards
and Trends in Religious Education* (New Haven, Yale University Press,
1933), p. 192.

36. Edgar W. Knight, *What College Presidents Say,* p. 357.

37. Hartshorne *et al., op. cit.,* p. 191.

38. See Galen M. Fisher, ed., *Religion in the Colleges.*

Religion and Education was held in Detroit,[39] both this and the Princeton affairs being sponsored by the Young Men's Christian Association, which has always been eager for larger administrative concern. Immediately following Detroit, the Conference of Church Workers in Universities and Colleges, meeting in Chicago, gave special consideration to the questions relating to "The Religious Self-Expression of a University." [40] The conference on "The Obligation of Universities to the Social Order," held in connection with the centennial celebration of New York University in 1932, discussed at length "The University and Spiritual Values." [41]

Since that time gatherings of college officials to discuss the relationship of religion to their institutions have grown tremendously in number and been held in all parts of the country. The Y.M.C.A. and Y.W.C.A., acting regionally and nationally, separately and together, have arranged many of these meetings. Significant groups have met frequently under the auspices of the National Council on Religion in Higher Education, the Edward W. Hazen Foundation,[42] and more recently the Danforth Foundation. All three groups have been of large influence in provoking interest and fruitful discussion.

Other organizations such as the Association of American Colleges, the American Council on Education, the American Personnel Association, and others, as well as religious agencies such as the Council of Church Boards of Education, the National Association of Biblical Instructors, and the Religious Education Association, have furnished increasing opportunities, both in their annual and other meetings and in their publications, for the discussion of religion on the campus. The practice of conferring and writing about the problem has become so widespread in recent days that individual chronicling is impossible. Mention should be made, however, of three especially important occasions at which the place of religion in higher education was given particular attention: the Bicentennial Conference of the University of Pennsylvania in 1941,[43] the Columbia University Conference on

39. For a report of the meeting see *Education Adequate for Modern Times* (New York, Association Press, 1931).

40. See M. C. Towner, ed., *op. cit.*, a report of the conference.

41. This conference was reported in *The Obligation of Universities to the Social Order*.

42. See *The Hazen Conferences on Student Guidance and Counseling* [Hazen Foundation], yearly editions.

43. See University of Pennsylvania Bicentennial Conference, *Religion and the Modern World*, pp. 63–87.

Religion in the Modern World, in 1942, and the Princeton Conference on Religion in Public Education, sponsored by the American Council on Education in 1944.

Immediately following the end of the war the American Council on Education, the Hazen Foundation, and the National Council on Religion in Higher Education undertook a joint sponsorship of a series of "Faculty Consultations on Religion in Higher Education." The first year of this new program, 1945–46, saw such meetings held on nineteen college campuses, with Edwin E. Aubrey, Theodore M. Greene, William E. Hocking and George F. Thomas serving as consultants.[44] During the last fifteen or twenty years, therefore, the increased concern of colleges, college executives and faculty has been recognized both by educators writing in the field and by the executives and faculty as they have met together to discuss their mutual problems. The time of profound interest in religion has arrived.

44. See John W. Nason, "The Program of Faculty Consultations on Religion in Higher Education," *Educational Record*, October, 1946. (pamphlet; reprint of magazine article.)

CHAPTER VII

RELIGION IN PHILOSOPHIES OF HIGHER EDUCATION

A PHILOSOPHY of higher education is implicit in the remarks of every college president on religion, or, for that matter, on any other aspect of the college program. Recognition of this fact does not mean that all administrators are philosophers. Like practical leaders in other fields, some are and some are not. Rather, the point for the purposes of this discussion is that the attitudes which college presidents hold toward religion grow out of their conceptions of the nature and function of higher education as a whole.

What, then, are the various philosophies of higher education? To what extent do they allow for, or even demand, a place for religion in the college scene? What sort of religion do they support, and what sort do they reject? Questions such as these must be answered if the interest in religion and the provisions for religion existent on college campuses are to be considered proper reflections of the institutions' purposes.

Before we proceed, however, the implication of the last question should be noted. The author is not interested in setting up his own definition of religion and in trying to harmonize it with the various philosophies. Nor does he conceive that it is part of his present task to do so. The final query suggests, rather, that the approach will be to examine the differing educational theories and to seek to discover what they mean by religion and consequently, what place they give to it in their total systems.

Though no precise definition will be attempted, it is obvious that the word carries a certain connotation in this study. Religion does not mean, for our purposes, either sectarianism or institutionalism. A dual usage of the term often causes confusion. The word is employed to denote both *a* religion and religion in the more inclusive sense of a way of life, of attitudes and ideals, of belief in God. The latter usage is the one followed herein.

Unlike the treatment in the three previous chapters, no division need be made among various types of colleges for a clear delineation of differing philosophies of higher education. Catholic colleges are the only ones having a precise philosophy of education to which all give allegiance, but they have arbitrarily been omitted from this discussion. For the rest, "Methodists or Presbyterians or Baptists would not proclaim a Methodist or a Presbyterian or a Baptist 'philosophy of education.' " [1] No more would the independent colleges promulgate an "independent" philosophy, nor the state institutions advance a concept peculiar to themselves. Since there is no necessary connection between philosophies of higher education and the types of institutions which espouse them, their differences must be discerned on the basis of content alone.

Doubt is expressed by some, however, as to the complete truth of this last statement as applied to religion. The doubt concerns what state-supported institutions can think and do. It springs from a misconception of the meaning of the old principle, the separation of church and state. Since this problem has important significance not only for the state universities but for other colleges as well, the laying of the ghost will be reserved for special treatment in the following chapter. Suffice it to say now that this doubt has no basis in fact. Philosophies of education do not differ among the various institutions by virtue of their type—church-related, independent, or tax-supported.

But the problem of analysis is not thereby less difficult. Theories concerning college education are almost as numerous as the host of theorizers themselves. They cover a tremendous range and represent all shades of opinion within that range. Educators who have attempted surveys have usually contented themselves with drawing the general outlines of two completely contradictory positions, one at each end of the scale, and herding the vast remainder into the cavernous no-man's-land between.

For the sake of convenience some such oversimplification seems necessary. But division into only two groups leaves unclassified those in between, and implies unjustly for them a fence-sitting attitude, an inability to make up their minds. The fact is that many of those who have sought a golden mean are as positive and definite in their educational philosophy as those who represent the more extreme positions. For the purposes of this discussion, therefore, the various theories concerning higher education will

1. Robert L. Kelly, *The American Colleges and the Social Order*, p. 281.

be classified generally into three groups which, for lack of more accurate terminology, will be called "progressive," "classical," and "liberal."

A. THE "PROGRESSIVES"

The progressives are more easily distinguishable than either of the other two major groups, for they have a core of adherents who call themselves by such a name and believe in what they term "progressive education." If the meaning of their self-imposed title is not always clear, at least the general lines of belief of the progressives are discernible. John Dewey, as the acknowledged spokesman for this group, is the natural authority to consult.

Dewey finds the center of gravity for his educational thinking not in the teacher or subject matter, but in the individual student. His philosophy is concerned primarily with the student's total personality. Formal education, as well as the informal which lasts throughout life, must consider the "whole child," and must rest upon a recognition of individual differences. Students should be interested in what they learn. The whole process of education must be creative rather than transmissive; learning takes place through activity, through participation in life situations, through the use of the project method. Teaching consists not of indoctrination but of guidance. Knowledge itself is viewed as life experience and is therefore evolutionary, and complete trust is placed in the scientific method for arriving at tentative truth. All education consequently is growth, and growth is social as well as personal. The end of education is not so much intellectual competency as it is personal and social efficiency. The educational institution should be a miniature community and bear a direct relationship to society as a whole. It must recognize the responsibility for training its students to adjust themselves to, and, if necessary, to seek to change, the social order. Education must be related to the ideals of the society in which it works, particularly the ideals of democracy. Thus the schools and colleges of the nation, while respecting the past, are moving in and concerned with the present, and are even more consciously directed toward and motivated by the future.

Such, in general, is the educational philosophy of Dewey and of his countless associates and followers. With different men and at different times, one or another of the items in their general philosophic pattern has received greater or lesser emphasis. But in the midst of minor variations, there run the consistent threads of progressive thought: "interest," "student-centered school," "learning by doing," "life experience," and "relation to society."

One immediately recognizes the source of inspiration for many of the changes and developments which have taken place in higher education in recent years, as indicated in Chapter II. The interest of college executives in the extracurricular activities of students, the establishment of programs of guidance and personnel work, the multitude of innovations in teaching method, examining and grading, the relationships fostered with the outside world—all these and many other developments are, at least partially, outgrowths of the progressive philosophy. The willingness of colleges to experiment, if partly attributable to the uncertain times and the general confusion in higher education, is also a product of the pragmatic thinking of progressives. At least two experimental colleges, founded in recent years—Sarah Lawrence and Bennington—rest wholeheartedly on the faith of John Dewey.[2]

The heightened interest in democracy manifested by all groups of educators today is especially characteristic of progressives, who relate it to their insistence upon the establishment of an organic connection between school and society. Thus among the recent profusion of books on the connection between education and democracy, an impressive number are from the progressives. This revitalized concern for democracy is an indication that the progressives have increasingly come to look upon their educational thinking as a branch of social philosophy. The extreme experimentalism of earlier days has, to this extent, been replaced by a definite commitment to the values of the democratic way of life. It is largely through their support that "the decade of the 'thirties has seen a steady growth in the influence of the theory of social aims in education." [3] Progressive education, therefore, fully accepts purposes that are "functional" and "practical" to meet the basic needs of the present day.

2. For Sarah Lawrence, see Constance Warren, *A New Design for Women's Education* (New York, Frederick A. Stokes, 1940); and *Sarah Lawrence College, Thirteenth Year*, October, 1940. For Bennington, see Robert D. Leigh, "The Newest Experiment in Higher Education," chap. xviii in P. A. Schilpp, ed., *Higher Education Faces the Future;* and *Bennington College Bulletin*, IX, 1 (September, 1940), 6–7.

3. R. Freeman Butts, *The College Charts Its Course*, p. 336.

It is easy to ridicule the progressive position by charging that it encourages a "bargain-counter" or "service-station" concept of education. Certainly many progressives would agree with President Lotus D. Coffman of the University of Minnesota when he said: "The state universities hold that there is no intellectual service too undignified for them to perform." [4] But for the progressives "intellectual" is a necessary qualification for "service." Those colleges which have completely sold themselves to a practical-minded public are not true mirrors of the progressive thought, even though that thought finds its primary loyalties in "method" and "function."

What are the implications for religion in the philosophy of the progressives? One discovers a curious omission of the word from many of their treatments. And the explanation is not far to seek. To John Dewey, as the father of the faith, religion is not much more than sectarianism, consisting of a "special body of beliefs and practices having some kind of institutional organization." [5] Education can have nothing to do with this, and Dewey calls for a laissez faire policy on the part of the schools.[6] He points out, however, a "difference between religion, a religion and the religious." [7] The adjective "religious" denotes "attitudes that may be taken toward every object and every proposed end or ideal." [8] Thus the "religious attitude" is sanctioned, and progressive education may seek to foster it.

But this concession does not mean much. A good naturalist, Dewey objects to any attempt to include the supernatural, and his use of the term "religious," in contrast with "religion," refers only to "the use of natural agencies." [9] He feels that "dependence upon an external power is the counterpart of surrender of human endeavor" [10]—an opinion astounding to any student of history. It is little wonder, then, that many of the progressives, who think of

4. Lotus D. Coffman, *The State University; Its Work and Problems* (Minneapolis, University of Minnesota Press, 1934), p. 205.

5. John Dewey, *A Common Faith* (New Haven, Yale University Press, 1934), p. 9.

6. John Dewey, "Religion and Our Schools," *Hibbert Journal*, VI (1908), 796–809.

7. John Dewey, *A Common Faith*, p. 3.

8. *Ibid.*, p. 10.

9. *Ibid.*, p. 81.

10. *Ibid.*, p. 46. For a detailed refutation of Dewey's whole thesis in *A Common Faith*, see Henry P. Van Dusen, "The Faith of John Dewey," *Religion in Life*, IV (Winter, 1935), 123–132.

religion primarily in sectarian terms and refuse to acknowledge the presence of a supernatural element, have ignored religion in their philosophy.

A recent example is furnished by Algo D. Henderson in his volume, *Vitalizing Liberal Education.* Chapter VII deals with the "Search for Higher Values" in which he points out both the failure of the church and the importance of "values." Yet all he can suggest for their furtherance is that the college encourage "general reading" and "writing . . . an occasional 'life aims' paper." He approaches the question of Chapter XVI, "Education for What?" with the recognition that "there should be an ethical aim in education." "Democracy" or "education for the good life" is, of course, his answer, but "what the good life is must be determined experimentally." And that is as close as he comes to religion, for nowhere is the subject discussed.[11] It should be added that Henderson's practice is better than his philosophy, for as President of Antioch he has shown keen interest in the development of a vital religious program for the college.

Others of the progressive school, however, have not followed in Dewey's neglect of religion. Many of them believe that religion must be included, for as Chapman and Counts said:

Socially a negative policy is disastrous, and educationally it can be attacked on the grounds that it provides no adequate unifying principle for the varied activities of the school.[12]

Writing particularly about the situation in the state universities, Searles made a similar plea, while criticizing Dewey:

The weakness in this [Dewey's] position, however, is that it is claimed that the public schools are serving the cause of religion by keeping silent on the whole subject of religion. Might it not be that both religion and education would greatly profit from a conscious and deliberate recognition of their common aims . . . ; for certainly education needs the religious ideal and religion needs more of the educational ideal. In view of the uncertainty of educational aims it would seem that a broad religious ideal in education would tend to unify and inspire education as a spiritual enterprise.[13]

11. Algo D. Henderson, *Vitalizing Liberal Education* (New York, Harper & Brothers, 1944), p. 195 and chaps. vii and xvi, *passim.*

12. J. C. Chapman and George S. Counts, *Principles of Education* (Cambridge, Mass., Houghton Mifflin Co., 1924), p. 465.

13. H. L. Searles, *The Study of Religion in State Universities,* p. 56.

George A. Coe found "the springs of democratic motivation" in religion. In answer to Harold O. Rugg, who turned to aesthetics and ignored religion,[14] Coe said:

Democracy where most we notice other persons and spontaneously experience their weal and their woe as our own . . . [is] more akin to religion than to art.[15]

After an exhaustive evaluation of present theories of higher education Mowat Fraser described an "adequate college," adequate in terms of his major criteria of "genuine interest" of the student and "inclusive aims" of the institution. He considered religion thoroughly, pointing out the consonance between it and his major principles, and concluded:

Thus, an adequate college would be vitally concerned with religion. In fact, as problems of living become increasingly complicated and as the significances of departmental or *ad hoc* knowledge incidentally become increasingly obscured, only by deep, absorbed reflection concerning the attainment of inclusive aims—religious reverence and idealism—can these complicated needs and this subject matter be studied in clear perspective. In all its teaching, the college would strive to encourage inclusive aims which correspond to religious ideals, to encourage deep genuine interest which corresponds to religious reverence, and to consider detailed requirements for attaining aims which correspond to the details of religious creeds and customs. Furthermore, because of the influence of religion, the college would have it considered specifically by name. In fact, because of the tendency today for the truth and power in religious traditions to be obscured by short sighted formalists or to be spurned by rash reformers at the very time when that truth and power are most needed, the college would make special effort to have those traditions considered fully; but it would not encourage any particular religious beliefs. Religious beliefs, like all others, it would encourage a student to accept only as they become genuinely significant to him in coping with problems of living. In religion as in all other fields, then, beliefs would be taught only incidentally. Primarily the college would strive to encourage genuine interest in inclusive aims in the various phases of living.[16]

14. See Harold O. Rugg, *Culture and Education in America* (New York, Harcourt, Brace & Co., 1931), Pt. IV.

15. George A. Coe, *Educating for Citizenship* (New York, Charles Scribner's Sons, 1932), p. 171.

16. Mowat Fraser, *The College of the Future* (New York, Columbia University Press, 1937), p. 480.

If such statements do not go as far as some religionists would desire, at least they serve to show that there are some progressives who grant religion a significant place in their philosophy of higher education. And among the few colleges which follow the progressive philosophy thoroughly, for every Bennington which seems to ignore religion, there are a Rollins and a Sarah Lawrence which give it large attention.

Among progressives, themselves, therefore, a disagreement exists as to whether religion ought rightfully to have a place in education; or, granted a place, as to the way in which it should be integrated into the life of the institution. Some would accept religion, as the word is being used in this discussion, but would hesitate to deal with it directly, preferring to provide for its nurture by indirect methods and to employ circumlocutions in its description. One suspects that much of this hesitancy springs from Dewey's own misapprehensions. It is often argued that the progressive philosophy preserves rather than destroys religious values,[17] but religion, if included at all, should be recognized by name—and on this point our examination of what progressives have said has been inconclusive.

But from their own principles the implications for religion, even though not always drawn by the progressives themselves, are unmistakable. In almost every treatment of progressive ideology, "religion" can be inserted for "education" or "democracy" without changing the fundamental message to be conveyed. This is not to say that education or democracy is, or ought to be considered, synonymous with religion. As Professor Brubacher points out, such a conception of religion "would be fragmentary; it would be worshipping the part for the whole." [18] The point, rather, is that religion supports wholeheartedly every major principle of the progressive philosophy.

Religion is interested primarily in personality and its development. It is creative and grows by means of life's experiences, for a person has religion only as he is religious. It believes in the scientific method. Its emphasis on the person is not separated from, but rather is complementary to, a social outreach. It seeks to

17. See, for example, J. S. Brubacher, *Modern Philosophies of Education* (New York, McGraw-Hill Book Co., 1939), p. 317; C. A. Hauser, *Latent Religious Resources in Public School Education* (Philadelphia, Heidelberg Press, 1924); I. B. Berkson, *Preface to an Educational Philosophy* (New York, Columbia University Press, 1940), chap. v.

18. Brubacher, *op. cit.*, p. 321.

change both men as individuals and men in relationship with each other, or the social order. And it gives profound allegiance not to any form of government but to the democratic ideal.

Progressive education and religion together, therefore, would make an excellent team. Progressive education seeks to give guidance to the intellectual, emotional, and experimental sides of man's life. The college adopting a progressive point of view, therefore, may include religion as subject matter in the curriculum, as worship, and as activity. If the college is to be completely consistent with its educational philosophy, it must include religion in such ways. And as the institution takes upon itself direct responsibility for fulfilling its other educational tasks, so must it be concerned not merely with seeing that religion is being adequately presented, but it must do the job, or at least a major share of the job, itself.

Progressive education, however, is not atomistic. The "sides" of the student's personality are distinguished for the sake of convenience, but the student is viewed as a "whole person." Similarly, educational aims may be separated arbitrarily, but are thought of as forming a unity. Progressive education is searching for a unifying influence and, as we have seen, is finding it at the present time in democracy. But since the ideals of democracy approach religion, religion might come to be considered as the desirable integrating factor. At present the complete faith of many progressive educators in a solely naturalistic philosophy would prevent them from regarding religion as anything more than a *part* in the life of the school, along with other parts of the educational whole. But in the future, as progressives overcome their fear of the supernatural element in religion, they might conceivably recognize the central role which religion could play in higher education, without at the same time sacrificing any of their cherished educational principles. The conclusion is inescapable that, for the present, religion must have a place in the educational plans of progressives; for the future, it may have an even larger place.

B. THE "CLASSICISTS"

The classicists, even more than the progressives, can trace their lineage far back into educational history. They acknowledge their debt to the scholastics and the humanists of the Middle Ages and the Renaissance, and beyond them to the ancient Greeks. In more recent times they are beholden to the early colleges of America, and claim to be carrying on their tradition of emphasizing classical learning. St. John's of Annapolis, the most thoroughly classicist of American colleges, has discarded the term "New Program" for the type of education inaugurated there in 1937, on the grounds that it is "neither novel nor experimental," but represents an attempt "to restore liberal education, of the sort once available in American colleges of liberal arts." [19]

But for all their rootage in the past, they owe their present revival and impetus to influences of much more recent date. At the turn of the century the elective system seemed to be the answer to the colleges' problems, but as years passed and hopes failed to materialize, it was blamed for the widespread confusion of the 'twenties. A general onslaught upon all the shortcomings was initiated, with an attack on the principle of free election as its center, and a host of objectors sought to lead education back to older and more solid ground. Opposition to the elective system and its attendant evils may thus be considered the provocation for the reassertion in the last two decades of the classicist point of view.

Though Nicholas Murray Butler would hardly be accepted as a representative of classicist thought today, he may be said to have announced the text of the corporate castigation out of which the classicists got their start. In the early years of his career, President Butler showed numerous signs of sympathy for the budding progressive philosophy.[20] But as time passed he was sobered by the responsibilities of his position as the executive of Columbia University. His own Teachers College was coming to be the feathering nest of the progressives, but he began to consider their movement as the "New Barbarism." In his *Annual Report for 1919–20* he cried in lusty exaggeration: "These new and numerous Philistines are concerned with displacing discipline for indiscipline, scholarship for deftly organized opportunities for ignorance, thoroughness for superficiality, and morals for impulsive and appetitive conduct." [21]

The theme was taken up by Abraham Flexner in 1930 in his famous volume, *Universities, American, English, German.* Scath-

19. *Report of the President, St. John's College, Supplement to the Bulletin,* April, 1940, p. 5.

20. See Nicholas M. Butler, *The Meaning of Education* (New York, Macmillan Co., 1907), chaps. iii and iv.

21. Quoted in Edward C. Elliott, ed., *The Rise of a University,* Vol. II, *The University in Action* (New York, Columbia University Press, 1937), p. 119.

ingly he denounced the American colleges for their superficiality, their stupidity, their exaltation of "service," and concluded: "No sound or consistent philosophy, thesis, or principle lies beneath the American university today." [22] During the 'thirties others pressed his thesis, notably President Robert M. Hutchins of Chicago in his provocative lectures originally delivered at Yale, *The Higher Learning in America*,[23] and in other writings. Professor Norman Foerster of the State University of Iowa condemned roundly the man who will "teach his students to learn by Deweying, and how to live in a Freudulent age." [24] And even Stephen Leacock, whose famous horseman riding off in all directions at once has been taken as a symbol of the present educational confusion, added his good-humored but not less authoritative rebuke.[25]

The critics of the status quo came from all points of the philosophical compass, for progressives and liberals as well as classicists were greatly dissatisfied with conditions as they were. Criticism alone, therefore did not serve to identify the classicist group. Their philosophical position began to be recognizable only when they addressed themselves to the problem of the changes that should be made in the system. The best-known proponents of the classical and humanistic philosophy, differing among themselves but with a large core of agreement, are Hutchins, who is considered the chief spokesman for the group, Mortimer Adler, Stringfellow Barr, Scott Buchanan, Abraham Flexner, Norman Foerster, Arnold Nash and Mark Van Doren.

The outlines of their general position are readily understood. Since colleges are too easy, a measure of discipline, of an intellectual nature, must return to their programs. Since colleges are shallow, then in contrast to the progressive emphasis on method and function, primary attention must be given to content, to rigorous subject matter, to the pursuit of knowledge. The progressives' preoccupation with the "whole person" is shadow-boxing;

22. Abraham Flexner, *Universities, American, English, German* (New York, Oxford University Press, 1930), p. 213.

23. Robert M. Hutchins, *The Higher Learning in America* (New Haven, Yale University Press, 1936).

24. Norman Foerster, *The Future of the Liberal College* (New York, D. Appleton-Century Co., 1938), p. 86.

25. See Stephen Leacock, *Too Much College* (New York, Dodd, Mead & Co., 1939).

the classicists enthusiastically support Leon Richardson's analysis made in 1924:

When we consider all aspects of the problem we must, I think, come to the conclusion that the purpose of the college is primarily intellectual. . . . After all, we come back to the idea of the development of the intellect as the conscious purpose of the college: other results may be gained and will be gained, but they must be "by-products," and not the direct aims of the institution.[26]

Though Flexner spoke particularly of the university, his conception of its "four major concerns" has been made to apply to all of higher education: ". . . the conservation of knowledge and ideas; the interpretation of knowledge and ideas; the search for truth; the training of students who will practise and 'carry on.' " [27]

To Hutchins and his following, education is not primarily but solely the cultivation of the intellect. Its content should be the study of the world's best books. Borrowing from Thomas Aquinas, he wrote: "Education implies teaching. Teaching implies knowledge. Knowledge is truth. The truth is everywhere the same. Hence education should be everywhere the same." [28] Since 1937 St. John's has served as a special laboratory in which the ideas of the classicists have been tested. The college ". . . has re-dedicated itself to developing, in those who come to it, their intellectual powers," [29] and all its program and methods are shaped toward the fulfillment of this one compelling purpose.

Thus far the classicists are substantially agreed: the major emphasis of the college must be the pursuit of knowledge and the training of the intellect. But when these aims come to be translated into actual programs, the counsel varies. Flexner, for example, would allow a place in the ideal university for real contact with society, while Hutchins and his sympathizers believe that the institution of higher education should be primarily a modern cloister, unspotted from the world.

On one other point they approach agreement: the wealth of subject matter which is available must be brought into some coherent unity by an integrating discipline which is related to

26. Leon B. Richardson, *A Study of the Liberal College* (Hanover, N.H., [Dartmouth College], 1924), pp. 17, 22.

27. Flexner, *op. cit.*, p. 6.

28. Hutchins, *op. cit.*, p. 66.

29. *Report of the President, St. John's College*, p. 8.

all other intellectual disciplines and which is presupposed in all. But when the determination of this unifying factor is attempted the harmony disappears. Hutchins, representing the neoscholastics, suggests what he calls metaphysics.[30] Foerster, speaking for the humanists, thinks not in terms of one particular subject but of humanistic studies as a whole.[31] William Adams Brown wants theology as the core of the intellectual program,[32] and the Catholics, of course, would agree with his position if it were Catholic theology.

Underneath this disagreement may lie greater concord than the words would seem to indicate. For example, in his preface to W. A. Brown's volume, *The Case for Theology in the University*, Hutchins implies that what he meant by metaphysics is similar to the meaning Brown gives to theology; [33] we have already noted in Chapter V other words of his of similar tenor. And Foerster, though disclaiming both metaphysics and theology, agrees with Hutchins that what he desires for the college can be gained by a study of the world's best books.[34] At any rate, in spite of discrepancies among the various points of view, the second general belief of the classicists stands in bold relief: the necessity of finding a unifying factor in the subject matter of the college.

According to the thinking of the classicists, the place of religion in a college adopting their philosophy is similar to the place of any other discipline or interest: it may be included, but only in its intellectual aspect. Great religious thought, as represented in the Bible and others of the world's best books, together with the history of such thought and its development and the story of the organized channels for its expression, all this may be treated in the classical college. But religion as an attitude toward the whole of life, as worship, as activity, is outside the responsibility of the college and enters into its program only incidentally if at all.

The consideration which St. John's gives to religion is instructive at this point. A number of the great books which compose the content of its curriculum are primarily religious in nature,

30. Hutchins, *op. cit.*, chap. iv.

31. Norman Foerster, *The Future of the Liberal College*, and *The American State University, Its Relation to Democracy* (Chapel Hill, University of North Carolina Press, 1937).

32. William Adams Brown, *The Case for Theology in the University* (Chicago, University of Chicago Press, 1938).

33. *Ibid.*, Preface.

34. Norman Foerster, *The Future of the Liberal College*, chap. iv.

and problems of religion form a not inconsiderable part of the intellectual fare. But other provisions are totally lacking. Even the "extracurricular" interest in religion is represented not by chapel services or by activities but by a theological discussion group,[35] strangely reminiscent of the early theological societies in Harvard, Yale and elsewhere at the close of the eighteenth century.

Certain writers of the classical school of thought have confused the issue by employing words of broad meaning, such as "religion" and "Christianity," rather than the more precise "metaphysics" and "theology." For example, Norman Foerster's praise of "religion" is with only slightly less enthusiasm than his advocacy of humanism. But when he addresses himself particularly to the question as to how religion is to be included in the college, it becomes obvious that he is thinking in terms of subject matter alone: "In a humanistic university, it would seem proper to include a sympathetic study of the place which religion has occupied in our Occidental culture—the history and literature of Judaism and Christianity." [36]

Similarly T. S. Eliot, in his proposal of "Christianity" as the element of "control and balance" in education, narrows the idea in his discussion to its intellectual content, Christian doctrine.[37] The present-day thought of most classicists, it seems clear, allows only the intellectual aspect of religion to be given a place in higher education.

But this may not always be true of their thought. Already their exclusive emphasis on the intellect is breaking down, as the necessity for their battling the progressives lessens, and the consequent necessity for their taking an extreme position disappears. The classicists are no longer loath to defend their philosophy on pragmatic as well as theoretical grounds. And they are gradually recognizing the legitimacy of other than purely intellectual pursuits on the campus. The influence of this tendency in classicist thinking may soon be to justify the practice of religion as well as its study in the college program.

Actually, such a development is possible for the classicists at the present time without doing violence to their philosophy. In

35. See *St. John's College, Official Statement of the St. John's Program, Catalogue for 1939–40*, April, 1940, pp. 40–41, 46.

36. Norman Foerster, *The American State University*, p. 264.

37. T. S. Eliot, *The Idea of a Christian Society* (New York, Harcourt, Brace & Co., 1940), pp. 22, 26, 35.

their emphasis on the great books, they provide, for example, not merely for a reading of Euclid but for a rehearsal of his problems. Similarly, it would be proper for the classical college to encourage not merely the reading of the Bible but the recapture of the personal religious experience about which the Bible speaks. When W. A. Brown sought to include "worship" in his suggestion of "theology" as the unifying factor, "religion" might have been at those points a more accurate word than "theology." [38] His argument for the inclusion of worship is sound and holds good no matter what integrating discipline is suggested.

Moreover, the determination of the identity of the great books indicates the possession of a scale of values in which the classicist believes and which he would seek to foster. Whatever these values may be—the open mind, the pursuit of reason, the love of truth and goodness—the classicist will find that religion too is concerned with them and that the practices of religion can undergird them.

Hutchins' most recent volume leads the classicist philosophy, at least by implication, in this direction. He makes clear that he desires the development of the intellect not for its own sake and not for the mere amassing of knowledge but for growth in understanding: ". . . the aim of education is wisdom and goodness . . . we must reconstruct education, directing it to virtue and intelligence. . . . The great problem of our time is moral, intellectual, and spiritual." [39] These words hardly indicate opposition to religion, and the quotations from Hutchins already given in Chapter V go even further. The following conclusion seems therefore to be justified: from a disinterested pursuit of truth which classicists desire for their students, religion would subtract nothing; to the intellectual conviction which that pursuit should produce, religion, as worship, would add emotional commitment, and as service, fruitful experience. Whereas at present the classicist philosophy permits an intellectual approach, in the future it may recognize every aspect of religion.

C. THE "LIBERALS"

What may be termed, for lack of a better word, the liberal point of view, is characteristic of the great majority of college educators in this country. Though a wide divergence of opinion exists among

38. Brown, *op. cit.*, p. 68.
39. R. M. Hutchins, *Education for Freedom*, pp. 26, 47, 92.

them, they are distinguishable as a group both from the progressives to the left and from the classicists to the right. For purposes of clarification the chief emphases of the progressives may be denoted as personal-social and practical, while those of the classicists may be called intellectual. Correspondingly, the liberals may be recognized as stressing the cultural aspects of education. Now "culture" is as indefinite and debatable a word as "religion" or "democracy" or "truth," or any other of the terms with which educational philosophers must deal. Suffice it to say that, for our discussion, the word carries a meaning broad enough to include both the personal-social and practical, and the intellectual emphases.

A reference to the time-direction of the philosophies may also be useful in delimiting the three groups. The progressives are intrigued by the future, the classicists by the past; the liberals look in both directions and seek, as well, to serve the present. Or again, if the progressives think in terms of the importance of creation, and the classicists stress transmission, the liberals give allegiance to both methods.

And lest it appear that the liberals hold nothing more than a mere compromise position, the differences may be illustrated by reference to William Ernest Hocking's "three great themes of education." [40] The progressives emphasize "adjustment," by which is meant both adaptation to one's world and willingness to change the society in which one lives. The classicists accent "truth"; or to change Hocking's term slightly, intellect, both its training and its fruit. The liberals include both and add something as well in their concern for "value," which "is simply a summary name for those goods which make life worth living, those things for which we act, the termini of all our striving." [41] If it must be admitted that "values have to be discovered rather than taught," [42] the college, according to the liberals, must be eager to facilitate such discovery on the part of its students, and must consider this its primary task. Many educators of the liberal group have not developed their philosophy this far, but while they themselves do not always recognize it, their thinking seems to lead inevitably to such a conclusion.

40. See the address of W. E. Hocking in *The Obligation of Universities to the Social Order.*
41. *Ibid.*, p. 332.
42. *Ibid.*, p. 339.

The liberal, or cultural, or value-stressing philosophy of higher education is the tradition in which most American colleges have moved, and continue to move with greater conviction than in the immediate past. Certainly there is nothing original about such a point of view, for it long preceded both progressive education and intellectualism. To implement its apparent deficiencies and relaxations of emphasis the other theories sprang into existence. But in recent years the liberal position has received more careful attention, as being not alone the golden mean of the past but also the corrective for the present and the harbinger of a more abundant future. Among philosophers no one name, such as Dewey for the progressives or Hutchins for the classicists, has come to dominate the thinking of the group; but those who find themselves somewhere within the general liberal tradition far outnumber the disciples of the other two.

First of all the liberals seek to train the intellect, but they deny that this is the sole purpose of higher education. The opinion of President Burton of the University of Chicago could serve as a rebuttal to a successor in his office, Robert M. Hutchins. Emphasizing that one of the tasks of the college is to teach students to think, Burton yet proceeded:

. . . any definition of the function of the college in purely intellectual terms, however broad and inclusive, or however rigid and exacting, is fatally false by defect. Unless to whatever it does for the student by enlarging his horizon and by sharpening his power of intellect it also does its best to see that he acquires sound principles and right habits of action, it has failed at a point where failure is fatally serious.[43]

Both President Ernest H. Wilkins of Oberlin and Alexander Meiklejohn, formerly President of Amherst and chairman of the Experimental College at the University of Wisconsin held similar points of view. Wilkins said, it is true, that "The central purpose of the college is the training of the minds of the students," [44] but his development of the idea showed that he conceived of other important purposes for the college, and that even this purpose was directed to much broader than purely intellectual ends.[45] And Meiklejohn, almost a classicist in content and almost a progressive

43. E. D. Burton, *Education in a Democratic World*, p. 64.
44. E. H. Wilkins, *The Changing College* (Chicago, University of Chicago Press, 1927), p. 15.
45. See *ibid.* and his *The College and Society*.

in method, began his inaugural at Amherst in 1912 by saying, "The college is primarily not a place of the body, nor of the feelings, nor even of the will; it is, first of all, a place of the mind." [46] But he made his meaning clear by showing the relationship between an intellectual emphasis and practical matters:

Knowledge is to be sought chiefly for the sake of its contribution to the other activities of human living . . . the college is intellectual, not as opposed to practical interests and purposes, but as opposed to unpractical and unwise methods of work. . . . If there be no essential connection between instruction and life, then there is no reason for giving instruction except in so far as it is pleasant in itself, and we have no educational policy at all.[47]

President Henry M. Wriston of Brown University upheld what he called the "Liberal Ideal," as opposed to its classicist critics:

. . . distinguished educators have been known to insist that the function of a college is to train the mind, and that other aspects of experience, and specifically the emotions, are irrelevant. The statement does not make sense. . . . No one would seriously support that as a sound view of biology or of psychology. . . . [For a liberal education], emotional sensitiveness and spiritual awareness and power are as essential as a hospitable, though critical, mind.[48]

Facing in the other direction, the liberals agree with many of the tenets of progressive education, but temper their agreement with a critical appraisal of the whole. For example, they accept wholeheartedly the doctrine that education must be concerned with the whole person. Moreover, they adhere to the idea that freedom is necessary and reject a completely standardized subject matter. But they contend that the program of the college must contain aspects of stability as well as of change, and that the heritage of the past must not be neglected. They too know the importance of preserving actual contact with society; they speak of the social aims of education and of training for democracy; and they may even refer to "service" to the community as being one of the functions of the college. But such aims, however "practical," never lead to pure vocationalism, and they think primarily not in terms

46. A. Meiklejohn, *Freedom and the College*, pp. 157–158.
47. *Ibid.*, pp. 171–172, 174. See also his *Education Between Two Worlds* (New York, Harper & Brothers, 1942).
48. H. M. Wriston, *The Nature of a Liberal College*, pp. 7–8.

of mass education but in training for leadership. Wriston spoke against the progressives as impartially as against the classicists:

Those who want the college to get onto the firing line of business or make it an apprenticeship to public life are like the barbarians in establishing material over nonmaterial values. . . . The liberal college should eschew the foolish and self-defeating idea that only useful things are of value. . . . The modern world has seen many changes. Education has taken, and must continue to take, cognizance of them, but its major problem, stimulating the growth of personality, is not profoundly altered. The essence of the educative process is still self-discipline under guidance and encouragement.[49]

Thus the liberals find something to approve and something to reject in both classicist and progressive philosophies. They welcome the progressives' emphasis on method and function and the classicists' on content. But a liberal point of view makes a positive contribution of its own as well. As Wriston said:

The liberal college encourages the student to establish certain values as dominant in his life.[50]

These "certain values" go the whole round of creation. Educational philosophy to the liberal is not a branch of social philosophy, but subsumes it, together with all other interests, for education is as broad as life itself and its values are life's values. Stated another way, the interests and values which the college supports are the ideals of higher education. And these ideals are more inclusive than either intellectualism or democracy. In their delineation by many different educators religion is mentioned explicitly. With particular reference to the university, Burton discovered six ideals:

The University stands for scholarship . . . for the ideal of a symmetrical and well-balanced life . . . for interest in and concern for the individual. . . . On the other hand the University aims to create a community consciousness. . . . The University stands for character—high moral character. . . . Finally, the University stands for religion . . . religion is something more than morality, and . . . the University stands for both.[51]

49. *Ibid.*, pp. 22, 135, 140–141.
50. *Ibid.*, p. 142.
51. Burton, *op. cit.*, pp. 50–52.

Stewart G. Cole's list of similar objectives of liberal education also numbered six:

. . . the educator should aim: (1) to extend the democratic process until it leavens and controls every relation of man to man; and (2) to inspire within the personality of every youth the development of intellectual, social, and moral qualities of character that make the diffusion of democracy possible . . . [(3) to develop] the scientific method, or the exercise of intelligence, and [(4)] the artist's genius, or the cultivation of the esthetic sense . . . [(5)] personal religion . . . [and (6)] versatile language. . . .[52]

Do not the quests for (1) social democracy, (2) integrity of personal character in its members, (3) scientific method, and (4) esthetic sensitivity—as instruments of structural orderliness for man and society—and (5) personal religion or meaningful *Weltanschauung* represent the characteristic cultural forces of the American people? Does not each of these suggest a significant strand in the history of Western civilization? Has not the college of liberal arts sponsored one or more of them at every stage in its history? How inadequate its witness is to them today the educator knows but too well. The voice of prophetic culture joins that of chartless youth and imposes upon collegiate conscience a mandate to rethink the principles of educational philosophy and refocus the core values of American civilization.[53]

Even more significant than the general theories of individual philosophers are the statements of committees in various colleges which have struggled with the problem of purposes on the practical level of application to their own institutions. At the University of Illinois a Faculty Committee on College Policy stated:

The curriculum of liberal arts and sciences, with its several disciplines interrelated and overlapping, rather than sharply differentiated, is a process of liberalization, of freeing the mind from the prejudices and limitations of inexact and partial knowledge, of promoting a sympathetic understanding of the forces molding character, and of opening the eyes to see life steadily and see it whole.[54]

52. Stewart G. Cole, *Liberal Education in a Democracy* (New York, Harper & Brothers, 1940), pp. 64–68. See chap. iii, "Criteria of a Liberal Education."
53. *Ibid.*, p. 67.
54. Quoted in Frederick J. Kelly, *The American Arts College* (New York, Macmillan Co., 1925), p. 12.

The Dartmouth College Senior Committee said:

It is the purpose of the college to provide a selected group of men with a comprehensive background of information about the world and its problems, and to stimulate them to develop their capacity for rational thinking, philosophic understanding, creative imagination, and aesthetic sensitiveness, and to inspire them to use these developed powers in becoming leaders in service to society.[55]

During World War II numerous colleges, in forced examinations of their own programs, have had to pay thorough attention to their underlying philosophy of education. Out of such studies have come, on the one hand, a firm rejection of the partial emphases of both progressives and classicists, and on the other, a clear acceptance of liberal and value-stressing objectives. The "Report of the Alumni Committee on Postwar Amherst College" is a case in point:

In the educational confusion of our times it is possible to discern two main emphases. One group of educators tends to stress the importance of liberal education in passing on the heritage of the past. A second group seeks chiefly to adjust the student to his future social environment, whether this aim be stated in terms of "success," or "good citizenship." It is our contention that these two ends sought are not incompatible and that the means of attaining are the same.[56]

The liberal arts program can fulfill its function of preparation for life in society only if it accomplishes three things:
    (a) Helps the student develop into a well-rounded and well-integrated person with personal and social standards and values.
    (b) Enables him to understand the world and the society in which he lives.
    (c) Provides him with the intellectual training which will aid him in functioning effectively in his mature life. . . .
    Most important, surely, is the sense of standards and values. For the judgment which is not anchored to some secure basis of ultimate goals is ineffective in every field. Some may hold that values cannot be taught; but such is a counsel of despair which is at variance with human history. It is, no doubt, difficult to

55. *Report on Undergraduate Education of the Dartmouth College Senior Committee* (pamphlet. Hanover, N.H., [Dartmouth College], 1924), p. 10.
56. "Amherst Tomorrow, A Report of the Alumni Committee on Postwar Amherst College," *Amherst Alumni Council News*, XVIII, 3 (February, 1945), 50–51.

impart values today, because society is not agreed on its own standards as were the churchmen of the middle ages or the Puritan fathers of New England. But through the study of religion and participation in religious activities, through acquaintance with philosophy and philosophical methods, and through the informed study of history and literature, the student can be made aware of historic values and of the means by which a sense for values and standards is to be cultivated. It remains true, however, that the best way to teach values is through teachers who have them.[57]

A report of an Amherst Faculty Committee, working at the same time but not in conjunction, came to similar conclusions.[58]

The most widely heralded of all such wartime studies has been the "Report of the Harvard Committee" on *General Education in a Free Society*. Here again the same emphases are found. The classicist and progressive points of view must be combined:

The true task of education is therefore so to reconcile the sense of pattern and direction deriving from heritage with the sense of experiment and innovation deriving from science that they may exist fruitfully together, as in varying degrees they have never ceased to do throughout Western history.

Belief in the dignity and mutual obligation of man is the common ground between these contrasting but mutually necessary forces in our culture. As was pointed out earlier, this belief is the fruit at once of religion, of the Western tradition, and of the American tradition.[59]

Thus education should foster four "abilities . . . above all others": ". . . to think effectively, to communicate thought, to make relevant judgments, to discriminate among values." [60]

. . . the objective of education is not just knowledge of values but commitment to them, the embodiment of the ideal in one's actions, feelings, and thoughts, no less than an intellectual grasp of the ideal.[61]

57. *Ibid.*, p. 54.

58. *Report of the Faculty Committee on Long Range Policy* (pamphlet. [Amherst, Mass.], Amherst College, 1945). See especially Pt. I and Pt. II, chap. v.

59. *General Education in a Free Society, Report of the Harvard Committee* (Cambridge, Harvard University Press, 1945), p. 50.

60. *Ibid.*, p. 65.

61. *Ibid.*, p. 72.

It is already evident that religion has an important place in the liberal philosophy, and what is more, that this place is recognized by the liberals themselves. Nearly all of the educators quoted in the three previous chapters fall somewhere within the general bounds of the liberal group. Their interest in religion is the natural outgrowth of their general educational philosophy. The implication for the program of a college adopting the liberal point of view is obvious: that religion in all its aspects must be provided for and fostered.

But some liberals do not stop here. Like the progressives and the classicists, they seek an integrating discipline, a unifying factor, for the college. Democracy on the one hand, and metaphysics or theology or humanistic studies on the other, are too circumscribed. Something broader, more inclusive, more representative of all the ideals and values which the college cherishes, is necessary. Though many fail to go this far, an increasing number of liberal educators are coming to find that factor in religion.

In previous chapters reference has been made to the conviction of numerous administrators that religion should occupy a central place in the life of the college. Among other treatments of this idea, one of the most thoughtful and thorough is in the recent volume of Stewart G. Cole, *Liberal Education in a Democracy*. Here he contends that religion is the only one of his six major objectives of higher education which can bring unity into the college program. His argument is that

. . . formal education remains disintegrative for personality until the individual can discover within his divers experiences a unifying meaning and worth to his life; and that religion, functionally conceived, is the only compelling interest of man to insure the fulfillment of this high purpose.[62]

But what does it mean for religion to be taken as the integrating factor? Cole elaborates:

Has not youth a right to expect that a liberal arts college will: (1) introduce it to the history of religions, Christianity in particular, which are social movements that have had a profound effect upon American education and culture; (2) provide it with a realistic frame of reference adequate to give ultimate meaning and worth to human personality; (3) focus educational values to serve com-

---

62. Cole, *op. cit.*, p. 212.

manding personal ends of living; and (4) encourage it to articulate its personal faith in terms of an adequate philosophy of life? [63]

He considers other suggestions for the desired "adequate frame of reference" and is unconvinced. Democracy, he feels, is incomplete, is dangerously susceptible to being confused with an actual national pattern, and encourages a wholly homocentric view of life. He dismisses metaphysics and theology because they tend to omit the personal element which he believes necessary. In his discussion of religion, he does not minimize the practical problems which such a theory raises, but in spite of them he concludes:

. . . religion *may* be as indigenous to the educational process as science, art, or democracy on any college campus in America. Is not the time ripe to give this supreme human enlistment the central place in education as in life? [64]

If such a statement is still "extreme" among liberals, it may well prove to be the inescapable conclusion to which, as the years pass, the liberal philosophy will be led. For liberals, in their emphasis on values and on the totality of life experiences, must and do give large recognition to religion; and that recognition has become more conscious and widespread throughout the twentieth century.

It is apparent, therefore, that the increasing interest of colleges and administrators in religion, as discussed in the three preceding chapters, is consistent with any philosophy of higher education which they may espouse. Each one of the three rough divisions of philosophy—progressive, classicist and liberal—allows religion a legitimate place in the college, though in varying degree. At the present time the classicists admit religion only as subject matter, though the trend of their thinking may soon enlarge the bounds of their practice. The progressives are confused because of the hostile attitude taken toward religion by some of their leaders, but their philosophy necessitates in general its inclusion. The liberal philosophy demands the consideration of religion in all its aspects. It has long been the contention of leaders in religious education, and it is increasingly becoming the recognition of secular educators, that, in the words of Francis G. Peabody, written in 1903,

63. *Ibid.*, pp. 216–217.
64. *Ibid.*, p. 246. Italics are his.

. . . in their fundamental method and final aim religion and education are essentially consistent, coordinate, mutually confirmatory, fundamentally one.[65]

SELECTED BIBLIOGRAPHY FOR CHAPTER VII

The following books are suggested reading from writers of the three groups discussed above. From the wealth of recent material it is difficult to choose; particularly from the progressive and liberal groups is there a profusion of material. Many of the volumes already listed in the Selected Bibliography for Chapter II are also pertinent.

A. From the "progressives":

BODE, BOYD H., *Progressive Education at the Crossroads*. New York, Newson and Co., 1938. 128 pp.

CHAPMAN, J. C., and COUNTS, GEORGE S., *Principles of Education*. Cambridge, Houghton Mifflin Co., 1924. 645 pp.

COE, GEORGE A., *Educating for Citizenship*. New York, Charles Scribner's Sons, 1932. 205 pp.

COUNTS, GEORGE S., *Dare the School Build a New Social Order?* New York, John Day Co., 1932. 56 pp.

DEWEY, JOHN, *A Common Faith*. New Haven, Yale University Press, 1934. 87 pp.

——— *Democracy and Education*. New York, The Macmillan Co., 1916. 434 pp.

——— *Experience and Education*. New York, The Macmillan Co., 1938. 116 pp.

——— *The Way Out of Educational Confusion*. Cambridge, Harvard University Press, 1931. 41 pp.

FRASER, MOWAT G., *The College of the Future*. New York, Columbia University Press, 1937. 529 pp.

HENDERSON, ALGO D., *Vitalizing Liberal Education*. New York, Harper and Brothers, 1944. 202 pp.

KILPATRICK, WILLIAM H., *Education for a Changing Civilization*. New York, The Macmillan Co., 1927. 143 pp.

——— *et al.*, *The Educational Frontier*. New York, D. Appleton-Century Co., 1933. 325 pp.

65. Francis G. Peabody, *The Religion of an Educated Man* (New York, Macmillan Co., 1903), p. 12.

NEWLON, JESSE H., *Education for Democracy in Our Time*. New York, McGraw-Hill Book Co., Inc., 1939. 242 pp.

B. From the "classicists":

ADLER, MORTIMER J., *How to Read a Book: The Art of Getting a Liberal Education*. New York, Simon and Schuster, 1940. 398 pp.

BARR, STRINGFELLOW, "Report of the President, St. John's College," Supplement to the *Bulletin*. Annually.

BROWN, WILLIAM A., *The Case for Theology in the University*. Chicago, University of Chicago Press, 1938. 123 pp.

BUCHANAN, SCOTT, "A Crisis in Liberal Education," *Amherst Graduates' Quarterly*, February, 1938.

ELIOT, T. S., *The Idea of a Christian Society*. New York, Harcourt, Brace and Co., 1940. 104 pp.

FLEXNER, ABRAHAM, *Universities, American, English, German*. New York, Oxford University Press, 1930. 381 pp.

FOERSTER, NORMAN, *The American State University; Its Relation to Democracy*. Chapel Hill, University of North Carolina Press, 1937. 287 pp.

―――― *The Future of the Liberal College*. New York, D. Appleton-Century Co., 1938. 103 pp.

HUTCHINS, ROBERT M., *Education for Freedom*. Baton Rouge, Louisiana State University Press, 1943. 108 pp.

―――― *The Higher Learning in America*. New Haven, Yale University Press, 1936. 119 pp.

―――― *No Friendly Voice*. Chicago, University of Chicago Press, 1936. 197 pp.

NASH, ARNOLD S., *The University and the Modern World*. New York, The Macmillan Co., 1944. 312 pp.

VAN DOREN, MARK, *Liberal Education*. New York, Henry Holt and Co., 1943. 186 pp.

C. From the "liberals":

BURTON, ERNEST DEWITT, *Education in a Democratic World*. Chicago, University of Chicago Press, 1927. 165 pp.

COLE, STEWART G., *Liberal Education in a Democracy*. New York, Harper and Brothers, 1940. 309 pp.

GIDEONSE, HARRY D., *The Higher Learning in a Democracy*. New York, Farrar and Rinehart, Inc., 1937. 34 pp.

GREENE, THEODORE M., *et al.*, *Liberal Education Re-Examined*. New York, Harper and Brothers, 1943. 134 pp.

Harvard Committee, Report of the, *General Education in a Free Society*. Cambridge, Harvard University Press, 1945. 267 pp.

HENDEL, CHARLES W., "Agenda for Philosophers," *Fortune*, November, 1943.

KELLY, ROBERT L., *The American Colleges and the Social Order*. New York, The Macmillan Co., 1940. 380 pp.

MEIKLEJOHN, ALEXANDER, *Education Between Two Worlds*. New York, Harper and Brothers, 1942. 303 pp.

——— *Freedom and the College*. New York, The Century Co., 1923. 231 pp.

Obligation of Universities to the Social Order, The. New York, New York University Press, 1933. 503 pp.

WILKINS, ERNEST H., *The Changing College*. Chicago, University of Chicago Press, 1927. 132 pp.

——— *The College and Society*. New York, The Century Co., 1932. 173 pp.

WRISTON, HENRY M., *The Nature of a Liberal College*. Appleton, Wis., Lawrence College Press, 1937. 177 pp.

CHAPTER VIII

THE SEPARATION OF CHURCH AND STATE

ALL the interest of state college administrators in religion is meaningless if there exists definite legal prohibition against a partnership between public education and religion. All the propriety of including religion as study, worship and activity, attested to by educational philosophies, is inapplicable to state institutions if they are powerless to act. Before the conclusions of the two preceding chapters can be applied to publicly supported colleges and universities, careful attention needs to be paid to the legal status of religion in public education and to the principle of "the separation of church and state."

Does there exist, of necessity, a difference between what tax-supported and what private institutions can think and do concerning religion? As has been earlier noted in brief, many educators, both religious and secular, have felt, and some still feel, that state and municipal support and public control of education preclude automatically any inclusion of religion in the programs of such institutions. Their belief is based upon their misconception of the principle of the separation of church and state, which supposedly prevents any connection between religion and public education, and upon their lack of information as to what the law has to say on the subject.

John Dewey gave the weight of his reputation to the notion. In an early treatment of the subject he discussed as one the two separate questions,

. . . why the American tradition is so strong against any connection of state and church, why it dreads even the rudiments of religious teaching in state-maintained schools.[1]

The problem was pursued relentlessly by Alvin W. Johnson, whose judgment was that the state's

1. John Dewey, "Religion and Our Schools," *Hibbert Journal*, p. 800.

. . . attitude with respect to the public schools is one of absolute and impartial "neutrality" toward all religious doctrines, whether they be drawn from the Bible or another source. . . . In short, its purpose is secular education with no meddling in the province of the church. . . . It is only as such a position is taken that the principles and ideals upon which our government is founded, namely, the complete separation of church and state, may be maintained.[2]

If Dewey and Johnson are right, then the presence of religion in any form in a state institution is both illegal and inappropriate; and we would be forced, of necessity, to limit the present discussion solely to church-related and independent colleges. But, fortunately for those who believe the study and practice of religion should be fostered in all types of educational institutions, Dewey, Johnson and their followers are mistaken in their notions.

Their point of view can be refuted in several ways. First of all, a trend in educational thinking away from such a rigid conception of the separation of church and state is observable. This trend has already been noticed with reference to college executives in Chapter VI. Secondly, it is a fact that in tax-supported institutions at the present time there exists a great deal of religion, recognized as such, legally approved, and even in some cases required. We shall have occasion in later chapters to show the considerable extent to which state institutions of higher education make official provisions for religion. The presence of religious instruction in the public elementary and secondary schools has been thoroughly explored by numerous scholars, and the evidence is readily available.[3]

These arguments, however, would likely have had little effect on such strong objectors as Johnson. Admitting that there was often a connection between religion and public education he contended that any existing relationship was unconstitutional, since it involved a denial of religious liberty and represented a regression from the principle of the separation of church and state. With

2. Alvin W. Johnson, *The Legal Status of Church-State Relationships in the United States* (Minneapolis, University of Minnesota Press, 1934), p. 282.

3. See, for example, J. K. Jackson and C. F. Malmberg, *Religious Education and the State* (New York, Doubleday, Doran & Co., 1928); S. W. Brown, *The Secularization of American Education;* F. Ernest Johnson, "The United States," in I. L. Kandel, ed., *Educational Yearbook, 1932* (New York, Teachers College, Columbia University, 1933); and *Religion and Public Education,* American Council on Education Studies, Series I, No. 22, IX (February, 1945).

particular reference to the teaching of religion in the public schools, he said:

Occasionally we have failed to attain the high ideal which our constitution places before us in granting to every American citizen fullest protection in his religious belief; but such civic inertia has been no fault of the constitution and has been in violation of its spirit.[4]

A complete refutation of the views of Johnson, Dewey and others, therefore, must be based upon the history of the relations of church and state in this country. It is outside the scope of our discussion to deal with such matters in detail, but the general development of the principle can be outlined.[5]

The phrase, "separation of church and state," was first applied to the result of the struggle for religious liberty in the colony of Virginia. As a result of the Great Awakening, the dissenting denominations experienced a rapid growth in power and influence in the years immediately preceding and during the Revolutionary War. They rebelled against the restrictions imposed upon them by the established Church of England. Finding allies among such intellectual liberals as Madison and Jefferson, they succeeded first in securing the passage of the Bill of Rights in 1776 and later of the Statute of Religious Freedom in 1786.

It is important to note that, though Jefferson was the author of the latter document and is usually given credit for its passage, he was out of the country when it finally passed, and the real credit belongs to the dissenting denominations who rallied to Madison's leadership against the establishment. Jefferson, it is true, spoke of the "wall of separation" necessary between church and state, but to those who were most largely responsible for its actual achievement, "separation" never did mean such complete division of provinces.

These two Virginia enactments provided for the first real religious liberty on American soil. Maryland, Pennsylvania and

4. Alvin W. Johnson, *op. cit.*, p. 284. Others of a similar point of view are B. H. Hartogensis, "Denial of Equal Rights to Religious Minorities and Non-Believers in the United States," *Yale Law Journal*, XXXIX (March, 1930), 659–682; and Frank Swancara, *Obstruction of Justice by Religion* (Denver, W. H. Courtright Publishing Co., 1936).

5. For a full discussion, see Sanford H. Cobb, *The Rise of Religious Liberty in America* (New York, Macmillan Co., 1902); R. Kemp Morton, *God in the Constitution* (Nashville, Cokesbury Press, 1933); and M. Searle Bates, *Religious Liberty, An Inquiry* (New York, Harper & Brothers, 1945).

Rhode Island may have been the leaders in the movement toward toleration; but equality of all religious sects before the law, a very different thing from toleration, was secured first in Virginia. Those who are interested in the difference, which Madison and his followers recognized, will find illuminating his reasons for amending Patrick Henry's original Bill of Rights to provide not merely for toleration but for full religious liberty.[6]

The result achieved in Virginia became the precedent for the Federal Government when the Constitution was drafted by the Philadelphia Convention in 1787. Religious liberty was assumed in that document, as its protagonists made clear in the various state ratifying bodies. But to make assurance doubly sure the First Amendment, ratified in 1791, stated: "Congress shall make no law respecting an establishment of religion, or prohibiting the free exercise thereof." Each state, of course, was still free to maintain a religious establishment if it so desired, and several states did so, notably Connecticut until 1818 and Massachusetts until 1833. But as far as the Federal Government was concerned, establishment was doomed and religious liberty was guaranteed.

This achievement, first in Virginia and later in the Federal Government, was called "the separation of church and state." The fact is significant, therefore, that "separation" was synonymous with the struggle for the political equality of all religious sects. Such equality, or disestablishment, or "separation," had no intention of preventing the churches' giving opinions on moral and religious matters in politics,[7] for it was by way of giving opinions and implementing their opinions with action that the "separation" was achieved. Historically, the action

. . . was not . . . a blow aimed at religion, but a staff to support struggling multitudes as they sought liberty and happiness, by the aid of religious convictions concerning . . . these priceless objectives.[8]

Moreover, the doctrine has not prevented the *official* recognition, throughout the years and in numerous ways, that the United States is a religious nation.[9] There exists a common nonsectarian

6. See Cobb, *op. cit.*, pp. 490 ff.

7. For fuller discussion, see W. E. Hocking, *Man and the State* (New Haven, Yale University Press, 1926), pp. 435 ff.

8. Morton, *op. cit.*, p. 58.

9. See, for example, David J. Brewer, *The United States a Christian Nation* (Philadelphia, J. C. Winston Co., 1905); and Bates, *op. cit.*

faith among the vast majority of citizens to which the Federal, state and local governments attest. The evidence is large: the wording of constitutions and other official documents, oaths of office and in courts of law, Thanksgiving proclamations, observance of Sunday and other holy days as holidays, the use of prayer in legislative bodies, the presence of chaplains in the armed forces, the ascription in state and Federal courts, including the Supreme Court, that certain elements of religious faith are part of the common law of the land.[10] Large doubt may be thrown upon the first half of Dewey's statement above, that "the American tradition is . . . strong against any connection of state and church."

If the first half is doubtful, the second half is demonstrably false: "the American tradition . . . dreads even the rudiments of religious teaching in state-maintained schools." Not by the wildest exaggeration of the history of the principle could it be interpreted as dictating the separation of religion from all public education. Such an interpretation is invalidated not alone by the actual inclusion of religion in the public schools, which has already been referred to, but also by the *legality* of such inclusion, as tested in various courts of law—a much more convincing answer to Johnson's type of argument.[11]

The most famous case is that of *Board of Education v. Minor*, an Ohio action of 1869–72; and opponents of the inclusion of religion in the public schools have long seized what comfort they could from its decision. Alvin W. Johnson believed that in this judgment the Ohio Supreme Court drew a line of separation between Christianity and the law, and therefore between religion and public education,[12] but his notion is based upon an inadequate reading of the opinion of the presiding judge, Justice Welch. For the decision in the "Cincinnati case" was simply as follows: the community possesses a freedom either to exclude or to include religion in its schools, as it sees fit.[13] This freedom of the community with respect to religion in the schools is parallel to the

10. See, for example, L. A. Weigle, "Public Education and Religion," *Religious Education*, XXXV, 2 (April–June, 1940), 67–75.

11. As well as writings already cited, see also Ward W. Keesecker, "The Legal Status of Bible Reading and Religious Instruction in the Public Schools," *United States Department of Interior Bulletin*, 1930, No. 14; and Emerson O. Bradshaw, "Can Religion Be Taught in Our Public Schools?" *Religious Education*, XXXV, 1 (January–March, 1940), 32–40.

12. Alvin W. Johnson, *op. cit.*, p. 84.

13. See *Board of Education v. Minor*, 23 Ohio St. 211.

freedom which the Federal Constitution grants to any state with respect to a religious establishment.

Does this mean, therefore, that there is no such principle as the separation of church and state? On the contrary, it means simply that the principle, admittedly a sound one, has often been misunderstood. The misunderstanding has grown partially out of the unfortunate wording by which the principle has come to be known in common parlance, for no such "complete separation" as Johnson thought, or "wall of separation" as Jefferson wrote, was ever either intended or established. The doctrine which we have come to call "separation" is simply that, as Luther A. Weigle stated it,

. . . church and state are mutually free. It means a separation of control, so that neither church nor state will attempt to control the other.[14]

And it indicates, as a corollary, that since the "state," or Federal Government, can "make no law," the decision as to the inclusion of religion rests in the hands of the several states. This, of course, has brought upon us well-intentioned chaos of custom. As F. Ernest Johnson—his point of view is no kin to the Johnson above—wrote for the American Council on Education's recent conference on "Religion and Public Education,"

. . . the widespread discussion of the question . . . seems to assume, for the most part, that there is an "American way," defined by the doctrine of "separation of church and state." Undoubtedly this doctrine is subscribed to heartily by educators, by legislators, to a large extent by religious leaders—many of whom are among the most ardent advocates of the principle— and by the general public. But when it is asked, "What are the implications of that doctrine in terms of school policies?" there is no definite answer; rather, there is a wide variety of answers. Indeed, the question confronting us is not whether an established policy shall be set aside and some innovation adopted, but what choice shall be made among existing practices, which run all the way from rigid exclusion of religion to a broad accommodation to the religious views of the community. Another way to put it is that a study of education laws, state constitutional provisions, and administrative directives makes clear that the

14. L. A. Weigle, "The American Tradition and the Relation between Religion and Education," in *Religion and Public Education*, p. 33. For a fuller development of this point of view, see W. C. Bower, *Church and State in Education* (Chicago, University of Chicago Press, 1944).

principle of *public control* of the schools is strongly established, but there is no agreement as to what *public policy* should be in respect to the place of religion in education.[15]

The conclusion for the tax-supported colleges is obvious: there does not exist any nation-wide legal or constitutional principle which prevents such institutions from including religion in their programs if they so desire. Their own state laws or court interpretations may raise difficulties, but these occur in only a small minority of the states,[16] and there is no state in which nothing at all can be done.

The problem of including religion in the state colleges, therefore, is primarily not a matter of changing constitutions and laws. It is, rather, the necessity for overthrowing outmoded precedent and mistaken opinion as to what is constitutionally and legally permissible. But precedent and local interpretation are extremely difficult factors with which to deal. In actual practice, as we shall see in detail in the following chapters, state institutions have reacted to them in multitudinous ways, running from complete neglect to extensive inclusion of religion. And this variety of practice has its support in theory. The executive of one state institution may be convinced that trouble would ensue if he paid part of the salary of a Y.M.C.A. worker on his campus. His fellow executive in a neighboring state, however, may feel that the time is ripe for the establishment of a full-fledged department of religion. Though the actual legal status in the two states were substantially the same, yet each president might be right in his assessment of what local interpretation would allow or what his constituency would support.

He might be right, or he might be wrong. It is a problem in which hesitation and desire pull against each other, the temptation to do little or nothing, for fear the state law or public opinion would disapprove, wrestling with the desire to foster the religious growth of the students to the full measure of the institution's influence. Often the struggle as to which of these two wins the upper hand is based not on legal provisions nor even primarily on considerations of local interpretation but on the character of the executives themselves. In this regard, at least, the future looks bright, for though hesitancy is still widespread, yet sincere desire is growing, as witness the opinions of state college administrators

15. F. Ernest Johnson, "Policies and Practices of American Public Schools with Respect to Religion," in *Religion and Public Education*, pp. 48–49.
   16. See Keesecker, *op. cit.*

in Chapter VI. The presidents of tax-supported institutions are more eager to foster religion than ever before, at least in the twentieth century. What is more, they are progressively discovering that there are fewer handicaps in their way, and that often what they want to do they can do.[17]

One thing that they do not want to do, which is at the same time the one thing that they cannot do, is to encourage sectarianism. Here, at least, both the law and public opinion are clear and firm. It still remains, however, that what is considered sectarian in one place may not be so in another. In some states, notably Wisconsin in an oft-quoted decision of 1890, the Bible has been declared to be a sectarian book. But of the sixteen decisions on this point by 1930, the count stood twelve to four favorable to Bible reading, while in the same year eleven states actually required it in the public schools.[18] Here again, therefore, local interpretation is a key factor, for though sectarianism is universally condemned, there is no readily accepted definition as to what sectarianism is.[19]

The end of the matter, then, is simply that the separation of church and state is not a disabling principle, once and for all deciding the issue as to whether or not religion is to be allowed a place in public education. Tax-supported institutions may include religion in various ways in their programs, as long as that religion is not sectarian, and to the full extent to which state law and public opinion allow. State law is not nearly as prohibitory as has been thought in the past. Public opinion is not static: where skeptical or even hostile, it can be changed; and it is often more favorable than college executives have dared imagine. With all the progress toward the inclusion of religion which has been made in recent years, there is scarcely a state institution that cannot do more than it is now doing. And when college executives speak of their desire that religion be fostered, and when educational philosophers indicate the propriety of its presence in the college program, such statements may as legitimately be applied to the tax-supported institutions as to the church-related and independent colleges.

17. See Clarence P. Shedd, "Religion in State Universities," *Journal of Higher Education.*

18. See Keesecker, *op. cit.*

19. See F. Ernest Johnson, "Policies and Practices of American Public Schools with Respect to Religion," *op. cit.,* p. 61.

CHAPTER IX

CHAPEL

COLLEGES which profess an interest in religion and subscribe to a philosophy of higher education allowing a large place to religion are, consequently, impelled to make adequate provision for the religious growth of their students. We have considered what they say and what they believe; it remains for us to examine what they do.

Some have been criticized because their programs often fall short of fulfilling their religious aims.[1] But complete fulfillment is not to be expected if their aims are high. It is enough that they recognize the obligation which their purposes impose upon them to approach fulfillment as closely as possible. This many of them do. In the catalogues of hosts of colleges, for example, statements concerning their religious ideals are immediately followed by descriptions of the ways in which these ideals are implemented. Bethany of West Virginia says:

One of the expressed aims of the college is "To provide higher education in an atmosphere sympathetic to Christian ideals and Christian faith and to conserve and develop the moral character and religious life of its students." This aim is meant to bear upon instruction, counseling, and social life as well as formal religious services.[2]

Then follows a discussion of "Convocation," "The College Church," "Pre-Easter Services," and "Instruction." Similarly, Augustana of Illinois speaks of its aim:

To seek to stimulate every student endeavor by which an enlarged interest in and a more intelligent expression of the Christian life may be realized—as through participation in Bible classes, religious services daily in chapel, and regularly in services of worship, community and missionary enterprises of the Church, and the like.[3]

1. See, for example, Clyde A. Milner, *The Dean of the Small College* (Boston, Christopher Publishing House, 1936), pp. 27 ff.; and Laird T. Hites, *The Effective Christian College.*
2. *Bethany College Bulletin*, XXXIII, 3 (March, 1940), 76.
3. *Augustana Bulletin* (Illinois), Series XXXV, 1 (February, 1940), 22.

An interest in religion, therefore, is usually accompanied by numerous provisions in the total college program designed to encourage the religious development of the undergraduates.

The traditional provisions have been chapel services and courses in religion in the regular curriculum. These two, however, do not exhaust the methods for including religion. Ingenious ways of encouraging the voluntary religious organizations have been attempted. There has been provided official leadership for programs of worship and of religious activities. Religious counseling has been instituted. These and other methods will be considered in this and the chapters to follow.

A word of explanation is necessary concerning the facts and figures to which reference will be made. World War II put the various parts of colleges' programs out of normal balance one with another. Offerings in religion, like those in other fields of the humanities and social sciences, often suffered by reason of the necessary emphasis on the natural sciences. Heroic efforts were made to retain both curricular and extracurricular provisions in a state of health,[4] but these efforts produced widely varying results. Thus a survey of the actual situation in any of the war years or today would produce a distorted picture.

Moreover, this "actual situation" for any recent year is almost impossible to ascertain, for the custom of colleges varies in the extent to which they reflect the current picture in their catalogues. Some catalogues retain only what is actually to be offered during the year in question; others continue to include in their listings items which are held in abeyance until normality returns. Though today's situation is vastly different from that of the war years, it is still abnormal. A reliable picture can be gained, therefore, only by reference to the years immediately before the war, when the programs of the colleges were a fairly normal reflection of their aims and efforts. Consequently the following facts and figures will be based, for the most part, on the situation in the last full peacetime academic year, 1940–41. Tabulations of the figures, with explanations as to their sources, will be found in the appendices.

4. See Clarence P. Shedd and Granville T. Walker, "War-Time Adjustments in the Teaching of Religion," *Journal of Bible and Religion*, and Clarence P. Shedd, "The Movements of Religion in American Higher Education," *Journal of the American Association of Collegiate Registrars*.

From the beginning of higher education in this country colleges have taken time to worship. Until the latter years of the nineteenth century chapel services were assumed to be an indispensable part of the college program. And even as the element of compulsion characterized class attendance, so also chapel was required. As late as the 'eighties it was recognized as the "symbol of college unity and life." [5]

But by that time a different attitude was becoming noticeable. At the opening of Cornell University in 1868, chapel attendance was made voluntary. Compulsory services of worship were discontinued at the University of Michigan in 1871. The most publicized defection from the ranks was that of Harvard, which made its chapel voluntary in 1886. Unavoidably the question of compulsion came to be debated in numerous colleges, and here and there worship services were dispensed with altogether.

A few state institutions continued to provide chapel. For example, the Visiting Committee to the University of North Carolina in 1893 noted with approval the presence of "a Chapel for daily morning prayers." [6] In 1885 a student was actually expelled from the University of Illinois for not attending compulsory chapel, and the courts upheld the action. But the trend in the tax-supported institutions was toward abolition. In 1894, only nine years after the expulsion, the University of Illinois discontinued chapel. Purdue abolished such services in 1901. After the discontinuance of compulsory services at Michigan in 1871, daily prayers were held until 1895, then semiweekly vespers which were eventually abolished. Thus around the beginning of the century the time-honored institution of college chapel was feeling the liberalizing and secularizing pressures characteristic of the age.

But after the earlier period in which the tax-supported institutions discontinued their services of worship, the elimination of chapel from the programs of colleges has ceased almost completely. Moreover, throughout the twentieth century the trend away from compulsion has been gradual.

Here and there in the first two decades requirements were relaxed, so that a tendency toward the voluntary program was

5. C. H. Patton and W. T. Field, *Eight O'Clock Chapel* (Cambridge, Mass., Houghton Mifflin Co., 1927), p. 201.

6. Kemp P. Battle, *History of the University of North Carolina* (Raleigh, N.C., Edwards and Broughton Printing Co., 1912), II, 493.

discernible.[7] As early as 1893 DePauw had abolished compulsory chapel. In his *History of Dartmouth College* Leon Richardson said that

. . . in 1903, all compulsion in relation to Sunday church was abandoned on the ground that more required religion was then in vogue in Dartmouth than in most of the colleges in New England, and that the service tended "in the opinion of the president and faculty to be detrimental to the spiritual life of the students." [8]

About the same time Sunday chapel was discontinued at Illinois College. The historian of Davidson College reported that compulsory church attendance was discontinued there in 1913 on the promise of the students that they would attend voluntary Bible and mission study classes.

In the 'twenties the movement for a while gained ground more rapidly, and Harvard began to feel that its leadership was at last being recognized. Francis G. Peabody wrote in 1930:

It is reassuring to notice among the signs of the present time a manifest inclination on the part of other colleges and universities to follow, even if tardily, the way which Harvard University has gone, and to apply, with various modifications, the principle of voluntary worship.[9]

He referred approvingly to the recent developments at Amherst, Bowdoin, Brown, Williams, Chicago, Dartmouth and Yale. Amherst abolished compulsory church in 1927; a year later Chicago did away with compulsory chapel. All religious services at Dartmouth were placed on a voluntary basis in 1925. The struggle at Yale to which reference will be made later took place in 1926, which was the same year Vassar adopted voluntary chapel.

But the "inclination" of which Peabody spoke, while continuing, did not develop into any widespread adoption of the "principle of voluntary worship." Compared with the huge body of colleges which retained compulsion, the number of those making changes

7. See Isaac Sharpless, *The American College* (New York, Doubleday, Page & Co., 1915), p. 199.
8. Leon B. Richardson, *History of Dartmouth College*, p. 715.
9. F. G. Peabody, "Voluntary Worship," in S. E. Morison, ed., *The Development of Harvard University since the Inauguration of President Eliot, 1869–1929*, p. lvi.

was small, and in the main the patterns of the past persisted. While the rest of the educational program has undergone upheaval in recent years, college worship remains substantially as it was at the beginning of the century. As one investigator remarked in 1935: "It is interesting to note how little change there has been in the general plan and content of chapel services in the last twenty-five years." [10]

This opinion is confirmed by an examination of the various surveys of chapel programs made at different times in the past twenty years. At least seven such investigations have been conducted.[11] Though some of them are based upon an inadequate sampling of colleges and are limited to a particular type of institution, the group of surveys as a whole presents a comparatively unchanging picture and depicts consistently the following facts:

That a large majority of the colleges of the nation provide chapel services.

That church-related colleges, almost without exception, conduct such services, a large majority of which are compulsory in nature.

That independent colleges usually hold worship services of some sort, though the percentage is not as high as that of the denominational colleges, nor is the proportion of compulsory chapel as large.

That a minority of the state institutions provide chapel, only a few of which compel attendance.

These conclusions are sound for the present day. The actual figures for the last full peacetime academic year are given in the appendices. The results of the investigations summarized therein show that approximately 70 per cent of the non-Catholic colleges

10. Lura E. Aspinwall, "Status of Chapel Services in Forty-eight Colleges," *Christian Education*, XIX, 1 (October, 1935), 42.

11. See Edward S. Boyer, "Religious Education in Colleges, Universities and Schools of Religion," *Christian Education*, XI, 1 (October, 1927), 8–10; R. H. Edwards, J. M. Artman, and Galen M. Fisher, *Undergraduates*, pp. 253–257; Floyd W. Reeves *et al.*, *The Liberal Arts College*, pp. 411–414; Paul N. Elbin, *The Improvement of College Worship* (New York, Teachers College, Columbia University, 1932), chap. i; Hugh Hartshorne, Helen R. Stearns, and Willard E. Uphaus, *Standards and Trends in Religious Education*, chap. xiv; Aspinwall, *op. cit.*; and Gould Wickey and Ruth A. Eckhart, *A National Survey of Courses in Bible and Religion in American Universities and Colleges* (pamphlet. Bloomington, Ind., Indiana Council on Religion in Higher Education [1936]), pp. 31–33.

with which we are concerned provide some sort of worship services.

The ratio of compulsory to voluntary services, for those which sponsor chapel at all, is roughly a little over two to one among those institutions accredited by the Association of American Universities. The percentages are: compulsory chapel, 48 per cent; voluntary chapel, 20 per cent; no services at all, 32 per cent. But when the reference is broadened to include the host of smaller colleges lacking such national accreditation, the proportion of those providing compulsory chapel rises from about 48 to over 55 per cent of the total number of colleges involved. Clearly the smaller and weaker colleges are more loyal to the principle of compulsion than their larger and stronger neighbors.

For the different types of colleges the figures vary appreciably. All of the church-related colleges provide some sort of worship program, and attendance is compulsory at approximately 90 per cent of them. Among independent colleges around 85 per cent have chapel services, the majority, possibly as high as two thirds, being compulsory in nature. Only 27 per cent of the state institutions hold chapel, and the majority of these services are voluntary. An even smaller proportion of municipal colleges provide services of worship.

An effort to distinguish among men's, women's, and coeducational institutions yields only slight variations. The independent colleges of these three types return strikingly similar figures. Among the state institutions, those for women seem to provide more opportunities for worship than men's or coeducational colleges, but the numbers involved are too few to lead to any definite conclusions.

Though this discussion is not concerned with Negro, Catholic and teachers' colleges, it is interesting to notice that the first two have larger requirements for chapel than any other group except the denominational colleges, and that the last excels in this respect the state and municipal universities while still falling below the others.

Previous studies of chapel programs have not been concerned sufficiently with the frequency of services to enable any clear trends in this particular aspect of the question to be discernible. At the present time the most common number of compulsory chapel services is four a week, but frequencies of one, two, and three a week are all well represented in the college scene. State institutions provide chapel less often than independent and denominational colleges. The average length of time of the services in church-related colleges varies from fifteen to fifty minutes, the majority being approximately twenty to thirty minutes in duration.[12] The chapel hour is usually mid-morning.[13]

Traditionally "chapel" has signified a period of worship held on weekdays and led by some college official, often by the president himself. But Sunday services have also been common, and have been more nearly "church" than "chapel." When Harvard instituted voluntary chapel in 1886, a "Board of Preachers" was established at the same time. This Board was composed of ministers from outside the college, whose duties were to preach on Sunday morning, live on the campus for a few days for purposes of counseling students, and conduct daily chapel exercises.[14]

Though the whole of Harvard's plan has not been generally followed, the idea of visiting preachers has received wide acceptance in the twentieth century. Bowdoin, for example, began bringing visiting clergymen to the campus in 1904. Mount Holyoke instituted the practice in 1905. Chicago followed Harvard's plan rather closely in 1901, and still sponsors a large visiting-preacher program. By 1914 a number of eastern colleges were inviting preachers for Sunday services, for Henry S. Coffin's volume of *University Sermons,* published in that year, contains sermons preached at Yale, Harvard, Princeton, Columbia, Brown, New York University, Chicago, Williams, Dartmouth, Wellesley, Vassar, Mount Holyoke and Bryn Mawr.[15] In more recent times a host of other institutions have adopted the practice, as the discussion of individual college programs will later make clear. In the present day Sunday services, led either by members of the college staff or by visitors, and held either at the regular church hour or at vesper-time, are provided by a goodly number of institutions.

A mere recital of statistics however does not picture adequately the significance of chapel services as a means by which the colleges evidence their responsibility for religion. Certain other considerations concerning the nature of those services require at-

12. Aspinwall, *op. cit.,* p. 39.

13. Elbin, *op. cit.,* p. 64.

14. John H. Gardiner, *Harvard* (New York, Oxford University Press, 1914), pp. 64, 155.

15. Henry S. Coffin, *University Sermons* (New Haven, Yale University Press, 1914), Preface.

tention. First of all, the relatively unchanging character of chapel throughout the century does not imply a lack of serious questioning or a stagnation of interest in the subject. The problem of voluntary versus compulsory chapel, for example, has received intense study, and arguments pro and con have often been marshaled.[16] While one commentator points out that "it is necessary to keep [chapel] compulsory if students are to be in attendance," [17] another argues that "compulsory worship . . . is a contradiction in terms." [18]

It is the opinion of many that students will come of their own free will if the programs are of sufficient worth. Others believe that valuable habits are often based on coercion.[19]

So the discussion proceeds, with no final decision being as yet in evidence. It is instructive to note, however, that the early flight from compulsion on the part of the larger institutions coincided in time with the widespread adoption of the principle of election in the curriculum. The continuing trend toward voluntarism in worship has been slight in recent years, indicative both of the shift from requirement to election in all the college's program and, at the same time, the latter-day hesitancy to adopt free election throughout the curriculum. And Harvard, it is no surprise to find, led the way in voluntarism for worship even as in free election for studies.

In this connection it is important to realize that, for many institutions, the change from compulsory to voluntary chapel represented not an effort to escape from responsibility but rather an assumption of larger responsibility. Harvard, for example, felt that its move was "not a surrender but an advance," and rejoiced in the "transition from religion as a discipline to religion as a privilege." [20] Other institutions in more recent years have accompanied their shift to voluntarism with increased provisions of other sorts for the religious development of their students; illus-

16. See, for example, Galen M. Fisher, ed., *Religion in the Colleges*, pp. 56–61; Edwards, Artman, and Fisher, *op. cit.*, pp. 253–257; Hites, *op. cit.*, pp. 222–226.

17. Aspinwall, *op. cit.*, p. 41.

18. E. H. Wilkins, *The College and Society*, p. 95.

19. Esther McD. Lloyd-Jones and Margaret R. Smith, *A Student Personnel Program for Higher Education* (New York, McGraw-Hill Book Co., 1938), p. 229.

20. F. G. Peabody, "Voluntary Worship," in S. E. Morison, ed., *op. cit.*, pp. lii, lvii.

tration will be furnished in the discussions of Yale, Syracuse and Chicago, to follow in Chapter XIII.

It becomes obvious, therefore, that the problem is deeper than merely the question of voluntarism versus compulsion. Underneath this surface disagreement lies a basic harmony of desire that the services, whether or not required, be vitally religious. But here is the core of past and present difficulties—the chapel services in numbers of institutions are not religious at all. A recent investigation concerned primarily with church-related colleges said:

Certain facts about college chapel seem to be self-evident. Colleges have greatly overestimated the value of maintaining regular chapel programs, just because they upheld tradition or suited administrative convenience. Reliance upon required attendance has doubtless encouraged planless drifting. The purposes of worship have not been reconsidered in the light of the problems of youth. There is only the vaguest notion as to results in character change and attitudes. Objective measures are not used. Programs that might be built around some single unifying concept, some historic occasion, or some impending task to be performed, are too often hodgepodges of Scripture, prayer, song, announcements, business, and pep sessions. The needs of youth . . . are not being met on a distinctively religious level through the characteristic chapel services of church colleges.[21]

It is claimed by another that

. . . little can be judged by the size of the college chapel or the existence of daily service. These may be the outward and visible signs of a strong spiritual life within the institutions, or again they may be, and frequently are, little more than conventional gestures.[22]

A study of 1928 reported:

The chief reasons for chapel exercises given to the inquirers in the interviews were not religious value, but tradition, social unification of the student body and administrative convenience.[23]

And at the present time many colleges frankly admit in their catalogues that chapel is for other than religious purposes. Two quotations, which might as well be anonymous, will suffice:

21. Hartshorne, Stearns, and Uphaus, *op. cit.*, p. 166.
22. Constance Warren, *A New Design for Women's Education*, p. 199.
23. Edwards, Artman, and Fisher, *op. cit.*, p. 253.

Unless excused for good reasons, all students are required to attend chapel and assembly not only because these gatherings seek to minister to the spiritual needs of the college community, but, also, because they conserve the unity of student life, and give an opportunity both for announcing college events and for promoting college interests.

All students are expected to attend chapel services. . . . This convocation is not only for the purpose of holding religious exercises, but also for hearing public announcements and for cultivating the college spirit and good fellowship.

Such a development, of course, is deplored by those who conceive of chapel as one of the primary methods for providing for the religious growth of students. Thus, much attention has been given in recent years to the problem of making the chapel services consciously and fruitfully religious.[24] The various studies have emphasized the importance of such factors as an adequate length of time, lack of conflict with other items in the college schedule, a correlation with the rest of the religious provisions of the college, student participation in planning and conducting the exercises, competent leadership, wholehearted administrative support, and, above all, careful preparation of the services themselves in the light of the religious needs of youth. The effort of DePauw in 1933 illustrated the increased concern of colleges to make their chapel exercises religiously vital:

The old type of emotional appeal had lost its validity among the students of this generation. To meet this change in religious interests, a new kind of chapel service has been developed. For many years the DePauw chapel service had been a combination of student "pep meetings" with a religious tinge, consisting generally of a hymn, a prayer, and a talk of any sort. A few years ago, beginning as an experiment, there was arranged for each Wednesday noon, a voluntary worship service to be held in the church auditorium. The service is a formal worship service throughout, with a processional and anthem by the University Choir, with appropriate prayers and an address not exceeding six minutes in length. This service has proven astonishingly popular, because the students have found it helpful, and they

24. See, for example, Hites, *op. cit.*, chap. vii; Aspinwall, *op. cit.*; Galen M. Fisher, ed., *op. cit.*; and Elbin, *op. cit.*

have shown their appreciation by their uniformly large attendance.[25]

Chapel, therefore, is one important activity through which colleges express their interest in and responsibility for religion. The author's own comments on the present situation will be reserved for a later chapter. Suffice it to say now that students of the subject uniformly agree that chapel must be made more meaningful than it now is if it is to fulfill the religious purposes of the college. As Paul Elbin concluded his investigation in 1932:

In a day when every item of the college organization is being scrutinized with a view to its usefulness, the chapel service can not hide behind the skirts of sanctity and tradition any inadequacies it may have. If the historic tradition of college chapel is to be continued, it will be because the chapel has not lagged behind the classroom and the laboratory in its devotion to truth and to the needs of a new generation.[26]

25. W. W. Sweet, *Indiana Asbury—DePauw University 1837–1937* (Cincinnati, Abingdon Press, 1937), pp. 258–259.

26. Elbin, *op. cit.*, p. 31.

CHAPTER X

INSTRUCTION IN RELIGION

CHAPEL may be said to represent the continuity of interest in religion on the part of colleges. Correspondingly, course offerings in religious subjects signify the changes and developments which have taken place within that continuity. Religion as a regular study in the curriculum is largely an outgrowth of the increased concern of the twentieth century.

This is not to say, however, that the study of religion had no place in the college during the previous century and earlier. Certainly in the early church-sponsored institutions religion was taught in numerous ways. Many people in those days believed the Bible was not to be debased by use as a textbook for critical study, but there were informal Bible reading and teaching in the homes of faculty members or in student groups. Moreover, actual courses in "moral philosophy" or "apologetics" or denominational doctrines and history existed here and there; and the religious convictions of nearly all professors of the time enabled them to do much teaching of religion, unofficially and often unconsciously, in the pursuit of their own subject matter, whatever it was. Thus religion was taught, in a sense, throughout the whole curriculum, but its status as a regular part of the course of study was not always proclaimed, and was often merely a by-product of the college program.

Significant as this work undoubtedly was, yet it was of such a nature as to succumb easily to the educational movements of the latter part of the nineteenth century. As professional education developed, the theological seminaries took over such studies as Hebrew, New Testament Greek, and doctrine. Then with the enlargement of curricular offerings in all subjects, the relative prominence of the religion that remained was reduced. The process of secularization eliminated the subject entirely from state institutions and had its effect on the whole college scene. And the growing spirit of secularism was of influence in numberless ways, not least in that, since education was now often thought of as an "impartial" presentation of "truth" without any effort at indoctrination, fewer and fewer professors cared or dared to bring religious concerns and convictions into their teaching of other subjects.

A combination of factors, therefore, was responsible for the fact that by the turn of the century the study of religion was missing from the curricula of hosts of colleges throughout the country, even from many affiliated with church bodies.[1] The work of religious instruction, when it existed at all, was most often on a voluntary and extracurricular basis, being provided by such agencies as the Bible classes of the Y.M.C.A. Actually the Y.M.C.A.'s efforts were prodigious, and from the late 'eighties until the first World War literally thousands were enrolled in their study groups, thus helping in a considerable way to fill the gap.[2]

But such a state of affairs obviously did not satisfy those who were interested in the place of religion in education. In the early years of the new century educators began to explore the possibilities of making religion a subject for study in the regular curriculum.[3] One of the motivating concerns of the Religious Education Association in its establishment in 1903 was this question. Many connected with the voluntary Y.M.C.A. study groups, students in local institutions as well as national leaders, were instrumental in pressing demands that religion be incorporated or reincorporated into official college programs.

Soon numbers of colleges were adding religion to their courses of study. For example, Haverford established a fund for Bible study in 1900. About the same time Illinois College instituted courses in Bible, when Sunday chapel was abolished. A chair of religion was established at Vassar in 1902. Following President Nicholas Murray Butler's report for 1903, in which he "stressed the needs . . . for courses in Biblical literature," [4] Barnard

1. See George A. Coe, *Education in Religion and Morals*, chap. xix; and W. R. Harper, *The Trend in Higher Education*, pp. 55–56.
2. See Clarence P. Shedd, *Two Centuries of Student Christian Movements*, pp. 313–314.
3. See, for example, the annual *Proceedings of the Religious Education Association* (Chicago, 1903 and following) ; Coe, *op. cit.*, chap. xix, and his *The Religion of a Mature Mind* (New York, Fleming H. Revell Co., 1902), *passim*, and *A Social Theory of Religious Education* (New York, Charles Scribner's Sons, 1917), chap. xviii; Henry C. King, *Personal and Ideal Elements in Education*, *passim*; and W. R. Harper, *op. cit.*, chap. iii.
4. A. D. Miller and Susan Myers, *Barnard College; The First Fifty Years* (New York, Columbia University Press, 1939), pp. 72–73.

began a program of religious instruction. At the University of Pittsburgh religious education has been a regular part of the college curriculum since 1913. The development in many colleges took the form of freeing the study of religion from other departments and setting up separate chairs of biblical literature. This whole movement paralleled, one notes, the general trend in higher education of the period, namely, the broadening of the fields and areas for study.

Since the first World War the institution of courses and departments of religion has been extensive and continuing. Exhaustive surveys dealing with the extent of religious instruction in the colleges have been undertaken from time to time.[5] As late as 1916 a committee of the Association of American Colleges, defining the "Efficient College," included in its suggested curriculum only four year-hours of religion, all in Bible, to be taught by the Professor of Latin.[6] But in the last thirty years "instruction in religion has had a phenomenal growth,"[7] as all surveys, and comparisons among them, have affirmed, and the actual offerings on the average far outnumber the minimum set by the 1916 report. This enrichment of instruction in religion has taken place in all types of institutions, state-supported as well as independent and church-controlled.

Particularly in the field of religious education has there been great expansion. As we have seen, courses in other aspects of religion were not unknown in the colleges of the previous century, but religious education as a subject for undergraduate

5. See, for example, Charles Foster Kent, "The Undergraduate Courses in Religion at the Tax-Supported Colleges and Universities of America," *Bulletin of the National Council on Religion in Higher Education*, IV (1923) ; W. E. Uphaus and M. Teague Hipps, "Undergraduate Courses in Religion at Denominational and Independent Colleges and Universities in America," *Bulletin of the National Council on Religion in Higher Education*, VI (1924) ; Lura Beam, "Classroom Instruction in Religion in Two Hundred and Fifty Colleges," *Christian Education*, VIII, 6 (March, 1925) ; W. A. Harper, *Character Building in Colleges*, pp. 136 ff.; Floyd W. Reeves *et al.*, *The Liberal Arts College*, chap. xliv; J. S. Armentrout, *Effectiveness of Presbyterian College Programs in Developing Leadership for Religious Education* (Scottdale, Pa., Mennonite Press, 1936) ; Hugh Hartshorne, Helen R. Stearns, and Willard E. Uphaus, *Standards and Trends in Religious Education*, chaps. xiii and xv; Gould Wickey and R. A. Eckhart, *A National Survey of Courses in Bible and Religion in American Universities and Colleges.*

6. Calvin H. French, "The Efficient College," *Association of American Colleges Bulletin*, II, 3 (April, 1916), 64–65.

7. Hartshorne, Stearns, and Uphaus, *op. cit.*, p. 147.

study is a product of this century. The first survey of courses of this nature, made in 1915, compared their incidence with that of courses in Bible. Of the 140 institutions studied, 67 offered 356 courses in Bible, whereas only 38 provided only 71 courses in religious education. The study further indicated that the majority of courses in religious education had a history of only three years.[8] But progress in the field has been amazingly rapid, as further surveys throughout the years have revealed.[9] Today a large number of colleges have departments of religious education separate from other departments of religion, and nearly all colleges offering any work in religion include courses in the particular subject of religious education.

Because of the tremendous increase in the inclusion of religion in the curriculum, the investigations made at different times during the last twenty years present no consistent factual conclusions as valid as those for chapel services. But general trends are observable, and the numerous surveys progressively approach the following judgments:

That a large majority of the colleges of the nation provide courses in religion.

That a smaller, but substantial, majority have departments of religion separate from other subjects.

That church-related colleges, almost without exception, offer such courses.

That independent colleges usually provide courses, though the percentage is not as high as for the denominational colleges.

That an actual majority of the state institutions give religious instruction, though the percentage is considerably less than for the foregoing groups, and only a minority have separate departments of religion.

That requirements in the study of religion range all the way from being fairly general in the denominational colleges to being nonexistent in the state institutions.

8. Walter S. Athearn, "Religious Education in Colleges," *Religious Education*, X, 5 (October, 1915), 413–414.

9. See, for example, A. A. Brown, *A History of Religious Education in Recent Times* (New York, Abingdon Press, 1923), pp. 235–236; Edward S. Boyer, "Religious Education in Colleges, Universities and Schools of Religion," *Christian Education;* W. M. Alderton *et al., Undergraduate Instruction in Religious Education in the United States*, Religious Education Association Monograph No. 2 (1927); Theron C. McGee, *Religious Education in Certain Evangelical Colleges* ([Philadelphia, University of Pennsylvania],

The picture for the last full peacetime academic year indicates the extent to which the movement for including religion in the college curriculum has progressed. Once again the reader is referred to the appendices for supporting data. Of the more than 700 colleges bearing some mark of accreditation almost 60 per cent have departments of religion. All Catholic colleges and slightly over half of the Negro colleges offer religious instruction in departments, but of the 149 teachers' colleges in the nation, only ten possess departments, and four of these ten are independent rather than tax-supported. Eliminating these three groups of institutions we discover that of the colleges with which this study is primarily concerned over 65 per cent offer religion in regular departments.

For the purpose of examining more thoroughly this latter group, according to the various types of colleges, consideration may conveniently be limited to the 263 institutions receiving at the time the approval of the Association of American Universities. Among church-related, independent and state-supported colleges, the percentages having departments of religion are, respectively, 100, approximately 85 and 30. With respect to the independent classification, a division of colleges into men's, women's, and coeducational, shows little variation from the total percentage; but a similar division for the state institutions reveals the interesting fact that all but one of those for women have departments of religion, while the proportions for the state men's and coeducational colleges are, respectively, three eighths, and only slightly more than a fifth.

Well over half of all colleges possessing departments of religion require students to take some work in the field, and a similar requirement is made by a few which, lacking a separate department, provide courses in religion under some other classification. Requirements occur most often in church-related colleges, and never in state institutions.

Figures with relation to departments, however, do not tell the whole story. The absence of a department of religion does not necessarily indicate that the total curriculum is devoid of all courses concerning the subject. Over two thirds of the colleges which lack departments provide religious instruction elsewhere

---

1928); Walter S. Athearn, *The Minister and the Teacher* (New York, The Century Co., 1932), pp. 242–245; as well as surveys of courses in religion, previously cited.

in their curricular offerings. These, together with the institutions which do have departments, leave a total of only 27 nationally accredited colleges, or a bare 10 per cent, which make no provision at all for the study of religion.

The distribution of the 27 is significant. Three are independent colleges of liberal arts, 8 are independent technological schools, 14 are state institutions, and 2 are municipal colleges. It is obvious, therefore, that from the point of view of those interested in seeing the inclusion of religion in the regular college curriculum, the most desperate situation at the present time, according to percentages, is that of the technological schools. Eight of the total of 11 such institutions not only have no department but also have no courses, and the remaining 3 have only one course each in religion.

The situation with respect to the state institutions is, by comparison, much more encouraging, for the group of 14 without any courses in religion still leaves, out of a total of 70, exactly four fifths offering some measure of religious instruction. If only 30 per cent of the state institutions have departments of religion, 80 per cent of them do manage to include religion in some way in the regular curriculum. This figure, however, should not be taken to indicate too much, for 25 of the 56 state institutions which do provide religious instruction limit their offerings to only one or two courses, and those of the most innocuous variety, consisting of "The Bible as literature" in the English department or "The psychology of religion" in the psychology department.

On the other hand these figures for state colleges do not take into account the religious instruction offered by extracollegiate agencies, such as "colleges" or "schools" or "chairs" of religion, usually representing the collaboration of several of the Protestant denominations.[10] Such establishments are present at 13 of the state institutions which do not have departments of religion of their own. In 12 of the 13 their work is given regular academic credit, and represents in fact the addition of religion to the regular curriculum. They are not included in the above figures, however, because they do not represent what the colleges themselves officially provide. The School of Religion at the State University of Iowa is not counted as one of the 13 because it is now a regular department of the College of Liberal Arts.

10. For a discussion of such work, see Hartshorne, Stearns, and Uphaus, *op. cit.*, pp. 179–191; Kent, *op. cit.*; and Boyer, *op. cit.*

Certainly the implication from figures concerning departments is not that all of them are equally strong or efficient. Some comprehend multitudinous offerings, while others limit themselves to only two or three courses. But at least partial compensation is made for the small departments in the fact that a number of colleges not grouping their offerings into a department of religion provide three, four, five, or even more courses in other departments. Ten of this group are state institutions. The fields most often including courses in religion are English and philosophy.

But even as with chapel exercises, so it is with religious instruction, that a recording of the status in facts and figures fails to elucidate all the pregnant information. No light is given, for example, on the important question as to the nature of course contents. Anyone well acquainted with the college scene is inclined to suspect that much of the study of the Bible, for instance, treats it "either from the historical or the literary point of view, rather than from the distinctly religious angle." [11] This is not to suggest that definite objectives in the teaching of religion are lacking, for the colleges seem to be in fair agreement as to the desired ends.[12] But the means for arriving at these ends are in doubt. One survey concluded: "There is little agreement among colleges . . . as to what courses constitute adequate preparation in religion, or as to the way these courses should be related to one another, or to other departments." [13] This uncertainty is reflected in the wide variety of titles by which departments of religion are called and the conglomeration of course offerings within most departments. The necessary readjustments in such departments incident to the second World War have provoked large experimentation in types of courses and their relationships one with another.[14] But much still remains to be done before the confusion as to what and how to teach in a department of religion is resolved.

A potentially even more dangerous factor is the low intellectual level characteristic of much of the religious instruction now being offered, and the consequent lack of respect in which religion as

11. Herbert E. Hawkes, "Religion in a Liberal Education," chap. xix in R. L. Kelly, ed., *The Effective College* (New York, Association of American Colleges, 1928), pp. 202–203.

12. See, for example, Hartshorne, Stearns, and Uphaus, *op. cit.*, pp. 159–160; and Wickey and Eckhart, *op. cit.*, p. 23.

13. Hartshorne, Stearns, and Uphaus, *op. cit.*, p. 159.

14. See Clarence P. Shedd and Granville T. Walker, "War-Time Adjustments in the Teaching of Religion," *Journal of Bible and Religion.*

a subject of study is often held by the rest of the college. All that glitters in the catalogues is not mentally respectable gold, and courses in religion, as any experienced observer knows, are often "snaps" or "crips." An illuminating example is furnished by a discussion of the effort at one large university to provide "safe" curricular transit for its football players:

We placed the beef in classes where they would receive "sympathetic treatment" and steered them clear of those old sour apples who still insisted on flunking a guy just because he didn't know anything. . . . Accordingly, the typical course with which we loaded down the freshman beefer consisted of classes in Bible, Psychology I, Astronomy, and Music Appreciation. All were "cripples" of the purest ray. Bible was taught by a lovable old gentleman who delivered lofty lectures and never bothered his sleeping class with details like questions or examinations.[15]

It appears therefore that at the present time the major problem concerning religious instruction is not, as in earlier days, to secure its introduction into the curriculum but is rather to improve its quality. Here great gains have been made in the past two decades, notably as a result of the work of the National Council on Religion in Higher Education. Professor Shedd wrote in 1943:

No other provision for the religious life of students has had such steady and hopeful growth. Each of the successive surveys since the first by Prof. Charles Foster Kent in 1922–23 has shown steady increases in number of colleges offering courses, a constant broadening of the range of courses, a raising of the standards of the teaching personnel, and increased enrollment of students. The National Council on Religion in Higher Education, founded by Professor Kent, has been one of the most influential factors in enlarging the conception held by the colleges of their responsibility in this field and in discovering and training a distinguished group of teachers of religion.[16]

This is not to say that the question of inclusion has been finally resolved, for a few colleges are still without religious instruction of any sort, as we have seen, and in a much larger number of others the amount of instruction is totally inadequate.

15. William B. Huie, "How to Keep Football Stars in College," *Collier's*, CVII, 1 (January 4, 1941), 20.

16. Clarence P. Shedd, "The Agencies of Religion in Higher Education," *Religious Education*, p. 292.

But the movement to institute courses and departments of religion has not stopped. Many colleges heretofore barren in the field, particularly state universities, are planning to inaugurate departments as soon as possible; and some, notably the University of Georgia and Louisiana State University, have done so since the end of the war. Moreover, the problem of inclusion is still being agitated by educators interested in religion.[17]

But as the percentage of colleges offering religion in the curriculum has steadily risen, those colleges eager to demonstrate their concern for the religious growth of their students have shifted their attention to other matters not so easily measurable in figures. Teachers in the field, it is realized, must be as well trained as those in any other, and there are grounds for believing that this is now true.[18] In order not to handicap fatally the teaching of religion, educators are seeking actively to counteract the attitudes of cynicism and agnosticism and the forces of materialism and secularism which have been prevalent in other departments in the past. Since religion and respect for religion can, in a sense, be taught in any department, some colleges are striving to procure, and agencies such as the National Council on Religion in Higher Education are seeking to provide, instructors in all fields who desire to preserve religious values in their work. These and similar concerns, to be discussed more fully in later chapters, are today receiving the careful attention of leaders in higher education.

Thus the battle for the acceptance of religion in the regular course of study is nearly won. But in the deepest sense the problem of the meaningful inclusion of religion is not drawing to a close; rather, it has just begun. The author's own comments on the present situation will be reserved for a concluding chapter; but

17. See, for example, Stewart G. Cole, *Liberal Education in a Democracy,* chap. viii, and his "The Place of Religion in Higher Education," *Religious Education,* XXXV, 4 (October–December, 1940), 205–209; W. C. Bower, "The Teaching of Religion," chap. xv in M. C. Towner, ed., *Religion in Higher Education; Report of the Special Committee of the Faculty on Religious Education, April 11, 1935* (pamphlet. Princeton University, 1935); Paul J. Braisted, *Religion in Higher Education* (pamphlet. Haddam, Conn., Edward W. Hazen Foundation, 1942); Theodore M. Greene, *et al., Liberal Education Re-Examined* (New York, Harper & Brothers, 1943), pp. 66–69; and Reinhold Niebuhr, "The Contribution of Religion to Cultural Unity," *Hazen Pamphlets,* No. 13 (November, 1945).

18. See Wickey and Eckhart, *op. cit.,* p. 17; and Alderton *et al., op. cit.,* chap. iv.

apart from any one person's opinions, the facts make it abundantly clear that the nature of course contents and the quality of teaching must be strengthened in the years ahead. Now more than ever it is being recognized that

Until the curriculum in the field of religion is given educational standing comparable with the work in the various departments it will not be regarded as an integral part of the life of the institution.[19]

But it is not merely that religion be *given* comparable educational standing with other departments; it is also that religion *merit* such standing on the basis of the quality of the work it is now allowed to offer. With all the problems remaining, however, the growth of religion in the curriculum in the twentieth century abundantly testifies to the importance of this method for demonstrating the colleges' interest in and assumption of responsibility for the religious nurture of their students.

19. Shailer Mathews, "The Religious Self-Expression of a University," in M. C. Towner, ed., *op. cit.*, p. vii.

CHAPTER XI

OFFICIAL LEADERSHIP

CHAPEL and courses, worship and study, represent the two-sided program by which colleges have traditionally cared for their students' religious needs. While the program has changed and expanded in this century, its roots are deep in the past. But the third major practice by which administrative responsibility for religion is implemented is, almost without exception, a development of the present century. This method is the provision of official leadership for the religious program of the college.

As we have seen, investigations concerning the nature and extent of worship services and religious instruction have been made by many individuals in recent years. But, so far as the author is aware, there has been no comparable study of college religious leadership. Several writers, it is true, have referred in passing to the development; others have pointed out its necessity, sometimes without realizing the extent to which it had already progressed; and a few in recent years have attempted short studies, which have served admirably to draw attention to the practice.[1] The purpose of this chapter is to supplement these references with a description of the movement up to the present time.

In the early days the religious leadership of the college was usually the responsibility of the president. The evidences that remain in college histories, reminiscences, and volumes of sermons indicate that on the whole he discharged his duties with vigor, efficiency, and consecration. He was generally a minister; even the executives of state institutions were often clergymen. Since his religious functions consisted simply of leading chapel exercises and counseling students, the task was not too burdensome as long

---

1. See, for example, Arthur C. Wickenden, "The Director of Religious Life," chap. xvii in M. C. Towner, ed., *Religion in Higher Education;* L. T. Hites, *The Effective Christian College,* chap. vi; Clarence P. Shedd, *Two Centuries of Student Christian Movements,* p. 414, *The Church Follows Its Students,* *passim,* and various magazine articles already cited; and Edward W. Blakeman, *The Administration of Religion in Universities and Colleges: Personnel.*

as the college remained small and his other administrative duties light.

Even into this century, and in small church-related colleges up to the present day, the president has often acted as the spiritual shepherd for his student flock. President J. H. Harris of Bucknell wrote: "I regarded myself as pastor of the students, and to them I gave a large part of my time and thought." [2] He preached thirty-one baccalaureate sermons at Bucknell from 1890 through 1919, and in 1924, though he himself was not a minister. The historian of Dartmouth said of President W. J. Tucker, who held office from 1893 to 1909, that "He regarded in a very serious light his responsibilities as the moral leader of the college," [3] a judgment borne out by the quotations from Tucker's own pen in Chapter V of this book. Though he was chief executive of a tax-supported institution, President W. O. Thompson of Ohio State preached the baccalaureate sermons from 1911 through 1925 with the exception of two years.[4] Illustrations could be furnished by reference to the practices of many another college president.

But with the tremendous growth of the colleges, the consequent enlargement of the president's academic duties, and the increased influence of student-sponsored religious activities, the leadership of the religious life passed to other individuals and agencies. The Christian Associations, and later the church-sponsored organizations, began to employ trained secretaries who had no official status in the institutions concerned. The beginning of adult leadership for the Y.M.C.A. was at Yale in 1886. Clarence P. Shedd wrote: "By 1910 Christian Association secretaries were employed in most of the larger state and independent universities." [5] The denominational "university pastors" and secretaries for church-sponsored groups are largely developments since 1910.[6] In the meantime the direction of chapel services and of other religious provisions of the college itself was often taken over by faculty committees. These various methods of religious leadership continue to be characteristic of a majority of institutions at the present time.

While these practices were developing, colleges themselves were

2. J. H. Harris, *Thirty Years as President of Bucknell* . . . , p. 77.
3. L. B. Richardson, *History of Dartmouth College*, p. 744.
4. T. C. Mendenhall, ed., *History of the Ohio State University*, II, 279.
5. Clarence P. Shedd, *The Church Follows Its Students*, p. 62.
6. *Ibid.*, pp. 62–64.

forced to enlarge their administrative as well as their teaching staffs to take care of the new flood of students. The office of dean was instituted and there came to be deans of undergraduate instruction, deans of men and of women, and deans of the professional schools. Directors of athletics, of student activities, of health and housing were employed to give closer supervision to the different phases of student life. What more natural than that, in those colleges possessing a profound interest in religion, there should likewise be established positions of leadership responsible for the religious expression and growth of the students.

One of the first developments, therefore, was that individual colleges began to foster some official connection with the Christian Associations. This usually took the form of supplying part or all of the salary of the employed secretary, or of making contributions to the organization's budget to be used for salary expense. Among early examples of this practice were Mount Holyoke's employment of a Y.W.C.A. secretary in 1901 and Smith's appropriation of $100 to the Y.W.C.A. secretary's salary in 1903. Through the years the custom has spread widely, though in local situations it is difficult to discover when, why, and to what extent the administration assumed the responsibility. Many colleges list among their administrative officers a secretary of the Christian Association, but in any one instance such listing does not necessarily indicate that the institution contributes the whole, or even a part, of his support. Moreover, college policy with reference to this practice may vary from year to year. It is impossible, therefore, to say with any assurance how many colleges at present follow the custom. But that it is widespread is shown by reference to Edward W. Blakeman's listing of college religious leaders, as of 1942, in his volume *The Administration of Religion in Universities and Colleges: Personnel.*[7]

The inauguration of such a procedure has often been the result of careful planning, involving a thoughtful acceptance on the part of the administration of an obligation for furnishing guidance for the religious activities of students. Particularly has this been true of the considerable number of state universities which have adopted the policy. Because of the bogey of the separation of church and state, the problem on tax-supported campuses has been difficult of solution. Rather than either doing nothing at all or

7. Blakeman, *op. cit.*, pp. 29–135.

establishing official positions of leadership, they have often followed the middle course of aiding some nondenominational voluntary program which was already functioning. Among state-supported institutions which bear all or part of the salary expense of Christian Association secretaries are the Universities of Florida, Kentucky, Maine, North Carolina, Oklahoma, South Carolina, and Tennessee, and the Citadel, Georgia School of Technology, Kansas State, Louisiana State, Pennsylvania State, and Winthrop.

But careful planning and thoughtful acceptance of obligation have not always been present. In some instances the procedure was the outcome of a purely local and temporary situation which demanded an immediate improvisation. The method of aiding the already existing voluntary program recommended itself as easy and practical, but on occasion stood for the relinquishment rather than the assumption of larger administrative responsibility, coupled here and there with a desire to gain more effective control of the voluntary groups. Wherever the method has been used, and from whatever motives, it has served as an encouragement to the voluntary organization, but not as the creation of the college's own religious program.

But the result, as distinct from the intention, of such a development has been that the Christian Association secretary has become an officer of the college administration. He may not be considered so by others on the college staff, and even he may prefer to think of himself as independent from the college. But whenever the college pays part or all of his salary he is, in effect, an employee of the institution, no matter what his title. Thus it becomes clear that "Secretary of the Christian Association" may signify an official relationship as intimate as "Dean of the Chapel" or "Director of Religious Activities," though the sound of the title implies an unofficial status. To point out such a fact is not to criticize or praise it; it is merely to indicate that the secretaries of the Christian Associations in the state institutions named above, or in such colleges as Oberlin, Randolph-Macon Woman's College, and Vanderbilt, are not, as their titles might indicate, the independent employees of voluntary groups voluntarily supported, but are in actuality administrative officers.

Many colleges, however, have not been content merely to assist existing organizations or, for other activities, to rely upon the work of faculty committees. They have felt that the need of students for religious direction and counsel called for a more definite expression of administrative responsibility. Voluntary religious groups were expanding rapidly in number with the entrance of church-sponsored organizations into the field, and it was impossible to aid them all. Coördination was needed badly in the total religious program, not only among the Christian Associations and the various church programs, but also between these groups and the worship and curricular provisions of the college. The tremendous growth of the colleges themselves demanded an enlarged and unified approach to the subject of religion. These and many other factors of general or local significance have been responsible for the development in the twentieth century of officially sponsored religious programs and for the establishment of officially designated positions of religious leadership.

The position of chaplain has a long history in American colleges, but it largely disappeared with the coming of the Christian Association secretaryship in the 'eighties and 'nineties of the last century. For example, throughout much of the nineteenth century Yale labeled one of its professors "Chaplain," but in 1887 the position was discontinued because of the growth of the voluntary religious work and the institution of a secretary for the Christian Association. The return of the title "Chaplain," and of the office under various titles, is a development of this century and particularly of the last twenty years. Soon after coming to the presidency of Columbia in 1902, Nicholas Murray Butler led in the securing of a "Chaplain" for Columbia and Barnard Colleges. Motivated by the gift of a chapel by the founder's wife, Stanford employed a "Chaplain" in 1902. The growth of Maryville College made urgent the need for a "College Pastor," who was secured in 1917.

In the 'twenties the movement was greatly enlarged. Colby provided for a "Director of Religious Activities" in 1922, who was to offer courses and to counsel students and organizations on religious matters. In 1925 Columbia added to its leadership by the provision of three "Religious Counselors," for Catholics, Protestants, and Jews. Mount Holyoke appointed a "College Chaplain" in 1926, the same year in which Muhlenberg established its chaplaincy. Since 1927 Cornell has aided its unified program by furnishing the salaries of the executives of Men's and Women's Work, and at present also pays the salary of the "Executive Director of the Cornell United Religious Work." Strictly speaking, this was an acceptance by the administration of a voluntary program rather than the institution of new official positions.

But the late 'twenties were rich in new official positions, by which the colleges consciously departed from the patterns of the past. Yale secured a full-time "Chaplain" in 1927. Both Princeton and Chicago established the position, "Dean of the Chapel" in 1928, Princeton adding an "Assistant Dean." That same year Northwestern employed a "Director of Religious Activities"; this office was discontinued in 1933, but official leadership was reëstablished in 1937 with the inauguration of a "Director of the University Board of Religion." The title "Director of Religious Activities" was also applied to a new officer at Miami of Ohio in 1927 and at Alfred in 1929. Since the programs at every one of these institutions have proved of wide influence in the general spread of the movement, they will be discussed in detail in Chapter XIII.

The decade of the 'thirties witnessed a growth larger than at any previous time. The first "Dean of the Chapel" at Syracuse was installed in 1930, the same year that Colorado College created the office of "Dean of Shove Memorial Chapel." At the University of Pennsylvania there had long been an efficient and well-known program of united work, organized around the Christian Association and winning progressively the participation of the different denominations. But the administration had made no provision for official leadership of the religious life until, "In the spring of 1932 the Trustees, feeling that religion should occupy a more prominent place in the broad educational program of the University, approved the appointment of a full-time, resident Chaplain of the University, who would also serve as Boardman Lecturer in Christian Ethics." [8]

Rollins, also in 1932, established the position of "Dean of Knowles Memorial Chapel." In the following year, under the leadership of President Alexander G. Ruthven, who felt that "The University should recognize and honor all creeds and religions and place no obstacles in the way of the spiritual growth of the student," [9] the University of Michigan provided for a "Counselor in Religious Education," followed by a "Director of the Student Religious Association" in 1937. This large development has

8. Cornell M. Dowlin, ed., *The University of Pennsylvania Today* (Philadelphia, University of Pennsylvania Press, 1940), pp. 189–190.

9. Alexander G. Ruthven, "Some Problems of the University . . . ," *University of Michigan Official Publications*, XXXI, 27 (November 16, 1929), 9.

especial significance because it took place on a tax-supported campus.

Southern Methodist University began a reorganized and united religious program in 1934 with the appointment of a "Director, Student Council of Religious Activities." In the academic year 1934–35 Washington and Jefferson established a "College Church," the leadership of which was entrusted to a "College Pastor" in 1936. That was the year Duke began its extensive provision of official leadership, with a "Director of Religious Activities," who was joined in 1938 by a "Dean of the Chapel." Also in 1938 the State University of Iowa assumed the full administrative expense of the School of Religion, including the salary of the "Director," and since then has undertaken the support of the "Executive of the Religious Activities Board." The year 1938 was further marked by the creation of the positions of "Faculty Adviser to the Community Church" at Vassar and "Director of Religious Activities" at the Woman's College of the University of North Carolina. Emory University established the position of "Director of Religious and Social Life" in 1939.

With the coming of the years of war the establishment of new positions in the college hierarchy necessarily slowed down; the surprise is that the movement did not stop altogether. In spite of the difficulty of finding money for anything other than the continuance of established programs, and in contrast to the wartime emphasis on scientific pursuits, numbers of colleges have been unwilling to postpone new ventures in the field of religion and the establishment or redefinition of official positions of religious leadership. Developments of this sort, differing from each other in a variety of ways, have taken place during recent years at Antioch, Denison, Emory and Henry, Ohio Wesleyan, Pittsburgh, Rensselaer Polytechnic, Rochester, Southern California, Union (New York), and Washington and Lee. Another group, unable to take action while the war was still on, have gone ahead with their planning; and the immediate postwar years are witnessing a further extension of the policy among colleges in all parts of the country.

But these are only a few of the colleges which have established positions of religious leadership. At the present time the exact number of institutions following such a practice is not known. Accurate information is difficult to obtain. Short of an intimate knowledge of each local situation, one is not always able to tell from catalogues or even from questionnaires whether or not some individual religious leader is, in fact, an official of the college. Often it is a matter of degree; and the percentage of his salary which the college itself supplies is not the only factor involved in a determination of the degree of his official status. Moreover, the scene is shifting rapidly from year to year, and even within the academic year. And during the war some officers had their duties changed materially, though they still retained the titles descriptive of their peacetime functions. The only sizable effort to identify names, numbers and locations of positions of religious leadership is that of Edward W. Blakeman, in the volume mentioned above, but his useful work suffers from a failure to distinguish consistently between leaders supported by extracollegiate agencies and college officers.

For any sort of reliable picture, therefore, one is forced again to take the situation as it obtained in the last full peacetime academic year. Limiting consideration to those institutions bearing the accreditation of the Association of American Universities, we find that 59 out of a total of 263, or over 22 per cent, were recognizing their responsibility for religion in this way in 1941. This percentage does not begin to approach the overwhelming majority of colleges which provide chapel services and religious instruction, but its significance is great because of the recent development of the movement. Figures for the various types of institutions will be found in Appendix II; the names of the 59 and the titles of their officers are:

College	*Title of Officer*
1. Alfred University	Chaplain
2. Amherst College	Director of Religious Activities
3. Antioch College	College Pastor
4. Baker University	College Pastor
5. Barnard College	Chaplain (who also serves Columbia)
6. Boston University	Director of Student Counseling and Religious Activities
7. Bucknell University	Director of Religion
* 8. Chicago, University of	Dean of the Chapel
9. Colby College	Director of Religion

* Indicates member of, as distinct from merely approved by, the Association of American Universities.

College	Title of Officer
10. Colgate University	Director of Student Activities (including religious activities)
11. Colorado College	Dean of the Chapel
* 12. Columbia University	Chaplain
13. Connecticut College for Women	College Preacher
* 14. Cornell University	Director of the United Religious Work
15. Dartmouth College	Fellow in Religion
16. Denver, University of	Director of Religious Activities
17. Drake University	Chaplain
* 18. Duke University	Dean of the Chapel
19. Emory University	Director of Religious and Social Life
* 20. Harvard University	Chairman of the Board of Preachers
21. Hiram College	Religious Counselor
22. Hobart College and William Smith College	Chaplain
* 23. Iowa, State University of	Executive of the Religious Activities Board
24. Kenyon College	Chaplain
25. Lafayette College	Chaplain
26. Lake Forest College	Director of Religious Activities
27. Lehigh University	Chaplain
28. Linfield College	Director of Christian Activities
29. Maryville College	College Pastor
30. Massachusetts State College	Director of Religious Activities
31. Meredith College	Religious Secretary
32. Miami University (Ohio)	Director of Religious Activities
* 33. Michigan, University of	Counselor in Religious Education
34. Mount Holyoke College	Director of the Fellowship of Faiths
35. Muhlenberg College	Chaplain
36. New Jersey College for Women	Religious Counselor
37. North Carolina, Woman's College of the University of	Director of Religious Activities
* 38. Northwestern University	Chairman of the Board of Religion

College	Title of Officer
39. Pennsylvania State College	Chaplain
* 40. Pennsylvania, University of	Chaplain
* 41. Princeton University	Dean of the Chapel
42. Randolph-Macon College for Men	Chaplain
43. Rutgers University	Chaplain
44. Smith College	Religious Director
45. South, University of the	Chaplain
46. Southern Methodist University	Director, Student Council of Religious Activities
* 47. Stanford University	Chaplain
48. Syracuse University	Dean of the Chapel
49. Trinity College (Conn.)	Chaplain
50. Tufts College	Chaplain
51. Ursinus College	College Pastor
52. Vassar College	Faculty Adviser to the Community Church
53. Wabash College	Chaplain
54. Washington and Jefferson College	College Pastor
55. Washington and Lee University	**Director of Religious Activities**
56. Wesleyan University (Conn.)	Pastor of the College Church
57. Williams College	Chaplain
58. Wofford College	Director of Religious Activities
* 59. Yale University	Chaplain

Furthermore, 59 is by no means the total of all institutions which provide official leadership. It omits, of course, those institutions which have adopted the practice during and since World War II, and those others for whom the author's information was inadequate. For example, though Blakeman's compilation of only one year later, 1942, omits several included in the 59, he refers to at least 10 more whose names are not found above: [10]

College	Title of Officer
1. Central College	Director of Religious Activities
2. Converse College	Chaplain

10. See Blakeman, *op. cit., passim.*

College	Title of Officer
3. Grinnell College	Dean of the Chapel
4. Grove City College	College Pastor
5. Mills College	Dean of the Chapel
6. St. Olaf College	College Pastor
7. South Carolina, University of	Chaplain
8. Southern California, University of	Director of Religious Activities
9. Union College (N.Y.)	Chaplain
10. Wooster, College of	College Pastor

These, together with those listed above, make a total of 69, or over 26 per cent of the colleges under consideration.

But even this is not the whole story. When the reference is broadened to include those possessing only regional accreditation, other names appear: American International, Bard, Carthage, Northwest Nazarene, Phillips, Rollins, Southwestern of Texas, and others. Moreover, the figures do not include either the considerable group which support, partially or wholly, adult secretaries of voluntary groups, or the even larger group depending for official guidance of the religious program upon faculty committees. When these considerations are taken into account, the proportion of almost one fourth of the nationally accredited institutions which had established their own positions of religious leadership by 1941 is impressive testimony to the rapid growth of the practice.

Some knowledge of the way in which the movement has developed can be gained by an examination of the 59 colleges according to their type. Only 9 are state institutions and only 11 are church-related colleges, while 39 belong in the independent classification. The percentages of the total number of colleges in each group are slightly more than 12 for the state institutions, less than 20 for the church-related colleges, and approximately 33 for the independent schools. It is obvious, therefore, that of the three types, the independent colleges have been most ready to establish positions of religious leadership.

This conclusion would be even more justified, and the percentage of independent colleges would be even larger, if a more strict definition of the independent college had been followed in making the tabulation. The "Lovejoy College Rating Guide," on which the classification of institutions was based,[11] includes in its independent group many colleges such as Augustana of Illinois, Bethany, Hobart, and Park, which have a very intimate, if unofficial, connection with the denominations that gave them birth. But the vast majority of the independent colleges supporting religious officers are not of this type; rather, they are those which, if a contradiction in terms may be used, have severed even their unofficial connections with the various churches.

Reasons for the preponderance of the independent colleges in the total group are not hard to find. First of all, the independent colleges, by virtue of their independence, usually possess and therefore exert more freedom in making experiments. Even as they have often been the leaders in other innovations of higher education, so it is not surprising to find them leading the way here. The state institutions, of course, would be expected to show the smallest percentage, particularly in view of what we have already discovered concerning their readiness to use the alternative method of lending support to Christian Association secretaries.

As for the church colleges, many of them are very small, and in such situations it is still possible for the president or a faculty committee to furnish all the religious guidance that seems necessary. Figures on the presence of faculty committees having responsibility for the religious program show a much larger percentage for the church colleges than for either independent or state institutions. Thus they, like the state institutions, have an alternative method upon which many of them have come to rely. That this method, with all its obvious possibilities of inefficiency and divided responsibility, continues to be followed is due in no small part to the fact that church colleges are usually less well endowed than their independent neighbors, and thus find it financially more difficult to add new officials to their staffs. The implication from our figures, therefore, is that the size, freedom, and financial condition of the colleges are undoubtedly among the determining factors in the establishment of official positions of religious leadership.

Of the group of 39 independent colleges supporting religious workers, 5 are for women only, 17 for men only, and 17 are coeducational. More illuminating are the proportions for the total number of colleges of each type. Whereas 5 represents less than a

11. See C. E. Lovejoy, *So You're Going to College*, pp. 267–340.

fifth of the women's colleges and 17 only a fourth of the coeducational colleges, the other 17 denotes that approximately three fourths of the men's colleges have instituted directors of religion. Men's colleges may be, on the whole, more financially healthy than others, but no ready explanation of a general nature is forthcoming for the astounding preponderance of this development in that type of institution.

Since men's colleges are situated largely in the East, the supposition is that the geographical distribution of the institutions participating in the development is ill balanced by an undue proportion of them in New England and on the Atlantic seaboard. To a large extent this is true, though representatives of the movement can be found in all parts of the country.

More significant than that a considerable number are men's colleges or Eastern colleges are the twin facts that a substantial proportion of the 59 are among the recognized leaders in higher education, and are making notable experiments in other fields. "Leading college" is, of course, a slippery phrase to define. For the university level a convenient classification is that of the list of members, as distinct from the list of approved colleges, of the Association of American Universities. The non-Catholic American membership of the Association is 30, of which 12, or 40 per cent, have provided official religious leadership. Thus the percentage for these leading universities, justifiably so called, is far greater than for the list of approved colleges as a whole. It would seem to be a reasonable conclusion that the more prominent the institution, the more likelihood there is that it employs an official religious worker.

Closely related to this judgment is the fact, already referred to, that a large number of the exponents of the practice are making significant experiments in other areas of higher education. In the list of 59 are such colleges as Antioch, Chicago, Colgate, Dartmouth, Harvard, Hiram, the State University of Iowa, Princeton, Vassar, Williams, and Yale, all of which are distinguished for their provocative departures, in various fields, from traditional procedures. The contributions which many of these institutions have made to progress in higher education have already been referred to in Chapter II. As we have seen, the provision of religious leadership also implies such a departure from the past. The conclusion seems legitimate that this recent development for caring for the religious life of the students will usually have occurred not in those conservative colleges bound by customs of long standing, but in others which are continually reëxamining and seeking to improve their total programs.

The movement, it begins to appear, is still largely experimental in nature. No clear pattern is being followed in the establishment of such positions. The only point of unanimous agreement is that religion provided for in this way must be nonsectarian, but even here a division is recognizable according to whether the approach is interdenominational or nondenominational in emphasis. The variety of titles by which the religious officers are identified attests to the different conceptions as to the nature of the work. The favorites are "Chaplain," "Director of Religious Activities," "College Pastor," and "Dean of the Chapel," named in the order of descending frequency. For a few institutions the responsibilities of a religious nature consume only a portion of the time of the administrative official thus designated. On the other hand, several colleges have established more than one religious office.

But with all its newness and experimental character, the movement to furnish official religious leadership in the colleges has come to be, for those institutions taking part in it, equally as important as the older, more established provisions of chapel services and courses in religion. In fact, its very novelty emphasizes its significance. Colleges can easily continue traditional customs without being overly concerned about their relevance or efficacy for the present day. But colleges cannot so easily or thoughtlessly make an innovation in their programs. The establishment of positions of religious leadership reflects, necessarily, conscious consideration on the part of the college administrations of the problem of religion on the campus and tacit recognition of their obligation to care for the religious growth of the students. As Arthur C. Wickenden has said:

Institutions of higher education which have included on their staffs officers to direct the religious life have simply extended the philosophy of responsibility already governing other phases of student life to include the religious. The action is an acknowledgment that ultimate responsibility for adequate provision for the stimulation and development of the religious life of students rests upon the administration, just as it does for physical, social, musical, dramatic, and intellectual life. This does not mean the assumption of sole responsibility to the exclusion of all other forces, but signifies a recognition on the part of the institution that it cannot evade responsibility in this area and place it wholly upon other agencies.[12]

12. Wickenden, *op. cit.*, pp. 192–193.

CHAPTER XII

OTHER METHODS

MANY colleges have discovered other methods than the three major provisions already discussed by which they may officially foster religion on the campus. Less important than chapel, courses, and leadership, these methods yet possess no small significance, evidencing the fact that the colleges are giving at least some attention to religious interests. And since they usually occur only in combination with one or more of the chief methods, they serve to implement the total religious resources which the colleges officially provide.

Sometimes college executives protest their concern for religion by pointing out activities which are utterly inconsequential. For example, a president of a large municipal university recently proclaimed the interest of the institution in religion, and as evidence cited the custom that "at commencement and other ceremonial occasions there are hymns and opening and closing prayers by clergymen of the city." [1] With such insignificant expressions of religious interest our discussion is not concerned. The methods which will be considered are: permission to use college buildings for religious meetings; sponsorship of special religious meetings; subsidization of the voluntary religious activities; and religious counseling. They shall be discussed in that order, with time out before the last one to make some comparisons among those methods which are measurable.

A. PERMISSION TO USE COLLEGE BUILDINGS

The first method represents the minimum recognition which colleges can give to religion—permission to use college buildings for religious meetings. More adequate assistance of this general sort consists of allowing religious organizations to occupy office space in the buildings. And the most advanced example is the provision of a separate building for exclusively religious purposes.

1. Raymond Walters, "Historical Sketch of the University of Cincinnati," *University of Cincinnati Bulletin*, XXXVI, 15 (November, 1940), 40.

In a general survey it is impossible to distinguish the several degrees of performance of this method, as represented in numbers of colleges. But information concerning its widespread use can be secured, and is contained in Appendix I. In a special investigation of 107 colleges of different types, conducted before the war dislocated the college programs, it was discovered that 101, or over 94 per cent, provide college rooms or a separate college building for religious meetings or the use of religious organizations.

The percentages for denominational, independent and state institutions are respectively 100, almost 98, and about 86. Possibly the only surprise occasioned by these figures is that all the percentages are not 100. Only 1 of the independent colleges considered refuses to permit religious services on the campus, while 5 state institutions make such a prohibition. But these 5 are a small minority, indicating that the hesitancy of tax-supported colleges to sponsor religion does not often go to this extreme.

The fullest development of the willingness of colleges to house religious agencies is the building of religious activity centers and chapels on the campus. Numbers of institutions have included them in their construction plans during the last forty years, and others are now contemplating the erection of similar buildings to serve as war memorials. Unfortunately their presence does not always testify to the institution's interest in religion. As Stewart Cole has said:

At the focal point of the campus of the majority of colleges and universities, there stands a chapel, capped with a spire or tower, to symbolize the primacy of religion in higher education. Frequently the symbol is meaningless as far as liberal philosophy and educational statesmanship are concerned.[2]

The chapel may even be an unsolicited gift of a well-meaning philanthropist, accepted by the college in order to retain his favor but allowed to serve no useful purpose.

Such instances, however, are rare. Most often the donation has provided an occasion for the college to make increased provisions for the religious life of the campus. For example, the University of Pittsburgh was presented a chapel by the Heinz family, concerning which Chancellor Bowman said at the laying of the cornerstone in 1934, "It is obvious, I think, that a great usefulness of

2. Stewart G. Cole, *Liberal Education in a Democracy*, p. 244.

the Chapel will be its presence." [3] The University historian wrote that the chapel ". . . stands on the University campus as a memorial to the faith of a Pittsburgh family in the University and as a symbol of the spiritual in education." [4] The symbol has been made meaningful by the subsequent appointment of a "Chaplain" and the development of a well-conceived program of worship. In the following chapter we shall note how the building of chapels at Chicago, Duke, Princeton and Syracuse provoked a similar response.

More indicative of genuine concern for religion are the structures which have been consciously planned by the colleges themselves in order to fulfill recognized needs. The Citadel, for example, pointed out in its catalogue:

It is significant that the college in planning its present building program thought first of a cadet chapel which in size, dignity, and beauty would be a fitting reminder to all cadets that education must be founded upon spiritual strength. [5]

Yet, at the best, the provision of rooms, office space, separate buildings, or even beautiful chapels, constitutes only a beginning, the least that the colleges can do to acknowledge their responsibility for religion.

B. SPONSORSHIP OF SPECIAL RELIGIOUS MEETINGS

A second method is the sponsorship of special religious meetings of many different sorts and the bearing of part or all of the financial expense involved. Such meetings or convocations are often in addition to the college chapel services, and differ from them in that chapel is part of the regular program, supervised and led by college officials, while the special meetings involve the importation of outside leadership.

In olden days these meetings were usually highly evangelistic in nature, frankly termed revivals. But with the passage of years and the liberalizing changes in the general field of religion, the

---

3. Quoted in A. L. Starrett, *Through One Hundred and Fifty Years, The University of Pittsburgh* (Pittsburgh, University of Pittsburgh Press, 1937), p. 283.

4. *Ibid.*, p. 281.

5. *Bulletin of the Citadel*, IV, 2 (May, 1940), 47.

character of the college religious meetings underwent similar alteration. A more sophisticated age scorned the word "revival" and often dropped the practice entirely. Of late years, however, there has been a return to the idea, if not the trappings, of the earlier convocations, and at the present time hosts of colleges sponsor such meetings. The term under which they are generally known is "Religious Emphasis Week," though many other titles are also employed. As an alternative to the practice of holding such services at a stated period in the academic calendar, some institutions bring in special religious speakers for occasional services spread throughout the year.

The extent of this activity is reflected in the following figures. Seventy-nine, or almost 74 per cent, of the total of 107 colleges, the subjects of the special investigation mentioned above, assume financial responsibility for visiting chapel speakers or leaders of religious convocations. According to type of institution, this total represents 92 per cent of the denominational colleges, almost 78 per cent of the independent colleges, and approximately 57 per cent of the state institutions.

The various colleges adopting the method fulfill their undertakings in widely differing degrees of thoroughness. Some provide only the barest minimum of financial underpinning for the venture. One state university, one municipal college and two church-related institutions, for example, report appropriations of only $25 to $50 a year. For the majority, however, the gift is much more substantial: $300, $500, $800, and on up. In not a few instances the allotments are amazingly generous. Two independent colleges, one in the East for men, the other coeducational in the West, contribute $1,200 each. Two comparatively large church-related colleges grant $2,000 and $2,350 respectively. And one state institution appropriates $2,500 each year for this purpose.

The inference to be drawn from these figures is not that a larger amount of money signifies always a larger degree of interest. Still less is it that the actual money expended is the only barometer of the college's recognition of its responsibility to provide for special religious meetings. First of all, too much reliance must not be placed in the figures themselves, for like other figures they are "subject to change without notice." Then, obviously, such factors as the size of the student body, financial condition of the college, and its religious heritage are often more determinative of the amount to be expended than the college's present interest in religion. The only justification for the recital of such figures is that they constitute the sole measurable evidence of the use of this particular method.

The only legitimate interpretation of them is that, where there occurs a large expenditure, there must necessarily have been careful consideration of the purposes which it is to serve. No college, no matter how well endowed or well supported by public funds, has money to throw away. In this connection it is significant that a number of the institutions making substantial grants are tax-supported; here certainly, it may be surmised, such action is not unpremeditated.

The adequacy of such a method is not easily estimated. If a few programs here and there seem to be superficial, others undoubtedly produce deep and lasting effects of genuine religious significance in the lives of students. Many ministers and other speakers are almost on a circuit which takes them to several "weeks" or series during the academic year. Their names constitute an honor roll of the outstanding religious leaders of the nation at large, for the colleges in the pursuit of this method are not content to use less than the best, both in intellect and in persuasiveness, which the world of religion affords. The widespread character of the practice is eloquent testimony to the conviction on the part of the colleges themselves that the sponsorship of series of religious meetings is one of the most fruitful methods for fostering the religious growth of their students.

C. SUBSIDIZATION OF VOLUNTARY RELIGIOUS ACTIVITIES

With very few exceptions there exist in the colleges at least one and usually numbers of student religious groups. Even in those institutions providing official religious leadership and sponsoring an official religious program, voluntary groups usually flourish side by side with the administration's activities. These voluntary organizations are of two general types: on the one hand, Christian Associations; and on the other, church-sponsored agencies, such as Wesley or Westminster Foundations, Newman or Roger Williams Clubs, and the like. Another method of encouraging religion which colleges have discovered is the subsidization of one or more of these societies and their programs. Most often the contributions are made to the budgets of those groups which are interdenominational or nondenominational in nature, that is, to the Christian Associations, or to some coöperative council of the various groups; but in a few narrowly sectarian colleges the subsidy goes to the denominational organization of the institution's parent church.

An examination of our group of 107 colleges shows that 58, or over 54 per cent, follow this practice. The percentages for the major classifications of institutions are: church-related, 64 per cent; independent, 60 per cent; and tax-supported, about 40 per cent.

This form of aid to religion is rendered in several different ways. Sometimes money is directed to specific purposes, such as to the defraying of expenses for sending delegates to student conferences. But usually the appropriations are for the total budgets of the voluntary groups. The origins of the funds are various. Favorite sources are the student activity fees, contingent fees, and student funds of the college. In most instances the total realized is subject to fluctuation in the size of the undergraduate body, since a definite proportion is taken from each student activity fee. For example, as long ago as the first decade of this century the University of Virginia set aside two dollars of each ten-dollar student contingent fee to be used for the support of religious work. But in a few instances the college, though taking the money out of the total collected from such student fees, manages to contribute a fixed amount each year to the voluntary program.

Another and more direct source is the regular college treasury. The making of grants to the Christian Associations from the total finances of the institution, rather than from some special fund, is a fairly common practice. For example, in the years just before the war $300 was the annual appropriation at two independent colleges and one denominational institution, located in three different parts of the country; at one of these institutions this sum represented the total amount of the Christian Association budget. Sometimes in coeducational institutions unequal amounts are given to the various groups. One Midwestern state university provides 16 per cent of the Y.M.C.A. budget and 24 per cent of the Y.W.C.A. budget, while a Southern state institution apportions $700 to the Y.W.C.A. and $1,620 to the Y.M.C.A. Among the colleges adopting this practice, it is significant once again to find a large number of tax-supported institutions; the procedure is quite common in the state universities and state women's colleges of the South.

Like other forms of encouragement shown by an administration to a voluntary activity, this practice may mean in one instance assumption or in another relinquishment of an obligation to foster religion. Even when it is relinquishment, buying the performance of a task for a measure of financial subsidy, it still indicates the desire on the part of the administration that the function be performed. In any case, the work of the student activity is undoubtedly strengthened, and thereby the total religious life of the campus is enhanced. Though the custom cannot be said to represent, in every situation, the administration's recognition of its own responsibility, yet it is always beneficial to the general cause of religion on the campus.

D. COMPARISONS

Thus far six different methods of sponsoring religion have been considered: chapel services; courses in the regular curriculum; official positions of leadership; the provision of rooms or separate buildings for the use of religious organizations; special religious meetings and convocations; and subsidization of voluntary groups. The study of the 107 colleges to which repeated reference has been made furnishes a basis for comparing the frequencies with which these various practices occur, as shown in the following tabulation. It will be noted that there is added a seventh item, having to do with the sincere interest of the colleges' presidents in religion, as evidenced by their participation and public statements. In each instance the estimate as to the president's interest was made by a person or persons intimately connected with the local situation on whose impartial judgment the author relies. Thus comparison is afforded not only among the different methods themselves but between them and the prevalence of favorable attitudes toward religion on the part of the administration.

The figures refer to percentages of the total number of colleges examined which subscribe to each method or in which there is discernible such interest. Presentation is in order of diminishing frequency.

Item	Per cent
Use of rooms or separate buildings	94.4
Courses	81.3
President's positive interest	79.4
Special religious convocations	73.8
Chapel (compulsory and voluntary)	72.0
Subsidization of voluntary groups	54.2
Official religious leadership	44.9

It is to be noted that figures for those methods discussed in the three preceding chapters differ from figures used therein. This is due, of course, to the fact that in those chapters consideration was given to all colleges on the approved list of the Association of American Universities—263 in number—or in a few instances to the even larger number receiving regional accreditation, whereas for purposes of the comparison above attention is necessarily limited to the group of 107 institutions for which figures for the other methods are available. The most obvious discrepancy between the percentages for the 107 and for the larger group is in the matter of "official religious leadership"; the explanations are two. In compiling the figure for the present group, secretaries of Christian Associations, if their salaries were paid by the colleges themselves, were counted as administrative officers. Moreover, though the group of 107 is typical of the larger group in most respects, it included a slightly disproportionate number of institutions which were sponsoring positions of religious leadership before the war.

When division is made among the institutions according to their three major types, the orders of frequency as well as the percentages are found to undergo change. For the denominational colleges the figures are:

Item	Per cent
Use of rooms or separate buildings	100
Chapel	100
Courses	100
President's positive interest	96
Special religious convocations	92
Subsidization of voluntary groups	64
Official religious leadership	24

For independent colleges:

Item	Per cent
Use of rooms or separate buildings	97.8
Chapel	88.9
Courses	88.9
Special religious convocations	77.8
President's positive interest	73.3
Subsidization of voluntary groups	60.0
Official religious leadership	55.6

For state institutions:

Item	Per cent
Use of rooms or separate buildings	86.5
President's positive interest	75.7
Courses	59.5
Special religious convocations	56.8
Official religious leadership	45.9
Subsidization of voluntary groups	40.5
Chapel	32.4

These comparative frequencies point to several propositions and conclusions of significance. First of all, the church-related colleges lead in every item except the provision of official religious leadership, in the use of which important new method they lag behind both independent and tax-supported institutions. Granting that other factors such as size and financial condition are involved, it would still seem to be true that the denominational colleges are less inclined to experiment, more satisfied simply to follow in the ways of the past, or are not yet convinced that the new method is either necessary for them or beneficial to religion.

The figures for the independent group are only slightly lower than for the church colleges. The relative occurrence of each method in the two types of institutions is almost identical. Only in the item of religious leadership, in which the percentage for the independent colleges is more than double that for the denominational group, is there any large discrepancy between the two.

The percentages for the state institutions suggest how different is the problem of religion there. The figures are appreciably lower for nearly every index. The exceptions are important: the sincere interest of the president in religion, and the provision of religious leadership. The actual percentages surpass, in the former, the percentage for the independent colleges, and in the latter, for the church-related group. Moreover, the relative occurrence of the different items is strikingly at variance with the order of frequency in the other two lists. Chapel, high on the list of the denominational and independent colleges, is at the bottom among methods employed by state institutions, whereas both the items, the interest of the chief executive and the presence of religious officers, are much higher in the state-college tabulation than for the others.

These considerations carry important implications for the status of religion in state colleges at the present time and in the future. It would seem to be indicated, for example, that to the extent to which attitudes can be measured, presidents of state institutions are just as, if not more, interested in religion than administrators of independent colleges, even though still falling short of the concern of church-college executives. This observation is further supported by our preceding inquiry into the statements of college presidents, as discussed in Chapters IV, V and VI. Since the interest of those connected with the tax-supported institutions was pointed out there as having risen largely in the last decade or so, and since such interest in religion must obviously precede responsibility for religion, the confident expectation is that the use of all the different methods for sponsoring religion will be substantially increased in the state colleges in the next few years.

Furthermore, the relative prominence in the tax-supported institutions of official positions of religious leadership, and the relative paucity of chapel and religious instruction, signify a deep concern expressing itself in a willingness to try new methods, coupled with a retention of their older policy of neglect, formed in more hesitant days and distrustful of traditional procedures. In this connection it should be noted that the proportion providing special religious meetings is larger than those holding the older type of chapel exercises. This fact is certainly explained in part by the practical difficulty of operating chapel successfully in an institution numbering its students in the thousands. But another explanation is that the time-honored custom of chapel has long been thought to be prohibited in tax-supported institutions operating under the restrictive principle of the separation of church and state. Thus the state colleges, eager to demonstrate their concern for religion in ways not suspect, have turned to newer techniques.

E. RELIGIOUS COUNSELING

The extent of the foregoing methods for including religion in the colleges can be measured more or less accurately. There remains to be mentioned, however, one way which is not so easily subject to factual treatment, namely, religious counseling. Many of the problems of college youth are naturally religious in nature. A "study in undergraduate adjustment" of 1930 concluded:

Those who are maladjusted academically tend to be those who are not well oriented, and those who are not well oriented either are so partly because of their failure to secure the aid of religious institutions or have tried religious institutions and found them wanting.[6]

The "study of the transition experience" from high school to college, conducted at Yale in recent years, conclusively demonstrated the importance and the need of religion for the solution of undergraduate problems:

Our findings present ample evidence that there is a fertile field within the lives of the students for helping them develop creative and triumphant religious living.[7]

In the summary of factors making for success, an important place was given to what was called dynamic integration. . . . We also suggested that this working together and mutual support of these various contributing elements occurred under the integrating influence of a vocational or life purpose, an ideal of some sort, or a philosophy as to a man's relation to his world. It seems to be a fact that for many students this integrating principle has been contributed by his religious training and experience. . . . Our interest in religion lies in its possible contribution at this point. . . . We find its significance, for the purposes of this study, to lie in its potential integrating and directive power, and in the fact that the sources of this power, which lie back in the earlier religious experiences and ideas of the students, are often in conflict

6. R. C. Angell, *A Study in Undergraduate Adjustment* (Chicago, University of Chicago Press, 1930), p. 84.

7. Lincoln B. Hale *et al.*, *From School to College; a Study of the Transition Experience*, pp. 283–284.

with the "intellectual world" of the college, with the result that poise and stability are lost for lack of understanding and guidance.[8]

From such statements the conclusion seems justified that the movement to give a place to religion in the college scene has, or should have, a definite relationship to the movement to inaugurate personal counseling programs for the students.

But such a connection has not always been recognized. Formal programs of counseling and systematic measures of orientation and guidance have arisen largely since the first World War, as a product of the increasing concern of educators for the whole person. And this organized personnel movement has, on the whole, ignored religion.

This movement has developed in different ways in different places, but the essential point of view is the same. It exists for the purpose of treating students as individuals and of developing them into normal, useful human beings.[9]

Yet the recent survey of the movement, from which this quotation is taken, did not greatly distort the picture of its development by a complete failure to mention the element of religion.

This neglect, however, has not passed unchallenged by those who, seeking to foster religion in the colleges, recognize the importance of religious counseling. In the 'twenties the embryo guidance programs were greeted gladly. A survey of college problems in 1928, made by R. H. Edwards, J. M. Artman and Galen M. Fisher, said:

Perhaps the most significant new approach to the moral and religious needs of students lies in a personnel counseling service which draws not only upon the historic contributions of religion but also upon all the resources of modern science, physiology, psychology, psychiatry and sociology. All of these will be placed by the personnel counselor at the disposal of the individual student in the reverent and sympathetic spirit of religion.[10]

But the movement did not develop in this way. In 1940 Edwards recognized this fact, pointed to one of the reasons for it, and

8. *Ibid.*, pp. 315–316.

9. Luella Cole, *The Background for College Teaching* (New York, Farrar & Rinehart, 1940), p. 118.

10. R. H. Edwards, J. M. Artman, and Galen M. Fisher, *Undergraduates*, p. 309.

called for a closer identification between programs of counseling and religion. At a conference of college administrators in North Carolina he said:

Fifteen years ago . . . some of the early leaders and sponsors of this movement brought to it a great religious hope and expectation. In light of their belief in the sacredness of persons they looked upon the guidance of growth to worthy levels as generically a Christian method . . . on the whole it might not be unfair to say that the religious hopes and expectations of the pioneers have not been fulfilled in college personnel offices by and large. . . . The movement for personal counseling fell under the spell of the psychological measuring and testing movements.[11]

[But] this significant thing [of counseling] must be done significantly—that is, religiously, and by well trained persons, whatever their titles.[12]

In the academic year 1941–42 Robert Rankin made a study of the "Relation of Student Personnel Work to Religion in Higher Education." His findings, embodied in a Master's thesis at Yale which has unfortunately not yet been published, revealed that there is ". . . ample evidence in many institutions indicating that the official personnel agencies and the religious organizations are operating within their own spheres, quite unaware of one another."[13] But he also discovered great changes taking place in the attitudes of personnel officers. His conclusion was: "As a more mature outlook has been achieved, personnel has become increasingly aware of the importance of religion."[14]

This "more mature outlook" is shown, among other ways, by the large attention, in contrast with former neglect, which the American Personnel Association has given to the subject in recent meetings,[15] and by the interest of the American Council on Education in its recent brochure, *Student Personnel Work in the Postwar College*:

The postwar college will need to be prepared to counsel students in all areas, but unless the area of religious counseling, inter-

11. R. H. Edwards, *What Can Make Higher Education Religious?* (Ithaca, N.Y., Cornell Cooperative Society, 1941), p. 16.
12. *Ibid.,* p. 19.
13. Robert Rankin, *Relation of Student Personnel Work to Religion in Higher Education*, M.A. thesis, Yale University, 1942, p. 15.
14. *Ibid.,* p. 115.
15. *Ibid.,* pp. 31 ff.

preted in its broadest definition, can be wisely and adequately cared for, the omission will be serious.[16]

Yet this realization on the national level is slow in seeping down to individual institutions. On the whole it is still true that the formal counseling programs of many colleges omit any reference to religion. Certainly they fail in most instances to consider counseling as primarily or even secondarily a religious task. As far as the author has been able to ascertain, there is not one college in America that consciously conceives its organized counseling, orientation and guidance program to be, first of all, a religious undertaking, an indivisible part of its total religious program.

This, however, is only part of the problem. A second part is the concern that religious counseling take place significantly on the college campus. Whether or not the official personnel agencies recognize the contribution which religion can make, whether or not organic relationship between personnel and religion is established, and whether or not the college thinks of its general counseling program as fundamentally religious in character, religious counseling may and should be present.

Here the historical record is happier. Such counseling always has existed in the colleges. Both before and after personnel programs became organized, the religious guidance of undergraduates was furnished informally by faculty members and other interested individuals. Though its extent and influence can never be measured, such work has undoubtedly been and continues to be of large significance.

But as time has passed and other areas of guidance have been consciously developed, it has become increasingly clear that the colleges dare not leave purely to chance the provision of adequate religious counseling, any more than they can assume that worship or instruction will be automatically cared for. The Yale transition study of 1939 pointed out:

The very fact that religion, no matter how much in need of revision, is deeply entangled with life purposes, places on the colleges a heavy responsibility. This does not transform them into churches. Nor can the colleges lightly pass on to churches the

16. Willard W. Blaesser *et al.*, *Student Personnel Work in the Postwar College*, American Council on Education Studies, Series VI, No. 6, IX (April, 1945), 49.

essential educational job that is involved. Just as they are finding necessary the incorporation of adequate counseling on practical adjustment problems, so must they broaden their concept of their task to include provision for religious stimulation and growth.[17]

A recent study of the whole personnel movement gave a chapter to a discussion of "helping students to discover values," and said:

The program of religion should include opportunities for individual religious counseling. Religious consultants and advisers are important in order that students may be able personally and individually to find help with religious problems and perplexities. The counselors must be carefully selected for their scholarship in religion, their personality, sympathy, understanding, and faith in a living and vital system of values.[18]

And in 1943 the American Council on Education called special attention to the need in a pamphlet dealing solely with the "Religious Counseling of College Students." It was there the point of view of Thornton Merriam and his associated authors that

. . . institutions of higher education of all types have an inescapable obligation to provide religious guidance as an integral part of their work.[19]

The pamphlet considered thoroughly both the nature of religious counseling and the place it has, or should have, in the college program.

Leading educators, therefore, are now recognizing the importance of planned provision for religious counseling. Moreover, colleges are directly seeking to fill the need. Much of the motivation behind the recent establishment of positions of official religious leadership was the desire that men who could serve as religious counselors be available on the staff. Such professional workers, as well as their counterparts supported by voluntary organizations, usually give a large share of their time to counseling. Once again the extent and effectiveness of such work cannot be estimated, but they are undoubtedly growing. The increasing awareness of organized personnel agencies that reli-

17. Hale *et al., op. cit.,* p. 316.

18. Esther McD. Lloyd-Jones and M. R. Smith, *A Student Personnel Program for Higher Education,* pp. 230–231.

19. Thornton W. Merriam *et al., Religious Counseling of College Students,* American Council on Education Studies, Series VI, No. 4, VII (April, 1943), v.

gion is important, coupled with the increasing attention being paid to the provision of religious counseling apart from those agencies, augurs well for the future development in higher education of a more adequate total counseling program.

Thus far we have purposely spoken only of "religious counseling," not of counseling on problems of religion. Needless to say, the second is important, but it is narrower than the first. Moreover, it is often performed adequately on the college campus, either through wholly informal channels or by the regularly appointed religious leaders. But religious counseling is harder to provide, and for all the fruitful progress being made, one still waits for some college to undertake a total program of guidance for its students which is fundamentally religious in its conception and performance. It is now being recognized that counseling must be at the heart of any vital campus religious program. It remains for the parallel realization to develop, that religion must be at the heart of any vital personnel program.

A final way in which religion might enter the college is as the unifying force and spirit of the whole institution. As we have seen in previous chapters, certain administrators and philosophers of education hold this to be the goal toward which they work. But here again the extent to which the ideal is consciously pursued, much less achieved, is impossible to estimate. If college presidents are beginning to talk about making religion central, the institutions at present doing so are difficult to identify. A discussion much longer than this one could profitably be devoted solely to this problem. As it concerns what might be more than what actually exists, we shall postpone discussion of it to the concluding chapter. Suffice it to say here that the question is demanding attention at the present time, both as an inclusive strategy for unifying and vitalizing all the various methods of fostering religion which we have discussed, and as a motivating temper for the total life and program of the institution.

CHAPTER XIII

SIGNIFICANT PROGRAMS

AMONG colleges assuming large official responsibility for the religious life of their students are a number of institutions whose programs have particular significance. This may be true for several reasons. The importance of the official provisions may depend upon the educational prominence of the institutions, the length of time during which the programs have been established, the degree of conscious planning which went into their adoption, their unique characteristics, or the measure of imitation which they have evoked. Because of the presence of these and other factors in their development, the official religious programs of the following nine colleges and universities demand detailed examination: Yale, Princeton, Syracuse, Duke, Northwestern, Chicago, Miami of Ohio, Alfred, and Denison.

Nine is, of course, an arbitrary number. Others might as readily have been chosen. For example, the University of Connecticut, the University of Florida, the State University of Iowa, the University of Michigan, and Pennsylvania State College are leaders among tax-supported institutions concerned about religion. Of large import for the development in the smaller colleges are the programs at Bucknell, Colby, Colgate, Colorado College, and Rollins. Prominent among the provisions of the larger independent institutions are those of Columbia, Cornell, the University of Pennsylvania, and Stanford. Recent developments of special interest have taken place at Occidental, Pittsburgh, and Rensselaer Polytechnic Institute.

The omission of many of these colleges and universities from this discussion does not therefore imply that their programs are of less consequence than the nine to be considered. The choice of illustrations has been based not only on the significance of the religious provisions, but also on such practical considerations as the availability of information, the stability of the programs, the consequent accuracy with which they can be described, the consonance between the president's interest in religion and the actual offerings of the college, and the absence of earlier thorough treatments.

In some instances no effort will be made to carry the descriptions through the years of war. The purpose in describing these programs is to throw light upon the ways in which some colleges, comparatively free from extraneous pressures, have gone about the serious task of nurturing the religious life of their students. The pressures of war immensely complicate a task which at best is not easy to accomplish. But certain factual material concerning present occupants of positions or plans for the future will be given; and for at least one college, Denison University, the description will depend entirely upon what has taken place in wartime.

1. *Yale University* [1]

Yale "is, and has been from the first, a Christian college," said President Arthur T. Hadley at his inauguration in 1899.[2] That conviction has continued throughout this century. The present executive, Charles Seymour, recognized anew the religious responsibility of the institution in his inaugural address in 1937:

Yale was dedicated to the upraising of spiritual leaders. We betray our trust if we fail to explore the various ways in which the youth who come to us may learn to appreciate spiritual values, whether by the example of our own lives or through the cogency of our philosophical arguments. The simple and direct way is through the maintenance and upbuilding of the Christian religion as a vital part of university life.[3]

If it were necessary, further quotations could be given to demonstrate that the religious program at Yale is founded upon the

1. Information on Yale was gained from: Noah Porter, *Fifteen Years in the Chapel of Yale College, 1871–1886* (New York, Charles Scribner's Sons, 1888); James B. Reynolds *et al.*, eds., *Two Centuries of Christian Activity at Yale* (New York, G. P. Putnam's Sons, 1901); Arthur T. Hadley, *Baccalaureate Addresses* (New York, Charles Scribner's Sons, 1907); *Minutes of the Church of Christ in Yale University*, 1922 to 1941, MS; and from catalogues and other publications of the college and of Dwight Hall, speeches and writings of college officials, annual reports of the presidents, questionnaires, interviews, and personal participation in the program.

2. *Inauguration of Arthur T. Hadley as President of Yale University, October 18, 1899* (pamphlet. New Haven, Yale University [1899]), p. 38.

3. *Inaugural Address of President Charles Seymour . . . , October 8, 1937* (pamphlet. New Haven, Yale University, 1937), p. 13.

administration's deep and abiding interest in and sense of responsibility for religion. A recent notable statement is the discussion by President Seymour of the recommendations of a faculty committee on religion, as given in his Report to the Alumni in December, 1945.[4]

As long ago as 1901 Anson Phelps Stokes, Jr. wrote of "The Present Condition of Religious Life at Yale":

The university church, at present worshipping in the Battell Chapel, and the Christian Association, with its centre in Dwight Hall, are the two most important factors in the student religious life. The importance of the former shows that the authorities of the university recognize the Christian religion as a powerful factor in education; that of the latter is evidence that interest in matters religious is strong among the students themselves.[5]

Though the years have wrought many changes, Stokes's statement is still substantially true. As to his first "important factor," the program of the University continues to center in the "Church of Christ in Yale University." A student-and-faculty campus church, it has had a continuous existence since 1757. During much of the nineteenth century one of the professors served as the college pastor, but in 1887 the President assumed the duties. More recently the former Dean of the Divinity School, Charles R. Brown, acted as chaplain. In 1927 the full-time position of "Chaplain" was instituted, with Elmore McKee as the occupant. The present Chaplain, Sidney Lovett, came to the post in 1932.

Another part of the move in 1927 toward increased responsibility was the enlargement of curricular offerings in religion. The causes were both general and specific in nature. There was the general recognition that, as the University had grown in size, it ought to do more than it was doing for the religious development of the students. Linked with this feeling was the practical situation caused by a student revolt against the compulsory chapel services. When compulsory chapel was abolished in 1927, therefore, the University assumed larger obligations of leadership and instruction, in order to insure that religion would have a continuing and growing impact upon the student body.

The Church of Christ has its own budget, but the administra-

4. *Report of the President of Yale University to the Alumni, 1944–1945* (pamphlet), pp. 21–25.

5. A. P. Stokes, Jr., "The Present Condition of Religious Life at Yale," chap. vii in J. B. Reynolds *et al.*, eds., *op. cit.*, pp. 117–118.

tion cares for the major portion of the expenses connected with the Church and employs the Chaplain as a regular University official, together with one or more assistants. Sunday morning worship services are provided throughout the academic year. For the large majority of these services leading ministers of the nation, whose honoraria are paid by the University, fulfill the preaching duties. A recent development has been the establishment of a "University Board of Preachers," composed of several of the visiting group who are assigned as Fellows of the various undergraduate colleges. The Chaplain fills the pulpit about once a month.

The Church of Christ is not a student church in the sense that the students control its policies. But there is a "Board of Undergraduate Deacons," which is responsible for such church duties as ushering and which advises the Chaplain concerning the services and the preachers. Full membership is accorded in the Church to persons of the faculty and the college community. Membership for the students is on an affiliate basis, and in no way affects their membership in their home churches, since it is only for the duration of their college career. The Church is nondenominational in spirit, though because of the heritage of Yale it is closely connected in form of service and in the provision of communion with the Congregational Church.

Voluntary chapel services are held every weekday except Saturday. In addition, during the winter months, weekly vespers are provided at which time guest speakers give a brief address. In the early years Yale had an annual series of "Special Meetings," but these were discontinued in 1918. This custom was revived in 1939, "because of the belief, based on evidence in colleges and universities throughout the country today, that the time is ripe for a fresh religious movement." [6] The expenses of such meetings are borne by the church budget and by the Christian Association, and the planning is entrusted to a committee of one hundred faculty members and undergraduates. For all of these various worship provisions of the University the Chaplain is primarily responsible.

Curricular offerings in religion are not extensive, but have grown in recent years, and a wartime study of the problem envisages further development. There is a Department of Religion in which undergraduates may major, and for many years the

6. *Yale Daily News*, January 13, 1939, in an article entitled, "Yale Corporation to Initiate Talks by G. A. Buttrick."

Chaplain has taught one course in this department. Recently the Chaplain was given the further title of "Woolsey Professor of Biblical Literature," to indicate the increased emphasis which the University was prepared to place upon religion as a subject for curricular study.

The Chaplain is also responsible for the religious counseling of students. Four separate agencies for personnel work exist at Yale: the Bureau of Appointments, concerned largely with vocational guidance; the Health Department; the freshman counselors (graduate students who live in the freshman dormitories); and the Chaplain with his assistants, the secretaries of Dwight Hall, and unofficial religious workers. Among these four there is friendly interchange but no organized coöperation. Other than through the work of the Chaplain and the secretaries of Dwight Hall, counseling at Yale is not conceived in specifically religious terms.

The second of the two major religious activities which Stokes noted in 1901 has also continued to hold its place of prominence in the University life, though it, too, has undergone development. The "Yale University Christian Association" has had a continuous history since 1879, and is one of the strongest member units of the Intercollegiate Y.M.C.A. Popularly known as Dwight Hall, by reason of the building which it occupies, it carries on a program of religious work comparable to that of student religious organizations on other campuses. The Christian Association is a voluntary, independent agency, supporting an adult "Secretary" out of its own budget. Its relation to the University is similar to that of other self-initiated student activities.

Denominational work is carried on by the Baptists, Catholics, Congregationalists, Episcopalians, Jews, Lutherans, Methodists, and Presbyterians. For many years a priest and a rabbi have ministered wholly to college students. In 1946 several of the Protestant groups began the employment of full-time "secretaries"; and other denominations provide part-time professional leadership. No official connection exists between the University and these religious societies, and coöperation is maintained largely through the personal contacts of the Chaplain. Plans are now under way for associating the various denominational workers more intimately with Dwight Hall. With all this activity, however, it remains true that the church-sponsored agencies at Yale have never developed to the extent common in most large universities, and the religious life continues to center in the Church of Christ and Dwight Hall.

Elements of strength in the Yale program appear to be:

The consistency between the administration's interest in religion and the official religious provisions.

The centering of the program in the Church of Christ and in the Christian Association (Dwight Hall).

The possibility of great influence of the chaplain, as indicated by his various duties.

The organization of students into a nondenominational church congregation.

The presence of a strong voluntary religious group, Dwight Hall, encouraged by the University, at the side of the official program.

The recent expansion of curricular offerings in religion.

The gradual and logical development of administrative responsibility.

A willingness to reëxamine the program, represented by the wartime planning for the future.

Other items of significance at Yale are:

The relative weakness of denominational student work.

The influence of undergraduate opinion in causing changes.

The absence of organized channels for coöperative work among the various religious groups, official and voluntary.

2. *Princeton University* [7]

Princeton has always had a large interest in religion, but that interest, as we noticed in Chapter V, has markedly increased during the last twenty-five years. In 1935 President H. W. Dodds specified the methods by which this interest was made manifest:

7. Information on Princeton was gained from: Edwin M. Norris, *The Story of Princeton* (Boston, Little, Brown & Co., 1917); The Endowment Committee of Princeton University, *Princeton; A Statement by the President Regarding the Place of Religion in the Curriculum and on the Campus; Report of the Special Committee of the Faculty on Religious Education;* [Trustees' Committee on Princeton's Religious Program], *Princeton's Program of Religious Instruction;* Robert R. Wicks, B. A. MacLean and Paul Ramsey, "Religion at Princeton," *Religious Education,* XLII, 2 (March–April, 1947) 65–69; and from catalogues and other college publications, speeches and writings of college officials, interviews, and personal contact with the program.

There are at least three distinct ways of approach to religion with which such institutions may deal. They are the intellectual approach through courses in the curriculum; the opportunity for applied religion through practical service; and the experience of worship in chapel exercises. Princeton University makes provision for all three.[8]

The first of these three ways to be developed by the University itself was "the experience of worship." In earlier years chapel followed the traditional pattern, with no official leadership. But in 1928 the University Chapel was erected, and that same year saw the creation of the office of "Dean of the Chapel" and the appointment of Robert R. Wicks to the position. Dean Wicks reaches retirement in 1947, and will be succeeded by Bishop Donald B. Aldrich. From the first, Sunday services were provided. The Dean preaches about twice a month during the academic year; on the remainder of Sundays the pulpit is filled by visiting ministers. Freshmen and sophomores are still required to attend at least half the number of these services in each quarter.

As to week-day chapel, it had been the custom for many years at Princeton to provide noontime services during Lent. In the spring of 1938 the students requested that these services be continued beyond the Lenten season, and in the following year daily chapel on a voluntary basis was instituted as a regular observance. This custom, however, did not survive the wartime years of decreased enrollment, but may soon be reëstablished.

After the coming of Dean Wicks, the planning and direction of the worship program were completely in his hands. But in the late 'thirties a significant change took place, again largely through the interest of students. The feeling developed that the offerings of the chapel should assume some organized form, and should provide for larger student participation. In 1939, therefore, the "Chapel Congregation" was established. Student membership, as at Yale, is on an affiliate basis. The "Chapel Council," composed of both students and faculty as members, advises the Dean and serves as a sort of church board. Many of the plans for the development of the chapel into a church body rested in abeyance during the war, but the step served to give the students a larger share in the planning of the religious program. The Chapel Congregation is, of course, nondenominational.

During the past twenty-five years the administration at Prince-

8. *A Statement by the President* . . . , p. 1.

ton has sought to sponsor a large part of the religious activity of the students. This second method to which President Dodds referred was also developed about 1928. The old Philadelphian Society, which in 1877 led in the creation of the Intercollegiate Y.M.C.A. and functioned as a unit of that movement, possessed a distinguished history, but internal dissension in the early 'twenties weakened it and finally forced it to disband. When Dean Wicks came to Princeton in 1928, an "Assistant Dean" was also employed whose duty was indicated by his alternative title, "Director of the Student-Faculty Association."

Though it was the intention that this Association take the place of the Philadelphian Society, its function through the years consisted almost solely of sponsoring certain social service projects and fostering better student-faculty relations. Thus it cannot be said to have been a religious organization according to the usual pattern, though much of its work, of course, had unmistakable religious value for its participants. During the war there was a growing recognition of the inadequacy of the Student-Faculty Association as a real substitute for the Philadelphian Society and of the need for some University Christian Association. Plans made by a faculty committee provide for the restoration of Murray-Dodge Hall as a campus religious center and the creation of a Christian Association which will function much as did the Philadelphian Society and will have its own director whose work will be correlated with the work of the Dean of the Chapel. To this task Burton A. MacLean was called in 1946.

In recent years student religious activity at Princeton has been more nearly represented by the voluntary societies of the Catholics, Episcopalians and Presbyterians, which at times have employed professional workers. They have had no organic relationship with the administration, although their work has been encouraged in informal ways by Dean Wicks. Princeton's plans for the future include a reorganization of the total religious resources of the University so as to bring these denominational groups into more intimate touch with the rest of the program. The Dean and other religious workers counsel students on religious problems.

The third way in which the University approaches its task is by means of courses in the regular curriculum. The secular trend in higher education in the early years of the century was reflected at Princeton in the elimination of all instruction in religion. Even when the Dean of the Chapel was secured, no move was made to inaugurate courses in the field. But gradually the need was felt and the omission was recognized. A faculty committee, appointed in 1935 to study the problem, made a forceful argument for its inclusion. A course or two was thereafter provided, and in 1940 a real beginning was made with the appointment of George F. Thomas as "Professor of Religious Thought." In recent years, even during wartime, the work grew steadily until it justified the employment of a second man in the department, Paul Ramsey, in the fall of 1944.

An interesting contrast with Yale is furnished by the philosophy behind the establishment of the new teaching position. Whatever was the original intention when Princeton embarked on its enlarged program in the 'twenties, the result has been that the worship and teaching functions are separated. Dean Wicks offers no regular courses, and Professor Thomas has no direct connection with the chapel program. The idea of the separation of duties was defended by the report of the Faculty Committee in 1935:

The study of religion and the practice of religion certainly supplement one another and aid one another, but each gathers strength and respect if their different functions are not mixed together in confusion. In fact the proper performance of these different functions requires the recognition of very important, if somewhat delicate, distinctions; but distinctions which do not necessarily imply antagonisms or opposites.[9]

This theory of separation, which until recently involved the activity program as a third separate sphere, is not unanimously defended at Princeton today. The planning for the future, to which reference has already been made, implies that an effort will be made to integrate the various provisions into an interrelated whole, without losing any of the gains which the programs have achieved separately.

Elements of strength, both present and potential, in the Princeton program are:

The consistency between the administration's interest in religion and the official religious provisions.

The centering of the program in the chapel and in the Dean of the Chapel.

9. *Report of the Special Committee of the Faculty* . . . , p. 1.

The organization of students into a nondenominational church congregation.

The recent revival of curricular offerings in religion.

The gradual and logical development of administrative responsibility.

A willingness to reëxamine the program, represented by the wartime planning for the future.

The reëstablishment of a University Christian Association.

Other items of significance at Princeton are:

The influence of the gift of a new chapel, leading to the creation of the chapel program.

The theory of separation among worship, activity and study.

The relative weakness of the Student Faculty Association as a substitute for a University Christian Association.

The absence of organized channels for coöperative work among the various religious groups, official and voluntary.

3. Syracuse University [10]

The recent large increase in official provisions at Syracuse came about suddenly and without anticipation. As with Princeton, the gift of a chapel was a key factor. In 1929 the University was granted a sum of money for this purpose. The building, dedicated in June, 1930, was named Hendricks Chapel in honor of the donor. Thus Syracuse was immediately faced with the practical question of determining its use. The original problem confronting Yale may be said to have been, "What is the best way to bring religion into education, and to provide for the religious growth of the students?" But the question before Syracuse was, "What shall we do with this new building?"

The answer was the establishment of the position of "Dean of the Chapel" and the development of a program of religious activities. The late William H. Powers, the first Dean, went to Syracuse in 1929 and spent his first year in studying the situation. He was formally installed in June, 1930. Though his position had been

10. Information on Syracuse was gained from: William H. Powers, "The Story of Hendricks Chapel," *Christian Education*, XXI, 3 (February, 1938); *Hendricks Chapel After Ten Years* (pamphlet. Syracuse, 1940); Dorothy Hayford, *A Follow-up Study of Syracuse University Students Active in the Program of Hendricks Chapel During the First Nine Years of Its Existence*, MS; and from catalogues and other college publications, speeches and writings of college officials, questionnaires, and personal interviews.

created almost by accident, the program which he inaugurated was the result of careful planning, the outgrowth of his attempt to answer the question, "Why am I here?" rather than "How did I get here?" The propositions on which he proceeded were:

In the first place a university should make adequate provision in leadership, physical equipment and finance for the development of the moral and spiritual life of its students. This demands nothing less than a complete religious program. In the second place along with this provision there should be a large place for student participation, the only limit placed upon student activity and leadership being the extent to which they are willing to accept and discharge such responsibility.[11]

Thus, though the University had originally been motivated by necessity and expediency, the responsible officer undertook the fulfillment of the obligation in the light of well-defined principles.

These principles have been observed in the development of the total religious program, centering in Hendricks Chapel. The approach has been fourfold. First of all, the chapel provides worship services. One of the understandings on which Dean Powers insisted at the beginning was that the program should be completely voluntary. At Syracuse, therefore, there is no requirement for either weekday or Sunday services. The weekday services are held for twenty minutes on every day except Saturday, and are planned largely by students. Sunday worship is conducted either by the Dean or by visiting ministers. In recent years the proportion of services led by visitors has declined, in order that a greater continuity and a more normal church life might be attained.

To aid in the supervision of this program the Dean has a staff of officers supported by the University, who have various religious functions to perform or who are private and office secretaries for the chapel. The governance of the chapel, however, is in the hands of the "Hendricks Chapel Board," a group of approximately sixty, drawn from the administration, faculty, alumni, and student body. The large majority of the Board are undergraduates, divided equally between men and women. The chapel with its Board is really a church in nearly every way, for it provides communion once a month, receives offerings every Sunday, and even has a women's "Guild" composed of older ladies of the University community. But the practice of Yale and recently of Princeton of affording affiliate membership to students has never been adopted

11. Powers, *op. cit.*, p. 1, from reprint of magazine article.

at Syracuse. All students, in a sense, are "members"; in a more narrow sense, the "active participants" form the membership.

The second approach is that of counseling. The Dean and his staff are responsible for the religious guidance of the students. Their work is in full coöperation with, though not organically related to, other personnel agencies on the campus.

A third avenue by which religion enters the University life is through the curriculum. The Department of Bible and Religion, together with related studies in other departments, offers a variety of courses in religion. The contact between the regular curriculum and the chapel is made by the Dean himself, one of whose duties is the teaching of a course in this department. The relationship is close even with other departments. Striking witness of this fact is the action of the School of Speech and Dramatic Art in 1941: unsolicited by the Chapel Board or the Dean, the School established a sequence of courses for training in "Religious Leadership," growing out of the recognition of the importance of the Hendricks Chapel program in the life of the University.[12]

The fourth method of sponsoring religion is that of encouragement and, in part, supervision of the religious activities. When the administrative program was launched in 1930, the Y.M.C.A. had already died, though the Y.W.C.A. still persisted. The new Chapel Board soon began to serve as a medium for the religious expression of the students. Then the Y.W.C.A. decided to merge with the Board, and thereafter the activities of the men and women were coördinated. At the present time the Chapel Board is a member unit of the New York State Student Christian Movement.

The work of the Board is performed through numerous committees, headed by co-chairmen, a man and a woman. The program includes such activities as are typical of other campus religious organizations: social service, deputations, discussion groups, Syracuse-in-China, and "world relations." By no means static, it is organized anew each year. Although sponsored by the administration, it is free to develop as the students choose. This is in line with the second major condition originally laid down by Dean Powers, namely, that students be allowed to exercise their initiative to the utmost.

Such a complete and centralized program does not eliminate the activity of denominational groups, though these are obviously

12. See *Syracuse University Bulletin*, LXX, 4 (September 15, 1940), 16, 34.

relegated to a secondary place in the total provisions. The chief function of most of the church-sponsored agencies consists in Sunday evening services for the students, and the schedule of Hendricks Chapel is arranged so as not to conflict with this practice. Great efforts have been made to incorporate the work of the denominations into the chapel program. Though not supported by the University, the leaders of the following church groups are considered part of the staff of the Dean, and are termed "Denominational Counselors": Baptist, Catholic, Christian Science, Episcopal, Jewish, Lutheran, Methodist, and Presbyterian. The Hendricks Chapel Board, therefore, considers itself inter- rather than nondenominational. The interfaith character which was sought in the beginning is now largely absent, owing to the failure to hold the Catholics in any sort of coöperative endeavor.

With the completion in 1940 of ten years of the administrative program at Syracuse, a survey of the effectiveness of the work was attempted by an outsider, a graduate student in the Department of Education. This, so far as the author is aware, is the first extensive effort to determine the results of official sponsorship of religion. The original and present aims of the program were used as criteria in examining the attitudes of students who had been active in the work of Hendricks Chapel during the first nine years of its existence. These aims are:

(1) To promote a sincere spirit of tolerance and cooperation.
(2) To include activities fitted to all types of personality.
(3) To develop the comradeship of faculty and students.
(4) To make possible the sharing of viewpoints and convictions on important questions.
(5) To foster the highest relationship between men and women.
(6) To develop individual and social integrity.
(7) To increase the scope of religious knowledge.
(8) To develop mastery over the forces of life.
(9) To ensure a richer, more abundant life.[13]

The conclusion of the survey was that these aims had been and were being well accomplished.[14]

Elements of strength in the Syracuse program are:

The centering of the program in Hendricks Chapel and in the Dean of the Chapel.

13. Powers, *op. cit.*, pp. 1–2.
14. Hayford, *op. cit.*

The unity of the total program.

The possibility of great influence of the Dean, as indicated by his various duties.

The preservation of student initiative in the midst of large administrative activity.

The large official sponsorship of student religious activities, coupled with the encouragement given to voluntary groups.

The interdenominational character of the program.

The effort to estimate the results.

Other items of significance in the development at Syracuse are:

The influence of the gift of a new chapel, leading to the creation of the chapel program.

The replacement of the earlier voluntary student religious organizations with the Chapel Board.

The sudden development of administrative responsibility.

The difficulty encountered in achieving an interfaith character.

4. Duke University [15]

Duke University is the outgrowth of Trinity College, a small Methodist institution. Originally religion was fostered in traditional ways, by courses in the Bible and chapel services. But in 1924 Trinity became Duke, and the institution underwent a tremendous expansion by reason of its newly acquired wealth. The building program for the new campus included plans for a large chapel. The chapel was completed in 1932, and Sunday services of worship, of a voluntary nature, were provided. To lead these services two professors of the School of Religion were designated by the additional title of "Preacher to the University."

A further step toward an administrative program of large scope was taken in 1936, on the initiative of the late President W. P. Few, whose interest in religion had always been pronounced. The Christian Associations and other student religious groups had never had any professional leadership. With the growth of the student body President Few realized that coördination and guidance of these groups were desirable. In that year, therefore, the office of "Director of Religious Activities" was instituted. The

15. Information on Duke was gained from: *Report of the Director of Religious Activities*, June 1, 1938, MS; [Frank S. Hickman], *The Duke University Church (Interdenominational)*, 1939 (pamphlet); and from catalogues and other college publications, reports of various college activities, questionnaires, interviews, and personal participation in the program.

Director's functions were to encourage the voluntary groups and to foster closer relationships among them, and between them and the worship provisions of the University.

In the academic year 1936–37 the Y.M.C.A. and Y.W.C.A. became actively interested in the chapel program. The first result of this interest was the preparation of joint reports to the administration embodying student attitudes toward the daily and Sunday chapel services and their hopes for the future. A second and unexpected outcome was the achievement of a new unity of effort among all the religious groups. Since the men and women were housed on separate campuses, a joint Student Christian Movement had never seemed practicable. But the combined efforts of the two Associations on the chapel reports showed the benefit of coöperation, and accordingly in 1937 a "Student Religious Council" was organized, including these and all other religious organizations.

The Council fixed as its primary objective the securing for the students of a larger share in the planning and conduct of the chapel services and through them of the total religious program of the University. This purpose became identified in the students' minds with the establishment of a campus church. Through their efforts and with the coöperation of the administration, the "Duke University Church (Interdenominational)" was founded in the winter of 1938. Both its name and its origin in the thinking of the student representatives of the different religious societies signify its interdenominational character.

With the establishment of the Church and the growth of the whole program, the necessity for an enlargement of the religious staff became obvious. In the summer of 1938, one of the Preachers to the University, Frank S. Hickman, was made "Dean of the Chapel," and assistants for the Director of Religious Activities were secured. Dean Hickman continues to do some teaching in the Divinity School, as it is now called, but the major portion of his time is given to the direction of the chapel program.

The Duke University Church is administered by an "Official Board" of faculty and students. The student Board members represent the different religious organizations of the campus, and all groups participate in the Church with the exception of the Catholics. Affiliate membership is offered to the undergraduates in much the same way as at Yale. Worship services provided by the University are now the direct responsibility of the Board. A Sunday preaching service, weekday chapel services, and occasional special meetings are held, and attendance at all of them is voluntary.

Unlike Syracuse, the Official Board has no large program of religious activities because the voluntary organizations, particularly the Y.M.C.A. and the Y.W.C.A., continue to be strong. It does take the lead, however, in the sponsoring of united programs, and since the change from chapel program to church organization, it has instituted such customary church practices as communion, offerings, and on occasion the participation in the services of "laymen," represented by the students. The Dean and other members of the Divinity School staff do most of the preaching, though Duke, like other institutions we have noted, occasionally brings in visiting ministers.

Though compulsion is absent from the worship services, the curricular requirements of the University include a course in religion. The undergraduate Department of Religion therefore is large. It has no official relationship to the worship and activity program.

Religious counseling of students is undertaken by the Dean and the other religious leaders. Their work of this nature has no organic connection with the personnel agencies of the University. It is significant that the "Freshman Advisory Council," organized in 1937 for the men, was the product not of the secular personnel agencies but of the religious program. This Council was composed of upperclassmen and graduate students who, having undergone a period of training, advised freshmen in the University. By extension of activity, therefore, rather than by conscious planning, Duke evolved a philosophy of the all-inclusive part which religion should play in the University life. A further evidence of this philosophy was the sponsoring by the religious leaders of better student-faculty relations, represented in the organization of a "Student-Faculty Committee" in 1938.

The provision of official religious leadership at Duke is much more recent than that at Yale, Princeton, and Syracuse. Changes have been rapid. Since the institution of a Dean of the Chapel the original position of Director of Religious Activities has been of secondary importance in the program. The forms which religion is to take, and the relative parts which the religious societies are to play, are by no means fixed. Though an evaluation is therefore difficult, *the elements of strength in this recently developed program at Duke seem to be:*

The consistency between the administration's interest in religion and the official religious provisions.

The influence of students in causing changes and developments in the program.

The preservation of student initiative in the midst of large administrative activity.

The organization of students into an interdenominational church congregation.

The centering of the program in the Duke University Church.

The presence of strong voluntary religious groups, encouraged by the University, at the side of the official program.

The interrelation between the worship services and the activities.

Other items of significance at Duke are:

The influence of the construction of a new chapel.

The sudden development of administrative responsibility.

The influence of undergraduate opinion in causing changes.

5. *Northwestern University* [16]

The significance of Northwestern for our study is not to be found in a description of the present situation. It is no secret that of late years there have been strong differences of opinion on the campus as to how the program should be developed, how coöperation among the existing groups could be achieved, and how the University might most effectively play its part. Undoubtedly the uncertainty characterizing the program at present will be successfully resolved, for the prime requisite for a solution is fulfilled—the University is interested in religion and eager to encourage the religious growth of its students. It is the history of the development of this attitude, rather than the present picture, which concerns us.

16. Information on Northwestern was gained from: Estelle F. Ward, *The Story of Northwestern University* (New York, Dodd, Mead & Co., 1924); Esther McD. Lloyd-Jones, *Student Personnel Work at Northwestern University* (New York, Harper & Brothers, 1929); Thornton W. Merriam, *A Plan for Northwestern University*, May, 1937, MS; and from catalogues and other college publications, speeches and writings of college officials, questionnaires, and personal interviews.

At the beginning of the century, in spite of its historic relationship to the Methodist Church, Northwestern seems to have had slight interest in official religious provisions. For years it had a strong Y.M.C.A. and Y.W.C.A. which employed secretaries. It was the desire of President H. W. Rogers, in the 'nineties, to secure a chapel for the University, but the project was unsuccessful. In 1902 President E. J. James brought to his position a deep concern for the religious life of the students, but he stayed at Northwestern only thirty months. If, in succeeding years, the University sought earnestly to provide for religion, its efforts seem to have gone unnoticed by the students. A survey of student religious attitudes, made some time during the 'twenties, reported that: "The attitude of Northwestern's student body toward religion is indifference, because the attitude of the University itself is indifference." [17]

The study suggested therefore that the University should recognize its responsibility:

The University requires a year of mathematics or Greek of every Liberal Arts student. Every student must take physical training. Each young man and young woman must register for English. Yet the University apparently does not care whether the student flounders in a mental sea of bewilderment on religious questions. Regardless of the humanitarian viewpoint, can there be "liberal education" without any training in religious judgment? . . . The eager young men and women who fill the classrooms of the University are seeking for religion. . . . They need it desperately and they don't know what they need. . . . Might not the University be logically expected to know how to help? [18]

Whether or not it was in answer to this suggestion, Northwestern instituted the position of "Director of Religious Activities" in 1928. Thus an official program was begun and official leadership was provided in the same year that Princeton established the position of Dean of the Chapel and the year after Yale employed a full-time Chaplain. But the experiment seems not to have been a success, and the office was discontinued in 1933.

Though Northwestern was once again without any large official sponsorship of religion, there had never been a dearth of voluntary religious activities. The Y.M.C.A. and Y.W.C.A. had been strong for many years. About this time, however, the church-

17. Lloyd-Jones, *op. cit.*, p. 200.
18. *Ibid.*, pp. 199–201.

sponsored religious societies rose in influence sufficiently to challenge the preëminence of the older Christian Associations; and the religious scene was thereby complicated. The University had been in the habit of making substantial financial contributions to the budgets of the two Associations, but with the depression the amounts were materially decreased.

These factors combined to produce general dissatisfaction with the religious situation. For a while things drifted along. Then in 1936 the University decided to ask a competent outsider to review the religious resources in their totality and make recommendations as to what should be done. Thornton W. Merriam, at that time Executive Director of the National Council on Religion in Higher Education, made such an investigation in the academic year 1936–37.

Merriam discovered that the old desire for a chapel was still alive; and he concluded that if a chapel were to be built, it should be the outgrowth rather than the antecedent of a program. He concurred in the earlier report that the students felt the University to be indifferent to religion. On the other hand, he held that true allegiance to its educational philosophy compelled Northwestern to include religion in other ways than merely by offering courses:

Religion is so definitely a part of American culture and has, in some form or another, so woven itself into the experience of every person that it cannot possibly be ignored by any educational institution in America that conceives its task as inclusively and broadly as does Northwestern.[19]

That the University already looked tentatively in the direction of greater responsibility was clear from its experiment with a Director of Religious Activities and its custom of subsidizing the Christian Associations. Merriam's judgment therefore was:

We conclude that the University does recognize a responsibility for the religious development of its members, that it does not think that responsibility discharged when it has offered courses in religion, and that it has recognized the necessity of providing a program going far beyond the traditional curriculum.[20]

On the basis of his findings Merriam drew up a plan for the religious life. Central in the reorganization should be a "Univer-

19. Merriam, *op. cit.*, p. 3.
20. *Ibid.*, p. 3.

sity Board of Religion," the "Director" of which was to be the responsible religious officer of the University. The Board was to be composed of all of the full-time religious workers in the University community, whether or not supported by the administration. It was suggested, however, that in order to give these workers a sense of belonging and an official status, Northwestern should provide at least a part of the salary for all of them, for those connected with the various church groups as well as for those related to the nondenominational societies.

The Director himself should be recognized as an administrative official of the University, with ex-officio membership in the "University Faculty" and the "University Senate," and on the "Board of Supervision of Student Activities" and the "Board of Personnel Administration." Thus the Director was to have definite contact with all of the important administrative units of college life, and in this way the danger of isolating the religious program was to be avoided.

It is important to note also what was not included in the plan. At that time no chapel services were held by the University, and Merriam's report did not propose their establishment, except as they should result from the desire of students and faculty for them. The curricular provisions for religion were already present, and they were not to be affected by the new development. Thus the immediate concern of the Board was not to be with worship or with religious instruction, but with the strengthening of the University's voluntary religious activities. Its function was to serve as a religious workers' council, though the various religious groups were, in every case, to keep their autonomy. The students were to have no place on the Board.

Merriam's report was presented to the University in 1937, was adopted, and Merriam himself was employed as the "Director of the University Board of Religion" to put the proposals into effect. But for a variety of reasons this turned out to be impossible on certain important points. The Board of Religion was soon composed of faculty and trustees appointed by the President, acting as a purely advisory group on religion to him and to the trustees. Those who were to have composed the Board as originally outlined became members of the subordinate "Association of Religious Counselors." The University did not undertake to provide part of the salaries of the religious workers. A third coöperative group, the "Student Religious Council," composed of student leaders of various groups, was organized.

Great gains came to Northwestern's religious life under this plan. The programs and religious influence of the voluntary associations were appreciably strengthened. Their work was unified not only because of better structure but also because of the leadership of the Director and their closer relationship to the University through him and the Board of Religion. The Director and other workers engaged in a strong program of student religious counseling. A beautiful center was provided by the University for the activities of all the religious groups. Faculty-student discussions were revived on the need for corporate worship and the desirability of a University chapel building. In the autumn of 1941 the first move was made toward instituting chapel services by the inauguration of monthly vespers.

Later Merriam resigned to enter war service, and because of the war and changes in the University administration the office of Director was discontinued. Recent history is confused, and the program is still in a state of flux, but one clear fact emerges. The plan, whatever its merits or weaknesses, was an expression of Northwestern's growing recognition of its religious obligation. A recent and hopeful development was the appointment, in 1946, of James C. McLeod to the position of "University Chaplain."

The elements of strength in the Northwestern plan appear to be:

The sponsoring of a careful investigation prior to the inception of large administrative responsibility.

The interdenominational character of the program.

The organic relationships of the Director with all the major administrative departments of the University.

The presence of strong voluntary religious groups, encouraged by the University, at the side of the official program.

A willingness to change plans and procedures when necessary.

The strong emphasis on religious counseling.

Other items of significance at Northwestern are:

The centering of the program in a council of religious workers.

The absence of provisions for religious worship.

The lateness of the administration's recognition of responsibility.

6. *The University of Chicago* [21]

Throughout its history the University of Chicago has had a vital interest in religion. Moreover, this interest has always been expressed in actual provisions. From its opening in 1892 the University sponsored compulsory chapel and courses in religion. In 1901 the experiment of bringing "University Preachers" to the campus was inaugurated. Even before that time one of the professors was designated "Chaplain" and put in charge of the worship services. Together with this administrative program there also grew up active student religious organizations which the University encouraged.

John D. Rockefeller, Chicago's most generous patron, approved highly of this aspect of the University life. In 1910 he made what was known as his "final gift" of ten million dollars to the University, and in the letter of designation he said:

It is my desire that at least the sum of one million five hundred thousand dollars ($1,500,000) be used for the erection and furnishing of a University chapel. As the spirit of religion should penetrate and control the University, so that building which represents religion ought to be the central and dominant feature of the University group. . . . In this way the group of University buildings, with the Chapel centrally located and dominated in its architecture, may proclaim that the University, in its ideal, is dominated by the spirit of religion, all its departments are inspired by the religious feeling, and all its work is directed to the highest ends.[22]

The Rockefeller Memorial Chapel was not completed until 1928. Rockefeller's desire that it be a symbol of Chicago's interest in religion was eminently fulfilled, for from the first it has served to remind the community of the long-continuing religious purpose of the University.

21. Information on Chicago was gained from: William R. Harper, *The Trend in Higher Education;* Thomas W. Goodspeed, *A History of the University of Chicago* (Chicago, University of Chicago Press, 1916) and *The Story of the University of Chicago* (Chicago, University of Chicago Press, 1925) ; E. D. Burton, *Education in a Democratic World;* Floyd W. Reeves and John D. Russell, *Some University Student Problems* (Chicago, University of Chicago Press, 1933) ; *Religion on the Quadrangles*, 1938–39 (pamphlet) ; and from catalogues and other college publications, speeches and writings of college officials, questionnaires, letters, and personal interviews.

22. Quoted in T. W. Goodspeed, *The Story of the University of Chicago*, p. 181.

Its meaning is not fully located by the utilitarian question which the University faced at its completion: "Here is a great new building given to us—what now shall we do with it?" For the Chapel, alike in its donor's thought and in its own structure and function, symbolizes an idea and ideal of education which have been characteristic of the University of Chicago from its beginning.[23]

But the University did not overlook the "utilitarian question." Even as at Princeton and Syracuse, the new chapel served to inaugurate increased administrative provisions for religion. Until that time the worship services had been compulsory for the students; now they were made voluntary. A "Board of Social Service and Religion" was created to administer the program. The University called Charles W. Gilkey to the new post of religious leadership, "Dean of the Chapel," and he became the executive officer of the Board. Dean Gilkey will retire from his position in the summer of 1947; at the present writing his successor has not been announced.

The Board is composed of faculty members and students who are appointed by the President of the University. The element of student participation in this, the central planning agency for the religious life, agrees with the composition of the Hendricks Chapel Board at Syracuse and the Official Board of the Duke University Church. The Board's purpose and function were proclaimed in its original declaration of policy:

The board will seek to cooperate, as far as practicable, with the churches of the neighborhood, but it conceives its function to be the discovery and expression of the religious life of the University itself. Recognizing that religious motives have played a large part in the development of the University, and that the education the University would impart is not complete until its sons and daughters have their own convictions as to the highest values of life, the board believes that its special task is to multiply opportunities for the acquisition, expression and deepening of every form of idealism worthy to command the respect of a University community.[24]

The worship provisions of the University consist of daily and Sunday services. Those on Sunday are similar to the services at

23. Charles W. Gilkey, "The Relation of the Chapel to the Religious Life of the University," chap. ix in Reeves and Russell, *op. cit.*, pp. 162–163.
24. Quoted in M. C. Towner, ed., *Religion in Higher Education*, pp. 195–196.

Yale, Princeton, Syracuse, and Duke; Dean Gilkey preaches on the average about once a month, and visitors fill the pulpit the remainder of the time. The Board assists the Dean in planning the worship program, but is not organized along ecclesiastical lines, and like Syracuse maintains no constituent membership, affiliate or otherwise. Its program is nonsectarian.

The Dean has the added duties of religious counseling and of part-time teaching in the Divinity School. The counseling of students on religious problems is considered one of his most important functions and consumes a large portion of his time, but is not organically related to the other personnel agencies of the University.

In former times a large number of courses in religion were included in the regular curriculum. During recent years many of these were dropped, but a new interest in the study began to be evidenced in 1940, following the development at Princeton. The work of religious instruction has no official connection with the rest of the religious program.

The Board of Social Service and Religion has interpreted its duty as going beyond merely the provision of worship services At its instigation the "Student Settlement Board" and later the "Chapel Union" were formed. These two groups offer an officially sponsored program of religious activities, the Settlement Board by acting as a link between the student body and the University Settlement, and the Chapel Union by building up the social and spiritual life of the University. A second religious officer, "Advisor to the Chapel Union," is provided for this latter group.

The growth of the Chapel Union is the result primarily of student interest and activity. The Union now has no official connection with the Board; its contact with the administration is maintained through the personal services of the Dean and the Advisor. After the chapel was built, the old Y.M.C.A. became the "Men's Commission for Social Service and Religion," which in turn was absorbed by the coeducational Chapel Union. In its program of activities, the Union is similar to a unified Student Christian Movement. The Y.W.C.A., however, continues a separate existence. Since the chapel staff includes no women, the University makes a contribution to the salary of the Y.W.C.A. secretary. Aside from this aid the Y.W.C.A. is not structurally connected with the official program.

Together with these official and semiofficial religious agencies there exist at Chicago a host of voluntary religious groups sponsored by various denominations. The Board, of course, has no authority over them, but from the beginning the Dean has sought to coöperate with them and aid in their coördination. The Protestant organizations have formed their own instrument of coöperation, the "Interchurch Council." With all the church groups and with the Council the Dean has close relationships of an informal nature. Recently the University has adapted a building adjacent to the Chapel, called "Chapel House," for the use of these voluntary agencies.

Elements of strength in the Chicago program are:

The consistency between the administration's interest in religion and the official religious provisions.

The centering of the program in the chapel and in the Dean of the Chapel.

The possibility of great influence of the Dean of the Chapel, as indicated by his various duties.

The preservation of student initiative in the midst of large administrative activity.

The large official sponsorship of student religious activities, coupled with the encouragement given to voluntary groups.

The presence of strong voluntary groups at the side of the official program.

The nonsectarian character of the program.

The gradual and logical development of administrative responsibility.

Other items of significance at Chicago are:

The influence of the gift of a new chapel, leading to the creation of the chapel program.

The limited offerings of undergraduate courses in religion.

7. Miami University [25]

Miami of Ohio is the first state institution to be considered in this chapter. Until quite recent times the tax-supported colleges have generally been slow to sponsor official provisions for religion except in minor ways. But the development at Miami is striking

25. Information on Miami was gained from: Arthur C. Wickenden, "The Director of Religious Life," chap. xvii in M. C. Towner, ed., *op. cit.;* and from catalogues, speeches and writings of college officials, questionnaires, and letters.

evidence of what they can perform when and if they recognize the possibilities of action and sincerely desire to foster the religious growth of their students. Miami proclaims its own concern in the following statement: "The original act establishing Miami University designates among its purposes 'the promotion of virtue, religion, and morality.' From the beginning, the life of the University has emphasized spiritual values and religious activities." [26]

In the early years of the century Miami's religious provisions consisted of courses in religion taught in the departments of history and philosophy, and chapel services conducted by the president. The Y.M.C.A. and Y.W.C.A. took care of the religious activities of the students. About 1915 these two organizations employed secretaries. The religious life, therefore, was provided for in merely traditional ways, though the program was substantial for a state institution.

During the early 'twenties President R. H. Hughes began to feel that more should be done. This is the same Hughes who later, as president of Iowa State College, expressed his deep concern for religion in the statement quoted in Chapter VI. While still at Miami he endeavored to interest several denominations in establishing some sort of united religious work on the campus. When his efforts did not succeed he decided that the University itself should undertake a heavier responsibility.

Accordingly the office of "Director of Religious Activities" was established in the autumn of 1927, and Arthur C. Wickenden was called to the position which he occupies at the present time. His salary is paid by the state of Ohio, through the regular University budget. Throughout the years no serious objection from any quarter has been raised because of the presence of a religious officer on the administrative staff.

As originally conceived and in its present functioning, the office carries four types of responsibility. First of all, the Director is responsible for the planning of the regular University vesper services, and for the conduct of the brief devotional exercises which form a part of the weekly student assemblies. Students are required to attend five or six assemblies a semester, but credit for assembly attendance is granted for presence at vespers. The scheme allows freedom of choice and yet insures that each student

26. *Miami University Bulletin,* Series **XXXVIII**, 6 (February, 1940), 41–42.

will have some opportunity for worship. A second duty of the Director is that of religious counseling. Thirdly, he teaches courses in religion in the regular curriculum. Miami now has a separate Department of Religion, the beginnings of which were laid when Wickenden came to his post in 1927. The Director, therefore, is also Professor of Religion.

The fourth responsibility is that most nearly signified by the title "Director of Religious Activities." In this capacity Professor Wickenden gives a general leadership to the work of the various voluntary groups on the campus. The Y.M.C.A. and Y.W.C.A. are recognized as parts of the official University program and normally employ secretaries. Several denominations sponsor active student societies, some of which are guided by full-time professional leaders. In recent years a "Student Religious Council," composed of representatives of the Christian Associations, the Protestant groups, and the Hillel Student League, was organized to undertake coöperative projects such as "Religion-in-Life Week." Professor Wickenden acts as the adviser of this Council. The duty of the Director, therefore, is that of coördinating the programs of the various voluntary agencies. Thus the full independence of such groups is preserved and student initiative is encouraged, while at the same time the University lends more than mere verbal blessing.

Elements of strength in the Miami program are:

The consistency between the administration's interest in religion and official religious provisions.

The fusion of the functions of Director of Religious Activities and Professor of Religion in one office.

The possibility of great influence of the Director, as indicated by his various duties.

The presence of strong voluntary groups, encouraged by the University, at the side of the official program.

The interdenominational character of the program.

The gradual and logical development of administrative responsibility.

Other items of significance at Miami are:

Evidence of the University's understanding the true meaning of the separation of church and state.

The recognition of the need for coördination among voluntary religious groups.

8. Alfred University [27]

Alfred occupies the anomalous position of being both independent and state-supported. The College of Liberal Arts is independent, while the College of Ceramics and the School of Agriculture and Technology are supported by the State of New York. The large measure of state support gives added significance to the official provisions of the University.

Alfred is proud of the fact that it has long been concerned with religion. "The religious life of the students has always received careful attention of the administration. While the University is non-sectarian it is distinctly a Christian institution." [28]

The first development of administrative responsibility beyond traditional procedures occurred in 1929. President Boothe C. Davis was at that time also president of the Council of Church Boards of Education. Through that organization's University Commission he was able to arrange the establishment on the Alfred campus of the position, "Director of Religious Activities." The project was supported jointly by the Baptist, Methodist, and Presbyterian denominations and by the University.

During the depression, however, the churches were unable to carry their full share of the financial burden, and the University has increasingly assumed greater responsibility for the Director's support. At the present time, therefore, the Director is an official member of the administration.

The man chosen for the position in 1929, James C. McLeod, served until the autumn of 1940; subsequently the position has been filled by William Genné, B. Davie Napier, and since the fall of 1946, George Ball. In McLeod's regime the duties of the office were continually expanded, and to indicate them he assumed the titles of "Chaplain" and "Minister of the Union University Church." He and his successors also undertook some part-time teaching. Alfred provides courses in religion in a regular department, but that work is largely separated from the remainder of the religious program.

27. Information on Alfred was gained from: [James C. McLeod] *The Religious Life on the Alfred University Campus*, MS; George H. Ball, *A Brief Religious History of Alfred University*, MS; and from catalogues and other college publications, letters and personal interviews.

28. *Alfred University Publication*, XVI, 1 (January, 1940), 26.

As Director the religious leader supervises and coördinates the various religious societies on the campus. For many years the two chief organizations were the Y.W.C.A. and the Alfred University Christian Association, or A.U.C.A., which was the local name for the Y.M.C.A. These two groups united in 1941 to form the "Alfred Christian Fellowship," which changed its name to the "Religious Fellowship of Alfred" in 1945, in order not to embarrass Jewish students who had begun to be active in the organization. The "Religious Fellowship" sponsors a varied program similar to a co-educational Christian Association, and is affiliated with the New York State Student Christian Movement. Denominational groups exist or have existed for the Catholics, Christian Scientists, Episcopalians and Jews. For all of these organizations the Director serves as adviser.

As Chaplain the religious officer counsels students on religious problems and leads the chapel services of the University. Chapel is voluntary, and is held once a week at an hour set apart from the regular class schedule.

As Minister he has charge of the Sunday services of the Union University Church. The small town in which the University is located was originally a settlement of the Seventh Day Baptists, and for many years the institution was under their influence and held its main service of worship on the old Sabbath. But as this element in the University population slowly decreased in numbers, a desire developed to organize a Sunday church. About twenty-five years ago President Davis led in the founding of the Union University Church, and since that time it has occupied on Sundays the building used by the Seventh Day Baptists on Saturdays. These two congregations are the only ones in the town of Alfred.

Though there is no organic connection between the University and the Church, a very close relationship exists. The Executive Committee, which is the governing body of the Church, is made up of students, faculty members and townspeople. Affiliate membership is offered to students. The Church is not supported by the University or by any outside agency, but raises its own budget by an every-member canvass, including students. Out of this budget it pays a small portion of the salary of the Director-Chaplain-Pastor. The Pastor preaches nearly every Sunday, though there are occasional visiting ministers. The Church, of course, is interdenominational in emphasis and spirit.

Elements of strength in the Alfred program are:

The consistency between the administration's interest in religion and the official religious provisions.

The centering of the program in the Director of Religious Activities, who is also Chaplain and Minister of the Union University Church.

The possibility of great influence of the Director, as indicated by his various duties.

The organization of students into an interdenominational church congregation.

The presence of a strong voluntary religious group, encouraged by the University, at the side of the official program.

The gradual and logical development of the administrative responsibility.

Other items of significance at Alfred are:

Evidence of the University's understanding the true meaning of the separation of church and state.

The recognition of the need for coördination among voluntary religious groups.

The opportunity created by the absence in the town of a church representing any of the large denominations.

9. Denison University [29]

Denison is a coeducational liberal arts college, independent in government, but with strong religious sympathies and possessing tenuous ties with its parent denomination, the Northern Baptists. Throughout the years it has preserved a keen interest in the religious growth of its students. A recent statement of its purpose, adopted by both faculty and trustees, reads in part:

The college shall strive to foster in each student ethical and spiritual qualities; to integrate each personality around Christian principles and ideals; . . . to cultivate adherence to the highest

29. Information on Denison was gained from: *Christian Emphasis Program of Denison University, Reports,* August 1, 1943, MS; *Campus Christianity, Denison University Bulletin,* XLIV, 6 (September, 1944); *The Story of a Campus Experiment in Christian Emphasis, 1942–1946, Denison University Bulletin,* XLVII, 11 (March, 1947); and from catalogues and other college publications, speeches and writings of college officials, interviews, and personal participation in the program.

ethical standards in economic, political and social living; and to animate the whole group with Christian idealism.[30]

Its present executive, Kenneth I. Brown, concurs in this purpose, for in 1940 while still President of Hiram he called upon "the small, privately endowed college of liberal arts . . . to scrutinize its educational program and . . . reorganize it about 'the supreme reality of religious faith.' " [31]

But until recent years Denison, like other colleges of its type, confined itself to the pursuit of traditional methods. President Brown, however, was not satisfied with the usual provisions of compulsory chapel, courses, and an annual "Religious Emphasis Week," and with lending encouragement to the voluntary religious groups, the Y.M.C.A. and the Y.W.C.A. Though his coming to Denison coincided with the beginning of the period of retrenchment characteristic of the war years, he was loath to wait until the end of the war to start an enlarged program. He secured the interest and financial support of the Danforth Foundation in sponsoring a four-year experiment, with the understanding that at the end of that period, if the program were deemed successful, the University itself would take over all expense.

The four-year term of the experiment was to cover the period from 1942 to 1946. In its establishment provision was made for judging its effectiveness by the appointment of a committee of three, two of whom were not connected with the University, who would review its progress from time to time, and at the end of the period submit a final appraisal. At the present writing this report is not yet available, but in the confidence that it will be favorable the University is proceeding to finance the continuance of the venture.[32]

The experiment was given carte blanche, as an effort to answer the question, "What ought a college do to foster religion in a

30. *Denison University Bulletin*, XLIII, 1 (January, 1943), 23.

31. Kenneth I. Brown, *A Campus Decade: The Hiram Study Plan of Intensive Courses* (Chicago, University of Chicago Press, 1940), p. 128.

32. Since the Denison description was written the report has appeared, the "general conclusion" of which reads: ". . . the Denison Christian Emphasis experiment has attained significant religious and social objectives and . . . the University should be encouraged to continue the program . . ." (*The Story of a Campus Experiment in Christian Emphasis, 1942–1946*, p. 38).

thoroughgoing way?" Two answers immediately suggested themselves: the provision of some sort of voluntary religious meeting designed to serve student interests and needs, as a mainspring for all the religious activities of the campus; and the sponsorship of a sound and far-reaching program of social service activities.

These two lines of endeavor necessitated the employment of professional leaders. Accordingly the experiment began, in the fall of 1942, with the addition to the Denison faculty of two people, a man for the former task and a woman for the latter. Since it was part of the original purpose to give these workers regular faculty status for their own protection and wider effectiveness, and since they were to teach a course or two in the regular curriculum, their titles did not reflect their functions in the experiment but were, respectively "Professor of Religion" and "Instructor in Sociology." The former position has had two incumbents, the present being Alvin Pitcher; the latter office was filled throughout most of the period by Mrs. Lauriel Eubank Anderson.

The voluntary religious meeting is unique of its kind, the closest thing to it being the Burrall Bible Class of Stephens (Junior) College. Among other points of difference, however, Burrall requires attendance, whereas the genius of the Denison development is in its voluntarism. In order not to conflict with the local church services, the program meets at the Sunday-school period, though its pattern is not that of a study class or discussion. Going under the catchy title of "Deni-Sunday," its normal order of service consists of hymns, Scripture, prayer, special music, all conducted by students, and a talk by the leader. On occasion the normal order is abandoned, and a religious play or faculty forum or complete musical program is substituted.

It is in the talk that the difference between Deni-Sunday and the normal college chapel or church service is most clearly discernible. The talk is not a sermon; it is based usually on the consideration of some student problem or interest upon which are brought to bear the insights of religion. Thus the attendance at Deni-Sunday, unlike that at most of the Sunday services of institutions previously discussed, is almost altogether composed of students, and no special effort is made to entice faculty or townspeople. Since it is a program for undergraduates alone, with a large measure of student participation, it purposely lacks the dignity characteristic of the services at Yale, Princeton, or Duke.

It is frankly an attempt to reach many students who remain untouched by more traditional approaches—chapel, courses on religion, and Christian Associations.

Deni-Sunday is promoted by an undergraduate committee, thus providing for student planning as well as participation. The committee also sponsors various other religious activities comparable to the programs of voluntary religious organizations on other campuses, and works in close conjunction with the local Y.W.C.A. The Y.M.C.A. at Denison was moribund in 1942 and with the beginning of Deni-Sunday voted to unite with the new program. Deni-Sunday thus acts for the men as the local unit of the Intercollegiate Y.M.C.A. The Y.W.C.A., however, remains a strong separate organization. Denominational student work has never developed at Denison.

The second area of new activity at Denison, that of a carefully conceived social service program, is not represented by any one student organization. Rather, Mrs. Anderson chose to work through any student group which might be persuaded to undertake such a function. Representatives of the various participating groups form a steering committee for the total social service program, thus avoiding duplication of effort. The groups involved include not only the religious organizations of Deni-Sunday and the Y.W.C.A., but also social fraternities and sororities, the Athletic Association, dormitory groups, and other student agencies.

The program consists of every sort of "Community Service" in the college town, neighboring city, and surrounding rural areas for which students can qualify. Since the director is a trained sociologist, the philosophy underlying the program is not that of high-handed largesse to the poor and unfortunate, but rather that of education through participation in various types of community living and problem solving. But the significant difference between this development at Denison and social service programs elsewhere is not so much its philosophy or the identity of its sponsoring groups, as it is the method of its organization. Rather than setting up one official agency whose function shall be that of social service, or establishing "projects" for their own sake, the University administration has provided professional leadership for the encouragement and guidance of the students, and then granted to both the leader and the students large freedom in finding and developing the various channels of service. This freedom has meant that no organic unity between the two parts of the experimental program has been established, though they have, of course, grown side by side in the harmony of their underlying religious purposes. For all these characteristics, the Community Service program, changing from time to time as the local scene shifts and student interests vary, is, like Deni-Sunday, a unique experiment among college religious activities.

For the brief length of time it has been undertaken, *the experimental program at Denison appears to show the following elements of strength:*

The consistency between the administration's interest in religion and the official provisions.

The willingness to experiment, even in wartime, in two different areas of religious activity.

The preservation of student initiative in the midst of large administrative activity.

The large official sponsorship of student religious activities, coupled with encouragement given to a voluntary religious group.

The presence of a strong voluntary group, the Y.W.C.A., at the side of the official program.

The provision of a means by which the program may be impartially examined and its results estimated.

Other items of significance at Denison are:

The sudden development of an enlarged official program.

The lack of organic relationship among the various religious activities and groups.

The absence of denominational groups.

10. Summary

From the description of the programs of these nine colleges, certain characteristics and trends in the development of large responsibility for religion become apparent.

First of all, one is impressed by the lack of uniformity among the practices. The organizational centers for the programs are varied, consisting of churches, chapel boards, activity boards, or student-dominated agencies; or there may be no center at all. The programs may be inter- or nondenominational. The religious activities may be partly or altogether officially sponsored; or may stem from completely voluntary societies, encouraged by the administration. Students may have great influence in the development, and student initiative may be preserved; or they may have very small place or none at all in the planning and direction. The total program may be separated into certain distinct compartments: curriculum, worship, activity, and counseling; or a more or less complete unity may be achieved. The official responsibility may have been assumed as the result of careful planning or without any planning at all. The growth may have been gradual or sudden.

Similar divergence of practice is discernible with respect to the provision of official leadership. This characteristic was noted in our discussion of the method of providing professional leaders, in Chapter XI, and the descriptions of individual programs only lend emphasis to the variety indicated there. The religious officers may or may not have an organic relationship with other departments and administrative units of the colleges. That is, their positions may or may not have high status, and may or may not be formally connected with all the areas of religious activity and with the rest of the college life. Moreover, their divers responsibilities exist in different combinations. The newness of the development, including both positions of leadership and official programs, is responsible for the lack of clarity and consistency in the total picture.

But in this welter of divergent practices there do exist common characteristics among these programs involving large administrative responsibility as well as among others of a similar nature which might have been discussed. The following observations apply to all of them:

1. The development is everywhere experimental in nature. All programs including those founded on the basis of thoughtful study, those which have simply grown by happenstance, and those established suddenly in their entirety have undergone change. Obviously no one institution is satisfied with merely the traditional methods of chapel and courses; yet no one of the group claims to possess all the answers to the problem of religion on the campus. Thus the spirit of experimentation at the heart of higher education is once again found to be present in a large measure in the field of religion in the colleges.

2. Whatever the relationships of the programs and of the colleges themselves to the different denominations, they are all nonsectarian in emphasis.

3. All of them, as we have noticed, have found it necessary to

provide some official leadership for their programs. It would seem that an enlarged program of administrative responsibility for religion means, automatically, the institution of positions on the regular college staff for trained professional leaders.

4. Methods are disputed but final goals are clear. All colleges of this group are desperately eager to foster the religious growth of their students. Even if sometimes the beginnings of the official provisions for religion were accidental or unplanned, the participating institutions are now consciously and intensely interested in the problem. Interest in religion may not always result in responsibility for religion; but large responsibility always presupposes keen interest.

CHAPTER XIV

MOTIVATING FORCES

COLLEGES have reasons, good or bad, for doing as they do. Forces of much more import than the notion of the moment account for the emphases of the times, the experiments which are being made, the changes over the years. And this is as true for religion as for any other collegiate interest and activity.

In the preceding chapters passing mention has been made of the motivations behind general developments and local experiments in the area of religion. It is time now to gather this material together and present in orderly array a picture of the forces and factors which have influenced the movement for good and ill. Even as the characteristics of college religious programs are various, so these forces and factors will be found to be numerous and differing in type and influence. They have operated not only in the colleges which have undertaken large responsibility but in all institutions irrespective of the degree of their interest in the religious life of their students.

The working of these motivating ideas and events is discernible, first, in the attitudes of college administrators and other educators. In many cases their statements indicate the causes for their interest or lack of it in religion. In others one must rely upon the implications of their remarks; but usually the implications are unmistakable. Similarly the inferences in the various educational philosophies for the place of religion can easily be drawn. And thirdly, the forces are evident in the history of the programs themselves, both official and voluntary. Repetition of actual statement and of description of program is unnecessary; the treatment will be simply to list the factors and discuss them briefly.

A. SECULARIZATION AND ITS ROOTS

First of all, reasonable explanations are available for the period of relative poverty which religion in education suffered in the latter part of the previous century and the years immediately following 1900. The general cause was undoubtedly the movement known as secularization; the factors responsible for this development have been identified by many scholars.[1] It seems that in the main no hostility to religion was intended. But the nation was committed to the principle of education for all, and such a task could be performed only by the state. The divisiveness of Protestantism, resulting in rampant sectarianism, worked toward the discredit of all religion. Thus as protection against such ills, the principle of the separation of church and state came to be rigidly interpreted and applied, and its influence spread to other colleges besides those supported by the state.

As a process within education, secularization gained support from other educational developments of the day. The discussion in the first part of Chapter II indicated ways in which the chief problems of the early years of the twentieth century exerted a secularizing influence upon the colleges. The need for academic standards, the desire for accreditation, the increase in size of student bodies and therefore in complexity of administrative organization, the development of specialization—all played their part in reducing the role which religion was given in higher education in times past.

But all of this did not take place solely as a result of the trends in education. Secularization was a process within education, it is true, but it was a product of many pressures from without. The reference to sectarianism above indicates that much of this pressure came from religion itself and from the trends of thought and practice among the denominations. The influence of various religious concerns of the time has already been noted in Chapter III. These years were full of the disputes of fundamentalism versus modernism and of religion versus science. If religious leaders could not agree among themselves it was reasonable for educators to say, "A plague on both your houses." Correspondingly, though religious leaders were unprepared for and afraid of the advances of science, educators dared not fail to participate

1. See, for example, L. A. Weigle, "The Secularization of Public Education," chap. i in Committee on the War and the Religious Outlook, *The Teaching Work of the Church* (New York, Association Press, 1923), and "Why the Principle of Public Responsibility for Education Has Prevailed in the United States," *Religious Education*, XXII, 4 (April, 1927), 319–332; S. W. Brown, *The Secularization of American Education*; E. P. Cubberley, *Public Education in the United States*; and Stewart G. Cole, *Liberal Education in a Democracy*.

in the forward march of learning. Thus the relative neglect of religion in the colleges could often be laid at the door of religion itself. Its protest against collegiate unconcern was of little avail while its own actions blocked the road.

Forces from other aspects of our national culture were also operative. Historical events such as the winning of the West and the Spanish-American and first World Wars often affected public morality adversely. The practices of big business, a new American phenomenon, and of high society, composed of a new and wealthy elite, often did not adhere to Christian ethical standards. These were the things that took the public eye; and thus religion suffered. Secularization was made easier in an atmosphere in which religious values seemed to be discredited or denied.

It was this atmosphere of secularism even more than the movement of secularization which made religion's task in higher education difficult. Secularization forced the exclusion of religion from tax-supported institutions. It had a parallel though much less powerful influence upon independent colleges and even upon a few church-related schools. Yet religion's real enemy was not the movement but its underlying spirit, secularism, a temper of thought that had begun to infect not merely education but the whole society. Though we have paused before to indicate its deleterious effects which continue to persist, a full discussion of the nature of secularism must await our final appraisal of the religious programs and the more intangible religious atmosphere of the colleges. Suffice it now to say that the two leading negative factors of the early years of the century were secularization and its more powerful ally, secularism.

B. THE STATE OF THE WORLD

But in view of the continuity of religious interest and responsibility which has characterized the college scene, secularization never approached the complete victory in higher education that it did in the lower school levels. In fact, in the last thirty years the trend has been completely reversed. Moreover, even secularism has not been finally determinative. Since approximately the time of the first World War, as we have seen, colleges have become increasingly interested in religion and have greatly enlarged their religious provisions. Powerful forces have brought such a change to pass. The following paragraphs will indicate the important positive factors which have served to give religion the significant place in higher education which it occupies today. The treatment will proceed from general to specific causes.

Fear for the future of society has been one of the most striking forces working toward increased concern and obligation for religion. Educators have been persuaded to give religion a chance as they have viewed the state of the world with increasing alarm. This state is, of course, secularism, but it is also much more—a general rottenness at the core of human life. Even before the devastation of World War II men had begun to despair that civilization could survive, and writers all the way from Spengler to James Thurber freely predicted the decline of the West. Things were in the saddle and would ride mankind to their ultimate doom.

Then came the war. Many people found they could be brave, unselfish, infinitely patient, and capable of bearing every ill which the foe could contrive. Such demonstrations of spiritual strength were possible because "liberty, equality, and fraternity" and a host of other half-forgotten words once again took on powerful meaning. But men do not live on such high levels when the days of peace return, and the winning of the war, we know, has not automatically guaranteed our escape from destruction. In fact, in victory itself our doom is brought closer. The *Reader's Digest* reports a recent newspaper editorial of only two sentences: "The atomic bomb is here to stay. But are *we?*"

Then what can save us from the wrath to come? Educators have observed the present scene and have asked the question. And like many other thoughtful persons, they are beginning to answer, Religion. By religion they do not mean denominationalism or creedalism. They refer rather to religion as a system of values and as a kind of life in consonance with those values. And so the thinking of numbers of educators has run: The world in its present state needs religion; thus the future leaders of our world must be men and women possessed by a consciousness of religious values. The colleges which prepare them for that leadership must therefore give more attention to their religious growth.

C. DEVELOPMENTS IN HIGHER EDUCATION

A multitude of positive motives for including religion arose out of higher education itself, from the problems it faced and the various solutions it proposed. In the final analysis, of course, the details of the local situation are largely determinative, for each college has its own special set of problems and must solve them in its individual way. A later paragraph will deal with some of these specific factors; the reference here is to the general developments influencing all colleges to a greater or lesser degree.

1. That there are general developments decisive for the place of religion in higher education implies that there exists no special disabling principle or practice dictating the exception of any one type of institution. But as we have seen, the principle of the separation of church and state did at one time act as just such a disability. The mistaken strictness in the interpretation of the principle worked toward the elimination or noninclusion of religion from tax-supported institutions and had its effect upon all types of colleges.

As the reasons for rigidity of application passed away, however, state institutions have begun to discover that the principle does not prevent their fostering religion; and this too is having repercussions upon other colleges. When a state institution shakes off the shackles of the past by inaugurating some new religious program, independent and church colleges are prompted to examine their own provisions more closely to be sure that they are doing at least as much. Here and there the old misconception of the principle still persists and practical difficulties remain; but the point is that, theoretically, it does not *need* to exist anywhere, and practically, it will without doubt be slowly overcome. Thus one of the influential factors in the growth of administrative responsibility for religion has been the gradual dawn of *a more correct understanding of the principle of the separation of church and state*. Its influence has been to reduce real or imaginary restrictions and thus to enable the following forces of a general nature to work in freedom toward the larger inclusion of religion.

2. The motivation which can be given the most widespread application is *the principle that higher education must be complete*. The discussion in previous chapters makes the line of reasoning familiar. No area of intellectual endeavor is foreign to the colleges. As true today as when Cardinal Newman wrote it is his statement:

. . . if a University be . . . a place of instruction, where universal knowledge is professed, and if in a certain University, so called, the subject of Religion is excluded, one of two conclusions is inevitable,—either, on the one hand, that the province of

Religion is very barren of real knowledge, or, on the other hand, that in such University one special and important branch of knowledge is omitted.[2]

Though speaking particularly of universities, Newman here touched the heart of the conviction which may be held by all types of colleges. Of his two conclusions the vast majority of colleges have not been willing to admit the former or countenance the latter. Thus their refusal to ignore any legitimate interest or field of study has impelled them to make place for religion and to give it the same status as other subjects and interests enjoy.

This consideration is, of course, directed primarily at the inclusion of religion in the curriculum. It represents at least one important conviction upon which the various philosophies of higher education all agree. Whether the philosophy be "progressive," "classicist," or "liberal," the belief is firm that any field which is intellectually rigorous and in which great thinkers have labored must be included in the course of study. This belief has led in numerous instances to the recognition of the omission of religion and to the effort to fill the gap.

3. Related to this factor is *the conviction that higher education must be unified*. As colleges have grown in size they have automatically lost the unity which was formerly theirs. Thus educators of more than one philosophical school have begun to seek for a unifying principle or an integrating factor. What discipline would be adequate? Numerous solutions, among them religion, have been suggested. The search for unity, therefore, has led in some instances to religion.

This force, it will be recognized, has operated on a level one step removed from the preceding factor. Its result has been not merely to foster the inclusion of religion but to suggest the possibility that religion become the central element in the educational program. As far as the author is aware no college can yet claim to have fully translated this possibility into actuality, but a number of colleges have taken the philosophers seriously enough to talk about it as a practical development. The working of this conviction is discernible, of course, only in those colleges which have already given an important place to religion.

4. Probably of largest determinative influence has been *the*

2. John Henry Newman, *The Idea of a University, Defined and Illustrated* (London, Basil Montagu Pickering, 1873), p. 21.

principle that higher education must be concerned with the "whole person." This conviction, it is obvious, is closely akin to the idea that education must be complete. The two, however, are not identical. Both spring from educational philosophy; but the factor mentioned before grows out of a consideration of the content of the curriculum, whereas this belief is based on an examination of the nature of personality and the psychological fact of its indivisibility. The latter, therefore, is broader than the former, for it has to do with more than the intellect and intellectual pursuits. Consequently it would be largely inoperative in persuading the classicists. But since the colleges following the classicist philosophy are few in number, this principle holds the allegiance of the vast majority of institutions in the nation.

The former and the present considerations differ also in their implications for religion. Whereas the former operates toward the inclusion of religion in the curriculum, the concern with the whole person leads toward providing for the whole religious life of the students. Colleges adopting this principle have enlarged their care of the students to include health, living conditions, recreation, and extracurricular activities. The logic of their position, as we have seen in the foregoing chapters, has been highly influential in persuading them to become interested in religion and to make provisions for worship, activity, and religious counseling as well as for instruction.

5. All of these general forces exist in the consciousness of administrators. That is, when a college decides to embark upon an enlarged program of religion, the president is likely to state as the reason any one or all of the three convictions we have just considered. But underneath these identifiable motivations lies a trend in educational thought, present throughout the century, which though seldom given explicit expression has actually been the mainspring for the others. This hidden motive is *the increasing concern of higher education with values.*

The discussion in Chapter II identified a number of collegiate developments illustrating this trend. Whenever a college began to be more concerned with quality than with amount in any area of its activity, then religion stood to gain at least indirectly. Thus the abandonment of the idea of free election, or more careful policies of admission and orientation of students, or the development of personnel work, or the supervision of fraternities, athletics, and social life—these things and more sprang from the desire of the colleges that certain values be preserved or rediscovered or newly affirmed in the educational process.

Those values are, of course, religious in nature. Educators who could have given reasons on this level for such developments as those mentioned above would have said they sought for their students "larger growth of personality," or "acquaintance with the best that has been thought, said, and done," or "allegiance to high moral standards." Of course many have said so with particular reference to their provisions for religion, but those values underlie the general policies of colleges in recent years as well as their religious programs. And the effort to establish them throughout the institutional life represents in fact, whether or not it is consciously recognized, the extension of the religious atmosphere in the colleges.

This, in turn, acts as a great encouragement to the work of the specifically religious activities. How much easier it is to teach the subject of religion or lead chapel services or counsel a Christian Association when one knows that the faculty and administration in their several and total concerns subscribe to the same fundamental values. Needless to say, the extent of the presence of this factor on any one campus cannot be measured; it can hardly even be estimated except by those who have long familiarity with the local scene. But that it is often present and that, when present, it is largely responsible for the success of the religious program, no one well acquainted with higher education can deny.

6. One of the concomitants of recent educational theory has been experimentalism, and of educational practice, the innovation of programs and methods differing from the ways of the past. *The willingness of colleges to experiment* has had its influence, as we have noted, in many religious programs. When no special concern for religion already exists, this factor is inoperative. Thus many of the colleges most thoroughly experimental, such as Bennington and St. John's, tend to omit or ignore religion. But when other forces have previously operated to produce a heightened interest in religion in such colleges, this characteristic of their general policy has served to persuade them to inaugurate new methods of fostering religion and thus to increase their total self-assumed obligation.

D. DEVELOPMENTS IN RELIGION

The discussion in Chapter III identified the major interests in the general field of religion during the twentieth century and indicated briefly the ways in which those interests impinged upon the college scene. It is necessary here only to recapitulate the conclusions there offered, for which the intervening chapters have furnished illustrations, and to set within the general framework of this chapter the motivating forces for which religion has been responsible.

To describe the influential changes in thinking since approximately the first World War one may use a positive or negative approach. For example, the negative aspect is that sectarianism has largely disappeared; the positive, that ecumenicity has flowered. The negative position is that anti-evolution, premillenarianism, and fundamentalism in all its forms are lost causes for the religiously mature and informed. The positive statement is that, once again for the religiously mature, modernism has triumphed and religion and science have begun to look upon each other as allies. The positive approach, it is obvious, goes further than the negative in each instance, for the positive indicates not merely a reversal of the past but also a new development.

Other developments of significance have been the rise of the social gospel, the birth of the religious education movement, and more recently, the increased theological inquiry.

The influence of such matters upon college religious programs has been twofold. First of all, they have dictated the emphases which the college programs made. Chapel, curricular work, and extracurricular activity have followed with eagerness the leading movements. Since youth is easily excited by the new and the "liberal," often college programs have not merely followed but been in the vanguard of the procession, particularly with regard to interdenominational coöperation and the social gospel. And nowhere have the trends away from fundamentalism and toward a revitalized theology been more evident than among college courses of instruction. Thus, throughout the years, the developments in religion have determined or paralleled the interests of college religious programs.

The second influence has consisted in giving to institutions of higher learning a better understanding of the true and abiding nature of religion and its functioning. In their various ways all these developments have indicated that religion is a demanding study, a fruitful activity, an invigorating personal experience. It is not sentimentality or illusion or magic. Its pursuit is intellectually challenging, emotionally stabilizing, socially productive of worthy accomplishments. These things have always been characteristic of religion in its essence, but were perverted by certain of the narrow and anti-intellectual emphases of fifty years ago. When colleges have not judged religion on the basis of outmoded characteristics but have come to appreciate the attributes of the religious movements of this century, they have accordingly welcomed it into their programs. For they desire closely related ends; and religion has been accorded a larger part in the campus life as a result of the colleges' recognition of the identity between latter-day religious and educational purposes and methods.

E. THE NEEDS OF THE STUDENTS

One of the most significant developments in higher education in the twentieth century has been the increased interest of colleges in the students and their general welfare. Since this concern has led to a thorough examination of student attitudes and needs, it has often been an instrumental factor in causing the enlargement of campus religious programs.

This motivation is similar to, but not the same as, the conviction that higher education must be concerned with the whole person. The difference is in the locus of the original impulse. Concern for the whole person arose primarily out of educational philosophy, while consideration of student needs is largely a matter of practical import. Thus the former may be based so completely on philosophical and psychological assumptions that it may ignore individual student needs and result in a purely perfunctory interest and program. On the other hand, the administrator who has never heard of the "whole person" may recognize and seek sincerely to meet the needs of his students from day to day. Such an effort may make up for its possible lack of philosophical basis by a possibly greater concern and care for persons as individuals. In actuality, however, the two factors operate side by side.

The attempt to understand the problems and needs of students has led to the realization that in the field of religion they are abysmally ignorant. For all the growth of the religious education movement, it has not resulted in sending to the colleges a body of young people well informed concerning their Hebrew-Christian heritage and their faith. On the contrary, students know next to nothing about the Bible, other religious classics, or ecclesiastical history and doctrine.

Moreover, the little they have picked up in terms of interpretation is usually mistaken. The discussion in the preceding section mentioned that fundamentalism and its attendant errors had long since ceased to be influential "for the religiously mature," but the great majority of undergraduates fail to qualify under this phrase. The decision in the fight of Charles Darwin versus Adam and Eve, for example, has long been rendered for the informed, but many students do not yet know the outcome. Anyone who has conducted discussion groups in the colleges knows to his sorrow how often there arise questions which reflect this basic misunderstanding. Such a situation has prompted various institutions to increase their curricular offerings in religion.

Related to the recognition of their ignorance is the discovery of their prevailing attitudes toward religion. They tend to be suspicious or, possibly worse, contemptuous of the church. They possess no profound reasons for allegiance to religion's ethical standards, though for social reasons they remain fairly conventional in their moral judgments. They have been infected by the agnosticism and cynicism of the sophisticated. Thus some colleges, unwilling that such attitudes go uncorrected, have encouraged and strengthened their religious programs in divers ways so as to counteract this body of immature opinion.

The attitudes of students toward religion is symptomatic of their total reaction to the world around them. They are often brash and insensitive, yet just as often fearful and lost. They lack a sense of security, and their tragic instability promises to be even more pronounced in the confusing days of peace. Their great need is to become usefully adjusted to the tasks of personal and social living. This means, simply, that they need something true to believe in, something good to live by, and something noble to work for. That is religion. And as colleges have come to realize, first, the needs of their students and, second, the ability of a high religion to meet those needs, they have made increased provisions for religious experience in worship, study, and activity, and for religious counseling.

F. OCCASIONAL FACTORS

The forces we have thus far enumerated are of a general application and have operated in differing degrees throughout higher education. There remain to be noted certain specific factors which here and there have been instrumental in the development of administrative responsibility for religion.

Some of them have grown out of the nature of the voluntary programs of religious activities at various colleges. At certain institutions the voluntary groups, such as the Christian Associations and the denominational societies, have found it increasingly difficult to care for the religious life of the students. In a few institutions they have completely failed. The inadequacy of such programs, therefore, has occasionally been influential in the growth of administrative provisions as substitutes.

This inadequacy or failure in certain situations has not always been the fault of the voluntary groups themselves; still less is it a condemnation of the voluntary idea in student religious activities. Other forces have often been responsible: the huge growth of the college enrollment, making the voluntary group's task much more difficult; the personal inadequacy of an adult leader; the opposition of an administration unsympathetic to some particular emphasis or activity of the voluntary program. Wherever the fault has lain, however, the result in terms of the lessened influence of the voluntary groups has produced, in its turn, larger administrative obligation.

Yet, strangely, other official provisions have sprung up for the exactly opposite reason, namely, the strength rather than the weakness of voluntary agencies. On some campuses several voluntary groups doing excellent work have nevertheless created a chaotic condition of rivalry among themselves. Thus the colleges have sometimes been moved to action because of the recognized need for harmony and unity in the total religious program. This need for unity has led to the establishment of coöperative agencies and programs under official leadership, a development often implied in the title of "Director of Religious Activities."

Student pressure has been a decisive factor for several institutions. The influence has operated in various ways. Sometimes undergraduate dissatisfaction with existing religious provisions has caused colleges to reëxamine their practices and adopt new methods. The pressure may have been constructive as well as critical. A few times students have sought professional leadership, which the colleges have been persuaded to supply. On other occasions they have forced the enlargement of the official religious program by reason of their hearty support and activity in it. Students, therefore, have been influential in the movement.

Among the occasional factors should also be listed those accidents which sometimes come the way of colleges. The gift of a chapel, for example, or the endowment for a chair in religion has not infrequently been the impetus for the increase of religious provisions. As we saw in Chapter XIII, some of the most fruitful programs of administrative responsibility today have received their start through some such fortuitous occurrence. For any such program to develop meaningfully, however, many other forces than this one must be operative.

G. SUMMARY

Throughout the twentieth century all the forces working toward the exclusion of religion from higher education have decreased in their influence. As we shall see, this statement holds true even for the most dangerous of all—secularism, which, though its debilitating influence is still potent, has begun to lessen its grip on the campus. Correspondingly all the factors fostering the place of religion in the colleges have gained steadily in extent and power. It has already been observed that many of these positive motivations represent a complete reversal of the previous causes of secularization. The total group of forces, therefore, explain the swing of the pendulum toward larger administrative interest in and responsibility for religion.

Some of the factors have been general, others specific in their application. Some have been much more widely and powerfully influential than others. For example, the various developments in higher education discussed in Section C have probably carried more weight in more different institutions than any other one group of forces. But a division of causes into groups, though necessary for purposes of identification, is essentially unreal and artificial, since all have worked together. On any one campus the explanations for the state of the religious program are legion.

One further force remains to be identified. In previous chapters it was pointed out that developments in college religious programs have occurred within a basic continuity of administrative interest and responsibility. No reference has been made in this chapter to that underlying continuity, for the sole intention has been to identify the forces responsible for the changes that have taken place. Yet the majority of colleges have always had an interest in and, at least in embryonic form, a responsibility for religion. The one most powerful influence in explaining the continuing presence of religion in the colleges, irrespective of the changes through the years, has been their wholehearted allegiance to the original purposes for which they were founded. Those purposes were nearly always religious in nature. Their support through the days of secularization and into the present, coupled with the motives operative in later times, accounts for the presence and growth of religion in higher education.

CHAPTER XV

AN APPRAISAL OF THE MOVEMENT

A. ADMINISTRATIVE RESPONSIBILITY

WE have seen how college administrators and other educators have become increasingly interested during the twentieth century in the problem of religion on the campus. We have noted how philosophers of education have revived a concern for values and their inculcation, and have been led to the door of religion. We have discovered that various traditional techniques for fostering religion among undergraduates have been strengthened and enlarged and new methods have been inaugurated. It is now possible to discern the degrees of expression of administrative interest and responsibility, as presented in the following classification:

1. Lack of, or tentative, interest in religion, coupled with a lack of, or slight, obligation, and a willingness for other agencies to perform religious functions.
2. Interest in religion, leading to the partial assumption of responsibility by means of traditional techniques such as chapel and courses, but still depending largely upon the activity of voluntary groups.
3. Keen interest, leading both to the adoption of traditional methods and to the active encouragement and financial support of voluntary programs.
4. Deep concern for religion, sponsoring traditional provisions, aiding voluntary programs and providing for newer techniques such as the establishment of positions of religious leadership.

The extreme positions at each end of the scale would be, on the one hand, "hostility to religion," and on the other, "religion as the central element in the college program." They go unmentioned because, though possible, they are virtually nonexistent at the present time. Unless the chart were immeasurably enlarged all shades of interest and responsibility could not be depicted. Those which have been expressed are the major steps of progress discernible in the movement.

This pattern serves as a fairly accurate picture in three respects. First of all, it depicts the process throughout this century. The first two items were more nearly characteristic of the period before the first World War when secularization was still at its height. The latter positions are the products of more recent years. The chart therefore has a time-direction, reflecting the progressive stages of the development in higher education generally since 1900.

Secondly, the table is a rough characterization of the development in individual institutions. Even as the movement in the group of colleges as a whole has proceeded from step to step, so the direction of progress in any one college has tended to follow the same pattern. Transition from one stage to another has in some instances been gradual, in others quite rapid. In direct contradiction to the opinion of R. Freeman Butts, that there has been an "actual decline in religious studies and religious emphasis in the curriculum of colleges throughout the country during the twentieth century," [1] the changes since the first World War have all been in the direction of greater interest and larger obligation. There is no recorded instance of a college once having adopted No. 3 which later reverted to No. 2 or No. 1; there is only one instance, and that one questionable, in which a college undertook the degree of obligation indicated by No. 4 and later turned again to No. 3. The history of the typical college shows the predominance of the two first items in the early years of the century and the steady approach to the second pair of attitudes and actions in more recent days.

In the third place the chart depicts the situation among all colleges for any one year. Whether in 1900 or today or in any intervening year, examples of institutions for each separate point of view can be found. It is true that around the turn of the century very few examples of No. 3 were available, and no more than one or two of No. 4. Correspondingly, the progress through the years has not yet eliminated all the followers of No. 1, for today there still exist colleges with little or no interest in religion. The chart reflects therefore not only the direction of the movement in all colleges and in the typical individual college, but also furnishes a picture for the present situation. The point of this study, however, is that as a reflection of the present the percentages of

1. R. Freeman Butts, *The College Charts Its Course*, p. 395.

colleges falling under 1 and 2 are smaller, and under 3 and 4 larger, than ever before.

The movement toward increased administrative responsibility has had two parts: interest in religion, and provisions for religious nurture. Of the two the first is much the more difficult to identify. In this instance a straw or two in the wind would be insufficient to establish the full force and direction of the blow. Fortunately, as we have seen in previous chapters, the day of only one or two hopeful straws is past. The rich testimony of recent years embarrasses the chronicler in his selection of examples. So much is being said so often by so many that no impartial observer could fail to appreciate the trend. And the trend is this: there has developed during the last thirty years an increasingly serious interest in religion on the part of colleges and their administrators. At the present time there exists a larger and deeper concern with the problem than ever before in the history of American higher education.

The second aspect of administrative responsibility, namely, the provisions for religious nurture, is more easily measured because it is tangible, but it is not thereby more easily appraised. Yet some effort at appraisal of the three major techniques adopted, chapel, courses, and religious leadership, is called for. A fourth primary method, that of religious counseling, has not yet developed sufficiently to admit of reliable judgment.

As to chapel, it was discovered that an overwhelming majority of church-related and independent colleges follow the practice, though the percentage of state institutions doing so is comparatively small. Both in occurrence and in the character of the programs little change through the years was discernible, though such questions as voluntarism versus compulsion and the strengthening of the religious character of the meetings have received thoughtful attention. This is substantially the factual situation at the present.

For the wide prevalence of the practice one may be properly thankful—a method already exists on which something real and vital may be built. But doubts arise as to the adequacy of the expression as it is at present being sponsored. No observer of the college scene can take undiluted delight in the mere fact that hosts of colleges go through the motions. The motions must be meaningful or they are worse than meaningless.

Yet it is here that the important question arises: What is the nature and effect of chapel as it is at present being held in most colleges over the land? It is at this point that little accurate data are available; and one must rest upon the appraisal of those competent to judge. Clarence P. Shedd recently wrote: "Chapel in far too many colleges is a discredit to the college and a disservice to religion." [2] The author must report that he has seen nothing to shake his confidence in this generalization and much to substantiate it. That there are fruitful programs of worship here and there serves only to cast into bolder and more tragic relief the numbers of ill-conceived and poorly conducted chapel services.

The explanations are several: inadequate leadership, lack of time, lack of money, lack of a suitable place of meeting, lack of any sensitivity on the part of those responsible as to what is lacking. Strangely enough, what is usually *not* lacking is an interest in the religious growth of the students. Rather, the trouble is that there exists an abysmal ignorance of ways in which to make this interest operative, of adequate methods for the accomplishment of the job. And so, too often, something that is called chapel is sponsored with the pitiful hope that at least the good intention will communicate itself to the students, and they will be helped thereby.

Thus if a survey could be made of the existence of only those chapel programs which truly served the cause of a high religion and resulted in the increased spiritual awareness of students, the figures would be much less encouraging than those offered in Chapter IX. But the faults are old faults, and the full factual picture would need to include, on the other hand, the growing recognition of the inadequacies in chapel and the earnest efforts being made to remedy the situation. The status of chapel is not as good as it looks on paper, but it is probably better than ever before.

Instruction in religion, we found, has grown tremendously in scope since the first World War, to the point where nearly all colleges, even 80 per cent of the state institutions, offer at least some curricular work in the field. Though course work in religion has always been present at least among church-related colleges, religious education as a particular study is wholly a development of this century. Since the struggle for the inclusion of the study of religion has been so nearly won, attention has

2. Clarence P. Shedd, "The Agencies of Religion in Higher Education," *Religious Education*, p. 292.

shifted to the related problems of the nature and quality of course content. Here the matter stands at the present time.

It is high time that attention did so shift. Even as with chapel, the bare figures of the presence of courses in religion are no reliable guide as to the value of the work offered. Anything which the college itself has thought of as religion has been included in the totals. Thus some colleges have assumed their participation in the development because "Psychology of religion" was offered in psychology or "The Bible as literature" was listed under English. Such courses may have value as studies in psychology or literature, but there is no guarantee that they possess merit as studies of religion. Too many colleges still depend upon such extradepartmental offerings as substitutes for a department of religion, and when that is true the instruction in religion of that college is suspect.

But this is not to say that the large number of institutions which have established regular departments in the subject have thereby escaped suspicion. Here as with chapel a full appraisal must depend upon impressions as well as factual data. From a study of course descriptions there often arise impressions of poor organization of departmental offerings, emphasis on technique rather than content, and even as with extradepartmental courses, concern with religious history or literature rather than with religion itself. For example, the staple of nearly every department is a course or courses consisting of a "Survey of the Bible." A study of the Bible as the primary textbook of religion and religious thought is patently fundamental; but too often the content of such a course is mere genealogy, military history, sociology, and biography.

Even less encouraging are impressions one often gains of the intellectual rigor of the courses. Reference was made in Chapter X to the fact that the quality of teaching in religion has been questioned. That it deserves questioning there can be no doubt. As was previously indicated, evidence exists that the training of teachers in religion is on a par with that of those in other fields. It is not so much a matter of relative intellectual preparation, therefore, as it seems to be a relative unwillingness to demand of the students their best performance. Put purely on the basis of grades, seldom is it as difficult to get an A in religion as it is in philosophy or biology or economics. Yet God is a God of judgment as well as of mercy.

Our conclusion with respect to instruction in religion, therefore, is similar to that on chapel: the facts of tremendous growth are both encouraging and delusive. The picture is not as pretty as the first glance indicates. But the knowledge that the shadows are being identified and gradually eliminated justifies hope in the future of the method as a powerful way of communicating to students their religious heritage.

The establishment of official positions of religious leadership is almost altogether a product of the last twenty-five years. The development is still too new to have spread to more than a minority of the colleges, but because of the nature of the obligation, the character of the sponsoring colleges and the ability of the men chosen for these first positions, the method possesses great significance for the total problem of religion on the campus. The wide variety in local custom has thus far prevented the emergence of any clear patterns in the duties of such officers or in the programs which they direct.

Appraisal in this instance is particularly hazardous because for many institutions insufficient time to allow for sound judgment has elapsed since the inauguration of the positions. This much, however, should be said, that almost without exception the colleges which have embarked upon such experiments consider them successful, resulting in a material strengthening of the religious life of the institutions. Even here, however, hopes and intentions have outrun performances. The establishment of a position of religious leadership on the regular college staff is no guarantee that the cause of religion will be furthered. Though the great majority of such leaders are undoubtedly capable, a familiarity with the work of at least one or two incumbents of such positions leads to the suspicion that the kingdom of God has, at those colleges, not yet come.

This disquieting note serves to introduce the chief question arising out of this development. It has been feared that too great an emphasis is placed upon the ability and personality of one man, the officer selected for the job. John Bennett phrased the objection as long ago as 1931:

Sometimes there is a college chaplain or dean of religion who is responsible to the administration or the faculty and has in his charge the religious life of the college. At present the best thing about this form of religious organization is that the men who have been chosen to be deans of religion in conspicuous cases have been men of great ability and obvious independence. . . . If in those cases the office should be continued, but occupied by men of a different calibre, one can expect very little from that kind of religious organization.[3]

That the intervening years have furnished only an occasional instance of the danger does not detract from the good sense in the warning. A mistake in choice of personnel here is hard to correct, probably harder than for a position with less status, such as a Christian Association secretary. "Small" men in any religious position hamper the work of religion; in a position of great possibilities the work can be killed, and the college may find itself saddled with an incompetent for life.

Mild rebuttal to the warning, however, is furnished by the experience of institutions using this method and by the reminder that if extreme care in the choice of personnel is necessary, it is necessary for all types of religious positions. The descriptions of extensive administrative programs given in Chapter XIII, all of which employ religious officers, serve as eloquent testimony to the soundness of the development.

We have witnessed, then, the growth of administrative responsibility for religion, which may properly be called a movement in both higher education and religion. It is a new movement which yet has its roots firmly imbedded in the past. In its present richness it is a development of this century, particularly of the years since the first World War. Its foci are two, the heightened interest in religion on the part of educators and the increased provisions for fostering religion on the campus. The various provisions show weakness as well as strength, but the faults are correctible and the benefits are unmistakable and progressively valuable. The future of the movement is bright.

The movement has two primary points of significance. First of all, it gives incontestable evidence of the turning of the tide of secularization in higher education. The spirit of secularism is another matter and will be discussed in the following chapter. But secularization as merely the withdrawal or omission of religion is at an end. However inevitable it may once have been for the elementary and secondary schools, it was always unnatural for the colleges, since the great majority were founded with religious purposes uppermost. With the exception of the state

3. John Bennett, "The Conference in Review," in *Education Adequate for Modern Times*, pp. 8–9.

institutions they never rested easy in their secular role. And when the forces causing secularization weakened and reversed themselves, and other opposing forces came into play, the colleges began once more to join hands with religion. With new interpretations and methods they are again consciously fostering the religious growth of their students.

The second is a corollary of the first. Professor Shedd has stated it:

On its positive side this development is a fresh and significant attempt to integrate religion with the total life of the university. It symbolizes the administrative conviction that religion and education are inseparable.[4]

Official provisions put the college unmistakably on the side of religion. The recognition of the incompleteness of higher education without religion has been, as we noted in the last chapter, a major factor in the growth of interest and responsibility. The circle is completed when that growth proclaims the integral place which religion occupies in the colleges.

B. THE TOTAL RELIGIOUS LIFE

But to speak of administrative responsibility, its achievements and its significance, as a movement within itself is to run the risk of emphasizing the wrong issues. It is a development within the total religious life of the campus, a totality that includes other resources and the working of other agencies. The orientation of administrative responsibility is not in contradiction to or contrast with voluntary programs, but in consonance with the interest and efforts of Christian Associations and church-sponsored groups. As has previously been recognized, the present discussion is undertaken not to underline the differences between the administrative approach on the one hand and non-official activities on the other, but to indicate the contribution which official concern and action can make to the general religious task in the colleges.

Differences between the two approaches do exist, but on examination they turn out to be largely matters of distinction between college and college or leader and leader rather than between one and the other type of approach. The question of

4. Clarence P. Shedd, *The Church Follows Its Students*, p. 291.

control is an instance in point. It goes almost without saying that a religious program should be free to develop as the dictates of conscience demand. Moreover, the religious leader should be uninhibited in his interpretation of what religion has to say to individuals and society. Following his statement of appreciation of administrative responsibility, quoted above, Professor Shedd added:

There are signs, however, that in some situations the university has favored a plan for the official direction of its religious program because of its desire for a "safe religion." Too frequently the discussions and activities of church and Christian Association groups on controversial social issues bring embarrassment to the university. The unification of the religious forces under a chaplain may make it easier to avoid discussions and incidents which the administration regards as embarrassing or dangerous.[5]

It would be idle to deny the danger. But the point for this discussion is that the danger exists for any religious program, whether it be sponsored by administration, church or independent group, and for any religious leader, whether or not his salary comes out of regular collegiate funds. The unofficial status of, say, the local Christian Association has not always insulated it against the devices of an unsympathetic college president. And its professional leadership still may be subject to administrative pressure which is no whit less effective because it is circuitous. In fact, if comparisons must be made, he may actually have less freedom than the religious leader employed by the college, whose tenure and official status may constitute lines of defense against arbitrary action.

But comparisons are odious and the fact is, simply, that the danger is present for all alike. Whether a voluntary or official program is freer depends, in the final analysis, upon the nature of the program itself, the immediate situation which calls forth the question of control, and the temper of the administration, rather than upon the supposed distinction between "voluntary" versus "official." And similarly, the freedom of a religious leader, no matter what the source and terms of his employment, hinges primarily upon the character of the man. It must be admitted and continually guarded against, that religion in any form and under any sponsorship may be controlled to its disadvantage.

The related problem of student initiative has a similar answer.

5. *Ibid.*, p. 291.

The ideal, of course, is that students possess the liberty to meet for religious purposes and to engage in religious enterprises as they themselves are freely moved to do. Seizing upon the word "voluntary" which is often used to describe nonofficial programs and agencies, some commentators have suggested that this ideal is realized in Christian Association and church-sponsored groups while at the same time being difficult of fulfillment in "official" activities provided by college administrations.[6]

But a "voluntary" group does not automatically preserve the students' freedom of activity. Nearly all local Christian Associations and church foundations have adult secretaries or, at the least, "counselors." It is not impossible—in fact, as anyone acquainted with such organizations knows, it has sometimes happened—that such leadership may result in a stifling rather than a liberating of student initiative. On the other hand, we have already noticed in the descriptions in Chapter XIII that one of the "elements of strength" in many of those "official" college programs was "the preservation of student initiative." Related to student initiative in religious activities is the college policy with respect to attendance at worship services. On this point it is significant that, as again Chapter XIII shows, those colleges in which administrative responsibility is most highly developed are also the institutions which have accepted most completely the principle of voluntarism.

But the argument is not that administrative programs allow a larger degree of student initiative than voluntary groups. Rather, the point is that either approach to religion may provide for and encourage, or may kill, the freedom of the students to follow their own religious bent. The point is, further, that student initiative depends not upon the source of sponsorship of religious activity but upon the nature of the guidance which students are furnished, once again primarily upon the character of the leadership.

While we are dealing with the dangers in administrative responsibility which are, at the same time, dangers in voluntary religious activities, attention should be paid to the matter of inadequate planning. Professor Shedd pointed out the problem in 1940:

6. See, for example, Richard H. Edwards, *Three Basic Realizations About Religion at State Universities* (pamphlet. [Ithaca, N.Y.], 1940), pp. 23–25.

. . . in too many cases, administrative good will for religion does not rest on the solid foundation of religious intelligence and social concern, with the result that, too frequently, new total plans for the religious life of students are hastily conceived and, in their functioning, may stifle creative religious and social pioneering among faculty and students. . . . We must be glad for all this new administrative interest, most of which is sincere, but from some source guidance is desperately needed in the development of criteria by which proposals for bettering the present situation may be judged. It is an interesting commentary on the present situation that, in too many cases, there has been no fundamental thinking about a plan for religion until some philanthropic friend has made a gift to the college of a chapel, and even then the solution is likely to be the easy one, "Let's appoint a chaplain." This is not a point against either chapels or chaplains—colleges have been luckier than they deserve on both of these matters— rather it is a call for the unhurried planning of adequate college programs of religion.[7]

The point is sound, for surely the official programs, in some instances, have been too hastily instituted. Yet administrative responsibility is not unique in this respect. Voluntary programs, for all their national affiliations and policy-forming boards, are sometimes set up hurriedly and unintelligently. The attitude has occasionally been, "The Moslems and Hindus have already got work started at So-and-So College; our denomination must organize something right away."

This is simply to say, once again, that the problem is universal. "Unhurried planning," as will be mentioned in the final chapter, is the *sine qua non* of every agency and every part of the college religious program, and of its totality.

These matters are reminders that the college religious program should be considered as a totality, not a conglomeration of unrelated and discordant activities. Narrow control, destruction of student initiative and inadequate planning are dangerous for both official and voluntary programs, thus for the college religious life as a whole. Correspondingly the benefits of any one part of the religious program should contribute to the strength of other parts and the total.

The traditional areas of religious activity—worship, study and

7. Clarence P. Shedd, "Religion in the Colleges," *Journal of Bible and Religion*, pp. 183–184.

service—mutually fortify each other. A college-sponsored worship program in chapel or church strengthens and receives strength from a voluntary worship or prayer group. A program of study in the curriculum, always provided by the college itself except in some state institutions, both provokes and receives impetus from informal study and discussion groups organized by Christian Associations and church foundations. Adult leaders, whether employed by official or voluntary agencies, guide the development of the various activities, whether the title of the students' organizations in whose name they are performed reflects official or voluntary sponsorship. The lines of communication between voluntary and official programs, and among worship, study and service activities, are multitudinous in their possibilities. Where they break down or are nonexistent, the fault lies with the local situation, or local personnel; for by the nature of the activities themselves or of their sponsorship no barriers are arbitrarily set to the development of a vital religious life for the whole campus.

The question therefore should never be, Which of the two approaches, official or voluntary, is the better? Rather the question is, What contributions can both official provisions and voluntary activities make to the total religious life of the institution? Since our primary concern is with the official provisions, our question becomes, Do the various manifestations of administrative responsibility strengthen the whole work of religion on the campus?

If religion is discipline of the mind, then regular instruction in the subject matter of religion, together with other voluntary experiences of study, contributes toward this end. If religion is commitment to the good, then guidance in and opportunities for service and selfless living provided by the college, as well as by other agencies, lead to this goal. If religion is worship of God, then thoughtful services in the college chapel, along with the ministrations of the local church, encourage the personal practice. The evidence of the movement toward administrative responsibility for religion is that such official obligation does not supplant but strengthens and in turn depends upon voluntary religious activities.

The whole religious life of the colleges, then, has profited by the resurgence during the twentieth century of administrative concern and obligation. If in such matters as chapel and courses more emphasis has thus far been put upon quantity rather than quality of offerings, the future promises correction. For the present the renewed recognition of the college's own responsibility has turned the tide of secularization, made religion once again an integral part of the educational enterprise, and strengthened the total religious forces of the campus.

CHAPTER XVI

THE ATMOSPHERE OF THE CAMPUS

A. THE RELIGIOUS ATMOSPHERE

THE last sentence of the preceding chapter bears repeating: ". . . recognition of the college's own responsibility has turned the tide of secularization, made religion once again an integral part of the educational enterprise, and strengthened the total religious forces of the campus." The movement has, indeed, achieved much. Is the conclusion then, that colleges are much more Christian now than in 1900? There is no certainty that the answer is Yes. Religion needed to run hard to keep from falling further behind. With the growth of administrative interest and responsibility it has run hard, but it has had stiff competition.

"What is a Christian campus?" "What makes it Christian?" Finding answers to those questions has been the sport of leaders in religious education for many a year.[1] We shall play the game with general and specific suggestions in the concluding chapter; in this chapter we must note the inadequacy for the crucial issues of all that has hereinbefore been said.

Specific and tangible things, we are easily persuaded to think, make the campus Christian—provisions, activities, techniques, opportunities for worship, study and service. All the resources which we have considered in preceding chapters have a part to play, but it is essentially a superficial part. They have brought about many desirable results, but those results are surface achievements. Turning the tide of secularization, as we have used the word; making religion integral in education; strengthening the total religious forces of the campus—these good developments

1. See, for example, W. R. Harper, *The Trend in Higher Education;* E. D. Burton, *Education in a Democratic World;* W. A. Harper, *Character Building in Colleges;* Laird T. Hites, *The Effective Christian College;* M. C. Towner, ed., *Religion in Higher Education; Education Adequate for Modern Times;* R. H. Edwards, *What Can Make Higher Education Religious?* Harrison S. Elliott, "Religion in Higher Education, A Syllabus," *Religious Education,* XXXVII, 1 (January, 1942); and C. P. Shedd, "Proposals for Religion in Postwar Higher Education," *Hazen Pamphlets,* No. 11 (June, 1945).

may actually occur in an institution which yet continues to be to a large degree pagan in atmosphere.

Specific and tangible things, then, cannot make the campus Christian, except in a superficial sense. The standing of religion in a college is not a matter of how many courses are offered, or of how often the chapel services are held, or of how large a membership is boasted by the Y.M.C.A. It is a matter of spirit: a tone to the teaching of everything, not just religion; an atmosphere surrounding and supporting chapel and other college occasions; a level of daily living approached and held high by all campus activities.

Religion, as it has herein been interpreted, is a knowledge of high values in living. It is, moreover, an appreciation of and a personal commitment to those values, a search for the eternal verities, a faith in God. A student may be said to "have religion" when, for example, he possesses personal integrity and what is more, knows why; or when he respects selfhood in those around him, the rights and needs and joys of others; or when through personal experience he knows reverence and sympathy and goodness; or when he is sensitive to his obligation to society and acts upon it. He may and probably will affiliate with some organized expression of these values, church membership here and activity in a campus religious group there. These are generally accepted and usually valid evidences of his "Christian character" but they are concomitants of his religion, not the religion itself. It is still possible—though the possibility is usually overemphasized among the religiously immature—for him to be truly religious and yet lack the usual religious affiliations, or on the other hand to join and be active and yet fail to know God.

Correspondingly, a "Christian campus" is, for example, one which possesses the spirit of the honor system, whether or not its examinations are held under an honor code; or upon which the teaching of all subjects is conducted in an atmosphere sympathetic to religion; or where, in the presence or absence of fraternities, group loyalties are democratically arranged and manifested; or in which the ethical principles recommended in chapel are the same as those practiced in the institution's public and private dealings. Such a college may and probably will sponsor worship services, courses, and positions of religious leadership, and encourage voluntary organizations. These are generally accepted and usually valid evidences of its "Christian character" but they are the

paraphernalia of religion, not religion itself. It is still possible—
though the existence of the possibility is often productive of an
institution's wishful thinking as to its own religious temper—for
a college to be truly religious and yet lack the usual religious
provisions, or on the other hand to sponsor any number of activities and yet fail to possess a religious atmosphere.

The presence of such religious attitudes and the pursuit of such
religious values are not automatic characteristics of the individual or the college. They are consciously fostered. If personal
honesty is not guaranteed by reason of church or Y.M.C.A. membership, neither is institutional integrity a necessary follow-
through of chapel services or courses in religion. Over and
above the sponsorship of programs and activities in which the
adoption of such values may be encouraged, the values themselves
need to be consciously pursued. This means recognizing them and
calling them by name. Religious functioning, for individual or
institution, is based upon religious thinking, the knowing-why
for the value-judgment. For the institution at least, this means the
saying-why as well as the knowing-why. A college which is truly
religious in spirit, and not merely in the extent of its religious
program, will not hesitate to proclaim its intention so to be and
its reasons therefor.

But of all college pronouncements these need to be most carefully conceived and most honestly examined. If the institution's
religious atmosphere is not a matter of activity, certainly it is not
a matter of language. All the piety which colleges profess and
all the unctuous rectitude which they rehearse for their students'
and their constituencies' edification are so much bootless breast-
beating, unless they are accompanied, in season and out, in the
religious program and elsewhere, by the conscious pursuit of
high ethical and spiritual values.

At this point it may be well to deal forthrightly with certain
institutional temptations which afflict the various types of colleges
when they face the subject of religion. For example, the church-
related college is not Christian merely by virtue of its denominational affiliation, any more than by reason of, in most instances,
its extensive religious provisions. But because of its organic
relationship it, more than any other type of institution, is supposed to be religious. Thus there is a great temptation to call
itself a "Christian college" when, in point of fact, it has never
examined what such a designation really means, and often even

worse, when in many aspects of its own functioning it is a living denial of those high values which Christianity stands for.[2]

The actual situation with respect to church-related colleges today is not a happy one. Most of them are small; most of them are inadequately supported. This means not only that many of them are financially unable to provide the kind of religious program which they themselves believe to be desirable. It means, even more, that they are forced to makeshifts and shortcuts in other areas of their institutional activity which their professed ideals do not countenance. Thus the small church-related colleges are tempted to pretend, if not to do worse. They may pretend that their educational offerings are on a par with that of their larger independent or tax-supported neighbors; they may pretend that they and only they combine their education with an adequate religious program; they may allege their "Christian Character" as their *raison d'être*. And if, as is often tragically true, they fail in any one or all of these aspects, then religion itself suffers because of the pretense.

State institutions, too, may say more than they mean or can justify. But another of their temptations is of just the opposite sort: they may say less than they mean. They may, and today often do, make large provision for religion in their programs, which indicates an underlying intention to foster religion. Furthermore, they may talk about the training of "character," the search for spiritual as well as intellectual "truth," even the inculcation of "values," but often they hesitate to say "religion." Their hesitancy has historical roots and some contemporary justification; yet for all of that the circumlocution which is required dilutes the testimony which they give and intend to give. And to that extent, again, religion suffers.

Independent institutions may partake of these and other temptations. For that matter, no one kind of weakness applies to only one type of institution. For all types of colleges the chief faults in this area are two in number: to confuse the sponsorship of a widespread religious program with the existence of a religious atmosphere, and to claim too much.

Lest this discussion be guilty of the same faults, we must return to the question of the first paragraph of this chapter. Rephrased, the question is: With all the development in religious interest and activity during this century, are religion and its values more

2. See Edwin E. Aubrey, "Do or Die: The 'Christian' Colleges," *Religion in Life*, Autumn, 1941, pp. 586–594.

deeply imbedded in higher education now than in 1900? The hopeful answer is Yes; the truthful answer may be No. Taking the element of comparison out of the question, it becomes: Is the atmosphere of the colleges at the present time sympathetic to the development of a high religion in the students? Or again: Does the climate of higher education encourage undergraduates to discover religious insights, to adopt religious patterns of living, and withal to do so with the conscious realization that it is religion they find and follow? For the broad sweep of higher education and for the great majority of today's college students the answer is probably No.

The latter phrasings of the question must be the ones to concern us. On the basis of available evidence the answer to them in 1900 was also No. But 1900 is irrelevant, except as the condition at that time was instrumental in producing the subsequent growth in interest and activity. The hope behind such increased concern and action was that the day would come when the negative would be changed into an affirmative. But that day is not yet. Why?

B. THE SECULAR ATMOSPHERE

The answer lies in the fact that the prevailing atmosphere of higher education today is secular. The terrific competition which religion has had to face throughout this century and with which it still does battle today is the spirit of secularism. If we center our attention solely upon the collegiate interest in religion and the religious programs of instruction, worship, and activity, we may hopefully conclude that the campus atmosphere is religious in quality and that students breathe clean air. But when we broaden our consideration to include all institutional interests and all aspects of college life, then we must perforce admit that the tone of higher education is secular and the total impact upon the majority of students is, if not anti-, at least nonreligious.

Before attempting an analysis of this secular spirit, it is well to indicate what is meant by the term. Secularism is the notion that man can live by bread. It places emphasis upon the material to the exclusion or denial of the intangible and upon the natural to the disparagement of the supernatural. In its various ramifications it is directly contradictory to the idea of a high religion as we have used the term, for such religion has consistently believed that bread alone is not enough.

Much of the secular atmosphere of the colleges can be laid to the impact of the modern world upon the college scene. There are two sides to this impact. One side is the pagan quality of civilized life which, far from having been diluted by the idealism engendered by the war, seems at least in America to be reaching new heights of selfishness and insensitivity. The obvious does not need to be labored, for evidences of our desire for comfort, financial prosperity and sensory pleasures exist on every hand. This materialism is combined with a confusion leading to cynicism and despair.

> The world is too much with us; late and soon,
> Getting and spending, we lay waste our powers; . . .

Wordsworth phrased the other side of the picture, too, that we are "suckled in a creed outworn," or so we have been led to believe. All around us we are reminded of what Professor Hugh Hartshorne of Yale calls the "growing irrelevance of religion to life," or of what Professor George F. Thomas of Princeton describes as the "fading out of the spiritual view." Figures of the growth of the denominations to the contrary notwithstanding, we have come to think that religion, or at least its organized expression, the church, has entered a period of declining influence. Certain it is that countless "civilized" people look upon its ministrations as only an embellishment to life, sometimes useful but often worse than useless.

The world, then, is selfish and confused, and the campus is part of the world. Moreover, much of the world believes that religion is illusory sweetness and obsolete light, and often the campus succumbs to this opinion. But the secular atmosphere of the colleges cannot be blamed solely, or even largely, upon the world outside. For the chief cause of the secularism of higher education is to be found within higher education itself, its modes of thinking, its attitudes in teaching, and its practices in everyday living. Apart from the baleful influences from without, the colleges are in themselves strongholds of secularism.

As to modes of thinking, Professor Thomas feels that "the real enemy of religion in the schools and colleges is the dominant philosophy of naturalism." [3]

3. George F. Thomas, *The Place of Religion in School and College* (pamphlet. Montevallo, Ala., Alabama College, 1941), p. 15.

Secularism is the theory that men should seek ends which are exclusively human and natural. Its sting is in its assumption that all ends which claim to transcend nature and human life are illusory. In this sense of the term, secularism is a corollary of Naturalism, which accepts as real nothing that is not embraced in nature, the totality of events in space and time. . . . [On the other hand] Idealism agrees with Supernaturalism in at least one important point, the affirmation that the human spirit and its values are rooted in an eternal spiritual life. Since Naturalism rejects this belief, it must also reject the belief that human ends should be understood in relation to an eternal will and purpose. Secularism is simply what is left after this rejection has been made.[4]

Paul J. Braisted of the Hazen Foundation points out that those who follow this philosophical bent—and their number is legion in the average campus community—are

. . . naturalists . . . not in the sense of acceptance of a creed, but in the fact that they are preoccupied with the natural order. Almost unconsciously they come to assume that the beginning and the end of all inquiry and experience is in the natural process. This assumption is frequently formulated and it is agreed that the processes of history, and of human activity, are self-contained, self-explanatory and self-sufficient. The source of this attitude and conviction is a dogma—the dogma that only the material has reality and that knowledge can be derived solely from sensory experience.[5]

This form of thought leads to a "scientism" which assumes that the only avenue by which truth may be approached is the scientific method. Such a position, of course, rules out revelation as nonscientific; and because religion relies upon revelation it is condemned as antithetical to science. It matters not that in those areas in which the scientific method is applicable, religion gives as wholehearted allegiance to it as any other intellectual discipline. What matters to those who think in this wise is that religion will not, because it cannot, limit itself to this method.

Here an aside may be inserted to indicate the new struggle being waged between science and religion. The present disagreement is far removed from the older battle, referred to in Chapter III, in which religion was on the defensive and its nonscientific

4. George F. Thomas, *Religion in an Age of Secularism*, p. 9.
5. Paul J. Braisted, *Religion in Higher Education*, p. 11.

dogmatisms were defeated. Today religion debates with science as an equal, not as an inferior. It has something aggressive to say on a critical question in which science finds itself powerless to speak. The question is the nature of man and his salvation. Science has discovered that it cannot save the world, though it is sometimes loath to admit that religion can. But the statements of leading scientists of the present day already indicate the way in which the battle will go, or at least must go, if civilization is to survive. A high religion which gives ungrudging respect to the scientific method in its proper sphere has nothing to fear in the outcome.

Our aside has point for our discussion since the present struggle raises the question whether the scientific method alone can be conclusive. The eventual resolution of the problem has not yet disturbed the misplaced confidence of large numbers of faculty men in the colleges. Professor Mortimer Adler believes that 90 per cent of the professors in America still go on the assumption that the use of the scientific method is the only way of arriving at truth.[6] Whether or not his percentage is correct, those who fall in the group are, consciously or unconsciously, raising science to the position of a religion.

Or it might be said with equal truth that many who follow this naturalistic thought possess a religion of humanism. They subscribe to the same general ethical principles to which the Hebrew-Christian tradition attests. They believe in the dignity of man and in the democratic ideal for society. But they part company with the mainstream of Hebrew-Christian thought when they refuse to orient these beliefs and values in a world of the spirit removed from the purely natural and human world. Their thinking possesses no roots in eternal verities, for their real object of worship is man, not God.

Or again, the naturalistic bent may result in a strict and cold rationalism which subscribes only to those beliefs which can be "proved" by the reasoning of man's mind. Obviously such a mode of thinking not only tears down religion but also humanism, for in the final analysis even the humanistic values are never demonstrable beyond the shadow of a doubt. Thus various ones of these substitute faiths, naturalism, scientism, humanism, and

6. Referred to by George F. Thomas, *The Place of Religion in School and College*, p. 11.

rationalism, may jar against each other, but together they make war against the kind of religion of which we have been speaking. And as they are found in abundance in our colleges today, together they contribute to the secularism which characterizes the modern campus.

These modes of thinking which render difficult the work of religion in higher education are linked with concomitant attitudes adopted in the teaching process which are often more far-reaching in their unfortunate effects than the philosophies underlying them. Many faculty members adopt the attitudes about to be described without ever having thought out the theories of human life and of values on which they are based. And it is often the attitude more than the basic assumption which impresses the student.

First of all is "objectivity," the pose of the pseudo-scholar. It is recognizable in the refusal of many professors to go beyond mere ascertainment and description of data. Any interpretation of the subject matter is rightly conceived as involving value-judgments, and thus often and wrongly eschewed because, it is supposed, the mention of values makes the treatment subjective. But in point of fact, of course, pure objectivity is unattainable. The hesitancy to deal with values is itself a value-judgment of a negative sort. Even if the professor consciously interprets his data for himself—and not all go merely this far—his unwillingness to do so for his students leaves unavoidably the impression that interpretation is unscholarly and that value-judgments are not only unnecessary but unsound.

Related to this attitude, but one step removed, is the false notion of "tolerance" which infests the academic halls. This attitude is manifest in those instances in which the professor rightly recognizes his responsibility to interpret his subject matter, but wrongly conceives his obligation as consisting solely of a "fair" exposition of all possible points of view. President Ernest C. Colwell of the University of Chicago has described this strategy as

. . . a toleration so negatively defined that it leads to indifference. If every man's opinion is his own business, the teacher has no right to influence that opinion even by reason. All the teacher can do is to say that truth is this to A and that to B, and that the student should have a clear understanding of both A and B. As the teacher scrupulously keeps himself outside the picture, the usual effect upon the student is to convince him that truth is neither A nor B nor anything else.[7]

Thus this "toleration of indifference," as Colwell calls it, breeds the feeling that if value-judgments are inescapable, yet all values are merely relative.

Relativism is not only an impression unintentionally created in the mind of the student; it is a conscious attitude on the part of hosts of professors, and even more, it is a mode of thinking which might properly have been discussed with the other "isms" above. Impressed by the fact that in actuality differences among men's thoughts and practices are voluminous, the relativist concludes that all points of view are equally worthy and that the differences do not matter. Intellectual ideals, ethical standards, spiritual values can be said to be neither "good" nor "bad"; you pay your money and you take your choice.

This is, of course, an extreme form of relativism from which the press of recent catastrophes has forced a retreat. A democracy cannot fight for its survival if it believes that totalitarianism is "just as good," even if only for Germany and Japan. Thus the scramble to discover the basic differences between democracy and its opponents has laid bare the weakness of relativism in the political field, and the danger of possessing no norms for our ideals, standards and values. The weakness and the danger are present in other areas than the political; the tragedy is that countless professors have not yet discovered them. Much of the teaching in our colleges is still conducted in an aura of relativism which necessarily denies the claims and disparages the commitments of a high religion.

"Objectivity," "tolerance," and relativism make up the agnosticism characteristic of much of the work of higher education. But there may be said to be two chief varieties of the agnostic temper which are unequal in their effects. One is the searching sort which holds in respect both those whose search has been successful and the ends of their seeking. This type of agnosticism is no enemy of a high religion and may well prove to be an ally. But the other is the static sort which scorns believer and seeker alike, and throwing doubt upon the ends and values of other men, offers nothing in their place. Wherever it exists, as it does exist in

7. Ernest C. Colwell, "Opportunities in American Education," in William K. Anderson, ed., *Protestantism* (Nashville, Commission on Courses of Study, The Methodist Church, 1944), p. 254.

faculties all over the country, it represents a bitter opponent to religion.

False objectivity and tolerance are attitudes whose enmity to religion is often unconscious and unintended. But the agnostic's scorn and doubt of religion are usually explicit and unmistakable. Paul Braisted notes

. . . among university faculties a widespread tendency to slur religion in and out of the classroom and the slurring attitude has been inculcated in countless graduates. One has only to discuss religion with undergraduates in any institution . . . to find ample verification for this assertion. . . . In the hands of a lecturer, a "recognized authority" in a specialized field, a slur becomes a vicious weapon against which the student has little or no defense. How long will we continue to regard as competent those specialists, however well equipped with their own skills, who carelessly or maliciously scoff at religion? [8]

It is sometimes thought that the secularist aspects of teaching theory and practice characterize only the natural sciences. Certain it is that scientism, rationalism, and false objectivity, to name only part of the picture, may easily infect geology or biology or mathematics, but subjects of the social sciences and the humanities may also succumb. When they do their comparable lack of preciseness may make their pretensions to it more absurd and thus their secular influence even greater. Moreover, the social sciences and humanities are more properly called upon for value-judgments; when these are ignored or are made inimical to religion, the harm is often irreparable. On one campus the stronghold of secularism may be the natural sciences; on another the social sciences; on still a third the humanities. There is no gain, therefore, in seeking to determine which of the three is generally the most guilty, for all may make hurtful contributions.

Modes of thinking and attitudes in teaching are supplemented by practices in everyday living which add their secularist increment. Reference has already been made to those colleges which claim too much and follow through too little in institutional functions. This is secularism of a sort, for though the college pays lip-service and even leg-service to religion, yet if it fails to live up to its own ideals in, say, the treatment of its personnel or its business dealings, then religion is weakened and a non- or anti-religious atmosphere is created.

8. Braisted, *op. cit.*, p. 12.

Similarly, the practices of responsible individuals in the college community, as well as of the institution itself, often enhance the spirit of secularism. Anyone acquainted with the modern campus knows the professor who subscribes to a belief in values, yet fails to associate with a local church or in any other outward way give evidence of his allegiance to them. There is too the other professor who slurs and scoffs, yet tacitly lives by the code he denounces. Thus justifiable confusion is aroused in the students' minds by such inconsistencies. Is it the statements or is it the actions which are executed with tongue in cheek? At least tongue is in cheek at one place or the other, and that much the students do understand.

The consequence is that the students in their extracurricular life often imitate the inconsistencies between profession and practice which they find in the college and its faculty. Or being franker, they drop all pretense of following the higher values and fix their sights on what is tangible, immediate, popular, and fun. A rare campus it is on which the religious or any other consciously value-seeking activities draw anything like as large a following as the organized, not to speak of the informal, pleasure-seeking activities. In a disturbingly large number of colleges the value-seekers are merely, as one religious group actually refers to itself, a "Master's minority" among the happy pagans. It is not that dances, fraternities, and athletics, much less dramatics, student government, publications, and other affairs, are lacking in religious values for their participants, in the broad sense in which we are speaking of religion. It is rather that when those values obtain they are often unconscious and accidental, whereas in the religious activities they are conscious and intentional. Thus the student life may be just as thoroughly secular, without a thought having been given to it, as the more reasoned paganism of the faculty world.

It would be unwise to conclude that these various roots of the present-day secularism are characteristic only of state and large independent institutions. Protagonists of the small church-related colleges would like to think so, but much of their thinking is based on intentions, not realities. We have already noticed how the religious programs in many church-related institutions are lacking in quality and how institutional practices in other areas often contradict their religious ideals. It is also true that secularism in some of the forms denoted above is present in denominational colleges, for church affiliation is not enough to insure the absence of secularist attitudes and practices, or even of naturalistic modes of thinking, on the campus. If comparisons are to be made, however, the average church-related institution is probably freer from secularist modes of thinking among its faculty than the average large state or independent university. But the "average" institution of any type is nonexistent, and the personal philosophy of faculty members is only one avenue by which secularism enters the collegiate scene. In any case there is no point in trying to estimate which type of college is more or less secular than another type, for the record is clear that all have sinned and fallen short.

And the effect has been critically serious. Many of the results of the various expressions of secularism have already been noted; it remains to summarize with one or two general results of the process as a whole.

The first of these is that secularism encourages undue specialization and makes for a lack of unity in knowledge and in its dissemination. Now specialization of a sort is, of course, necessary. No one with any pretensions toward scholarship can take all knowledge for his province. But specialization can and easily does go to excess, and every one of the modes of thinking and the attitudes in teaching mentioned above, with the possible exception of humanism, contributes to this end. Limiting consideration to the "natural," relying solely upon the scientific method and the rationalistic approach, pursuing a rigid "objectivity," proclaiming a "toleration" which is indifference, succumbing to relativism and the agnostic temper—these attributes of large numbers of professors lead to a withdrawal from life in its fullness and an effort at mastery of only one tiny segment of factual data. Thus this extreme specialization implies the "autonomy" of each separate area of intellectual interest, and produces a "fragmentation" in knowledge and its pursuit.[9] The tragic consequence of these various manifestations of secularism, therefore, is that higher education lacks homogeneity. No basic underlying discipline, no unifying frame of reference, binds together the various expressions of the educational enterprise.

A second general result is that the numerous aspects of secularism combine to ignore values. An insensitivity to high values in life and living, it has already been pointed out, is the root of the secular atmosphere of the colleges; it is also the result of that

9. See, for example, Thomas, *Religion in an Age of Secularism;* and Braisted, *op. cit.*

atmosphere. This being true, the expectation would be justified that the plight of the colleges is, to one interested in religion, not merely serious but beyond repair. Such undoubtedly it would be, were it not for the parallel presence on the campuses of the keen interest in religion and the extensive religious programs which previous chapters have described.

Thus another result of secularism in the colleges may be said to be the struggle in which religious interests and activities must everywhere engage, in order to hold high the belief that life is more than meat and the body than raiment. Colleges have sought religion in the twentieth century not to fill a vacuum but to try to counteract the impact of the secular atmosphere already present on their campuses. Once religion comes, in whatever forms, it finds unrelenting warfare on its hands, for though its ministrations are held in higher esteem and given more tangible support than ever before, the forces of darkness are strong and also continue to receive many encouragements.

It might be said that higher education plays, willy-nilly, a two-sided game. That it has dealt so many cards to religion in recent years has made the game close, but has not yet made religion the victor. Secularism is too widespread for one to be able glibly to conclude that colleges are more Christian in atmosphere than in 1900. Moreover, the strength of the secular spirit emphasizes the necessity that religion's cards be high cards, that quality as well as quantity in religious offerings and activities be given increasing attention.

But a comparison with 1900 was a phrasing of this chapter's question which was discarded. Our attention must be centered, rather, on whether or not the present "climate of higher education encourages undergraduates to discover religious insights, to adopt religious patterns of living, and withal to do so with the conscious realization that it is religion they find and follow." The primary reason for emphasizing quality in religious offerings is at the same time the most vicious result of secularism: Too many students fail to discover religious insights in their college careers; too many students adopt secular patterns of living. The product of the atmosphere of higher education is the paganism prevalent among hosts of today's college graduates.

The temper of extracurricular life, to which reference has already been made, is an aspect of the general secularism of the campus. But the beliefs and practices of the individual undergraduate who later becomes the graduate are not merely aspects but tragic results of that secularism. The remarks of Norman Foerster, made in 1937 concerning state universities, are applicable in the present day to institutions of all types:

Not without justice are they regarded as irreligious, when they receive freshmen who are eager for ideal values in which intelligent men and women can believe and four years later send them out naturalized, skeptical, or cynical. . . . The destruction wrought by professorial intellectuals . . . far more than offsets the construction accomplished by the university in its decent espousal of university sermons, denominational organizations, discussion groups, and the Y.M.C.A.[10]

Because of the havoc which secularism can and does work in students' lives, the counter forces of religion must be intelligent and strong.

The struggle continues and the outcome is uncertain. But to those concerned about the religious growth of students there are many signs of hope. Paramount among these is that secularism is increasingly being recognized by educators for what it is, namely, the potential source of destruction of values in education and thus of education itself. Quotations above from Braisted, Colwell, Foerster and Thomas are representative of many more to which reference might be made.

Furthermore, educators are beginning to see the positive as well as the negative side of the problem; that is, they are realizing that religious provisions, however extensive, are not enough and that the colleges must not only discourage the secular spirit but also consciously and directly foster the development of a religious atmosphere. In his *Liberal Education in a Democracy* Stewart G. Cole wrote:

The appointment of a dean of the chapel, the maintenance of a chapel service at which clergy preach sermons and faculty members deliver additional lectures, courses of instruction in the *Bible,* and kindred plans, good as they may be, are beside the point. They can never meet youth's dilemma, and may soon become a means of escape from the real problem. The American college requires a reconstituted philosophy of education at the heart of which is a revitalized faith in the spiritual integrity of life and of the educational process.[11]

10. Norman Foerster, *The American State University*, pp. 263–264.
11. Stewart G. Cole, *Liberal Education in a Democracy*, p. 244. See also

The authors of *From School to College,* a study of the transition experience, expressed a similar point of view:

It would seem that the only way by which this [religious] need [of the students] can be met is for the college to reorganize its entire life so as to provide the opportunity for religious development and experience as part and parcel of its *total life and purpose.* The implications drawn from our data do not present any easy steps to be taken to this end . . . religious meetings, services, and projects inside or outside of the college life . . . [are] of little avail unless the whole morale and spirit of the college is religious in a broad and deeply social sense. Here is the crux of the situation.[12]

Hope is justified not merely on the basis of the recognition now being given, on the one hand, to the dangers of secularism, and on the other, to the need of a vital religious tone to education. There is, as well, the encouraging fact that many of the manifestations of secularism are actually beginning to lose their hold upon higher education. It can hardly be maintained that the impact of the modern world upon the campus is less secular than, say, ten or fifteen years ago; but it is clear that the campus itself is not following so slavishly in society's patterns of thought and action as it was at a date not so far distant. The "isms" of secularist thought do not today go unchallenged; false notions of objectivity and tolerance are now being corrected; and agnosticism with its attendant poses is not as popular as in the past. Examples are plentiful. For instance, the Harvard report of 1945 on *General Education in a Free Society* offers many evidences of such changes in thinking:

It is impossible to escape the realization that our society, like any society, rests on common beliefs and that a major task of education is to perpetuate them.[13]

. . . ethical neutrality is a guiding rule for the historian as scholar. Nevertheless, the historian or social scientist, as *teacher,* should probably go further and present to the student the human

J. Seelye Bixler, "The Resources of Religion and the Aims of Higher Education," *Hazen Pamphlets,* No. 4.

12. Lincoln B. Hale *et al., From School to College: A Study of the Transition Experience,* p. 316. Italics are theirs.

13. *General Education in a Free Society,* p. 46.

past and human institutions not merely as facts but as attempted embodiments of the good life in its various phases.[14]

A free society means toleration, which in turn comes from open-ness of mind. But freedom also presupposes conviction; a free choice—unless it be wholly arbitrary (and then it would not be free)—comes from belief and ultimately from principle.[15]

The universal community of educated men is a fellowship of ideals as well as of beliefs. To isolate the activity of thinking from the morals of thinking is to make sophists of the young and to encour-age them to argue for the sake of personal victory rather than of the truth.[16]

The "Report of the Alumni Committee on Postwar Amherst College," also of 1945, submits many correctives to the various secularist trends, one of the most striking of which is its forth-right handling of the important question of "academic objectiv-ity":

In the first place, no teacher worthy of the name can avoid having convictions on vital issues, and no teacher can actually succeed in hiding these convictions from his students no matter how hard he may try to do so. Secondly, the student is much less likely to be victimized by the professor's beliefs if they are stated openly. . . . Thirdly, we believe that students should be made to realize that responsible men do make up their minds, however tentatively, on questions of importance and that men are under moral obliga-tion to do so. . . . We believe that it is one of the chief functions of a liberal education to teach young men the possibility of, and the need for, reflective commitment. . . .[17]

These quotations, and others like them, are important not only for what they say, but because such things were not being said a short time ago.

A final evidence of the swing away from secularism is the search for some integrating factor in higher education. Even as one of the results of the secular atmosphere was seen to be the fragmentation of knowledge and the educational process, so the

14. *Ibid.*, p. 73. Italics are theirs.
15. *Ibid.*, p. 77.
16. *Ibid.*, p. 72.
17. "Amherst Tomorrow," *Amherst Alumni Council News*, p. 96.

desire to find a cure by the adoption of a unifying principle represents a renewed search for meaning and value in education. The host of quotations in Chapter VII which denote that trend constitute significant evidence. That a number of those quotations name religion as the proper end of the search indicates the large degree to which the realization of the need constitutes a departure from secularism.

Thus if the voyage is not yet done, the wind has begun to blow from the right quarter. To the conclusion that now, more than ever before, colleges are interested in religion and are making large provisions for religious activity, can be added the judgment that prospects for the achievement of a vitally religious atmosphere in higher education were never brighter. Colleges are seeking religion not merely as mental discipline or as activity but as a spirit for the whole campus life.

CHAPTER XVII

AN ADEQUATE PROGRAM FOR RELIGION

IT is hoped that no reader will begin here. The suggestions to be made in the following paragraphs grow out of the history and present status of religion in higher education, as sketched in the preceding chapters. The development of a program of religion on any campus should be undertaken only in the light of that history and present status. Trends in education and religion, the attitudes and experiences of other institutions, the emphases of various educational philosophies, the needs of higher education, its weaknesses and accomplishments in the area of religion—all these considerations and more should go into the making of local patterns. The suggestions to follow will often seem irrelevant unless the reader has been over the previous terrain.

But this is not to imply that merely by a knowledge of general trends or by an acquaintance with other experiments, one can build an adequate program. The problem in each institution is unique; no absolute pattern can be laid down as a solution for all colleges. Thus the following suggestions are simply guide-lines; the details of the individual application must always be worked out locally.

It will also be clear that the intention is not to outline the "ideal" program for some "ideal" college, but to indicate the fundamental attitudes and activities necessary for actual colleges. Much is demanded; but it should be obvious by now to all who take seriously the task of making religion vital in higher education that much is imperative. If the day ever existed, it is long since past when an institution could adequately care for religion by traditional gestures surrounded by pious platitudes. The need of today is for a religious program that cuts deep into the heart of every college and university in the country, regardless of type, and for a religious atmosphere that imbues all of higher education.

The remarks to follow, then, will apply to church-related, state-supported, and independent institutions alike.

This discussion of what should be can serve as a sort of summary for what is, a reminder of the ground we have covered. No one of the aspects of the program is new; each has been thoroughly tested in many colleges and all together have been attempted in a few. No one of the principles to underlie the program is startling; many have been upheld in various institutions, and those which may never have been seriously tried have at least been seriously talked about. The descriptions of individual college programs in Chapter XIII closed with a listing of the "elements of strength" recognizable in each development; these elements, it will be noted, have anticipated, and furnish illustrations for, our present discussion. Actual plans for the future, too, are envisaging the major part if not all of what is to be suggested herein. Thus, though the full picture may be "ambitious" or "difficult," it is not impractical. It is to be hoped that many colleges in the years to come will prove its complete practicality.

What would be *an adequate program for religion* for any college today? The word "adequate" is used advisedly, for though the list of sixteen items to follow is broad in scope, yet anything less for an institution of higher education will not serve adequately the needs of the present-day campus. The list is a minimum.

A. UNDERLYING ASSUMPTIONS

An adequate program will be based upon clear thinking. The college does not exist which possesses religious vitality by accident. Facing the problem does not mean plunging into the midst of activity. "We ought to have courses in religion; let's hire a professor." "Codger gave us a chapel, bless his heart; let's start some services." Such reflexes may yet serve as God's opportunities, but God probably has a hard time using them. The college which engages meaningfully in instruction, worship, or anything else is one which knows why, which has thought out in advance the implications for its whole educational philosophy and has come to some well-considered understandings. These are among the underlying conclusions which the college must possess:

1. *Keen interest in, and a liberal conception of, religion.*

The necessity for a keen interest on the part of some responsible college official goes without saying, and our discussion has indicated the existence of a deep and serious concern among college presidents. But the necessary scope of this interest is not so easily taken for granted; nor is there conclusive evidence of its presence today. It is not enough that the college executive be concerned, for that way the religious program may depend solely upon his personal support. Thus with a change in chief executives an institution may discover that the nature and extent of the backing given to religion have altered considerably.

By necessary scope is meant the need for administrative officials other than the president, for the faculty and for the members of the board to share in the concern. We shall return to the faculty below; emphasis now should be placed upon the necessity for the informed support of the governing body of the college. No program of religion will ever be well and securely founded unless the trustees or overseers of the institution, as well as the president and deans, know about and thoroughly sympathize with the efforts being made. As boards are becoming increasingly composed of businessmen and nonacademic figureheads, this is no easy task to fulfill. But lacking it there is no guarantee that interest in the religious program will possess the needed continuity from one administration to another.

Linked with the question of interest is the matter of definition. Mere concern is not enough; the kind of religion in which the administration is interested is of critical importance. If "religion" to the president or some influential board member means something sectarian, something dogmatic, and something quiescent, then his interest in the subject is a millstone around the religious life of the campus.

The college which would have an adequate religious program must realize that religion relevant for the present day must be nonsectarian in spirit, no matter the possible denominational attachment of the institution; that it must be intellectually respectable, abreast of the best thought in its own and other fields; and that in its effects it will probably be disturbing and revolutionary as often as reassuring and stabilizing. This last may be the most difficult for an institution to digest; for it calls for a willingness on the part of the administration to foster a force always capable of causing "trouble." But if the administration does not want this element in its life, then it is not really interested in a high and vital religion, for such a religion is always the conscience of the college.

2. *A conception of the essential religious nature of the educational task.*

This is one step removed from keen interest. It is the recognition that the high values in which education believes are the same high values of which religion consists.

That much poses no difficulty for the colleges, but recognition of this fact is not all that is necessary. If it were, then an institution could argue, when challenged, that its educational ideals were proof enough of the presence of religion. Such a defense, however, would be the cart before the horse and the part for the whole. The inculcation of the ideals is the task of the school, as well as of the family and the church, but the ideals themselves are religion. Then education must proceed beyond mere recognition of similarity between its and religion's values to the realization that it is religion in its broad and true sense which the college seeks to support.

Realization must involve proclamation. A hesitancy to name as religion the ideal which the college adopts is as unsatisfactory as the hesitancy to adopt it. The college must needs certify publicly that its aim and function are religious, and then to explain in terms of values the meaning which it gives to the word. Not even state-supported schools are prevented from taking such a step if the explanation is thorough.

Here is the end of the search for a unifying factor in higher education. We have seen how educational philosophers of all points of view have sought for an integrating discipline and an encompassing loyalty. Many frames of reference, worthy in themselves but all suffering from incompleteness, have been suggested—metaphysics, democracy, esthetics, "the tradition of Western culture," the problems of contemporary life, and others. It remains for the college to seek its unity in religion, that one aspect of life which includes and illumines all others. Robert L. Calhoun has written:

Religion of the right sort can provide a dynamic unity of experience more inclusive even than the theoretic unity of a metaphysics, and vigorous enough to withstand even the disrupting forces of anger and fear. It can provide, moreover, a kind of motivation that will forestall any tendency to passive onlooking, and at the same time will tend strongly to keep the active participation of its devotees above narrow partisanships or selfish opportunism. Religion of the right sort; not lip-religion or ceremonies out of touch with everyday practice, nor yet tribal fanaticism of either the old or the newer types.[1]

Religion lends itself to such use. As a discipline of the mind which gives meaning to matter, it can furnish a basis of unity for the curriculum. As an appreciation of high values, including the supreme value, God, it can undergird all college assemblies and occasions, whether religious or secular. As a motivation for ethical living, personal and social, it can raise the level of all extracurricular activities. And as an atmosphere, it can suffuse the whole life of the college with love of truth, of beauty, and of good will. Religion, and only religion, goes the whole round of creation. That college which in its educational philosophy makes religion explicitly integral in its total purpose can be not only, as Arnold Nash would have it, a "witness to the glory of God," [2] but also an agent for the ennobling of men.

3. *A determination to foster religious values in all the affairs of the institution.*

This is the necessary accompaniment to its predecessor. The former has to do with making religion integral in theory; this concern refers to making religion integral in practice. The former alone can easily result in an unproductive piety; it must be joined with a resolve to make the college's actions speak in consonance with its words.

The religious program itself will hardly be undertaken in forgetfulness or denial of high ethical and spiritual values. But the nonreligious enterprises of the college may well be conducted in complete forgetfulness and even contradiction of its religious purposes, unless special attention is given to them. Such matters as the policies of hiring and firing, the general treatment of personnel, business dealings and financial manipulations, the conduct of dining halls and book stores, methods of admission, hous-

1. Robert L. Calhoun, "The Place of Religion in Higher Education," in *Religion and the Modern World*, p. 68.

2. Arnold S. Nash, *The University and the Modern World* (New York, Macmillan Co., 1944), p. 292.

ing and discipline of students, sponsorship of intercollegiate sports —these and a hundred other collegiate functions offer temptations for laxness in the application of standards or for unethical, if technically legal, behavior. Against such temptations the college must be ever watchful. But the full obligation is not discharged by a negative desire to escape scandal. The college must consciously use even the least significant and most secular of its occupations as opportunities for the affirmation of its high principles.

The danger in disparity between theory and practice cannot be overemphasized. Both theory and practice in conformity with religion's values must be achieved. Students will forget most of the facts which their college furnishes them, but they will not forget its attitudes. They will recall the principles which the institution proclaims, seeks to foster, and itself abides by, if those principles are made sufficiently clear. And they will hold in hurtful memory any divergence between proclamation and performance. The second and third items on our list must be undertaken together.

4. *A determination to combat those aspects of college life making for a secular atmosphere.*

The first three attitudes deal with the direct incorporation of religion into the heart of the college. Now we turn to an indirect, though no less necessary, approach. The college must continually strive to lessen the effect of today's widespread secularism by an attack upon those elements in its institutional life which support it.

Our discussion of the secularist temper indicated that its most heinous effects are usually to be observed in the classroom. Here it is that naturalism and its attendant "isms" have their breeding ground, that false notions of objectivity and tolerance are broadcast, that relativism and agnosticism get a dangerous hearing. If the college with its right hand would uphold religion, it cannot ignore what its left hand is doing. It must seek consciously to eliminate every source of the canker that would destroy its and religion's values. If necessary this calls for the invasion of its own classrooms and the inspection of its professors' beliefs and attitudes.

The approach, then, is not indirect after all. It involves a willingness to undertake two positive courses of action. First is *the effort to guarantee that, wherever religion and its values legitimately inhere in the subject matter, they be included, and that all subjects in the curriculum be taught in a religious spirit.* This is not a suggestion that the college take to bootlegging religion; it is only that the various departments not fail to mention it when such mention is justified. As Professor Shedd has said:

It is a great disservice to religion to lug it in where it does not belong, but it is an equally great disservice to avoid reference to a religious view of life and the universe at those points where subject matter seems to demand it.[3]

The point is that religion can be taught in every department; then, since it can be, it must be. President John H. MacCracken of Lafayette stated the problem as long ago as 1920:

A department of Bible, important and desirable as such a department is, will not make a college Christian, which is pagan in its department of Greek or agnostic in its department of Geology.[4]

But how would religion be taught in the departments of Greek or geology or anything else? Speaking before a state college audience, Professor George F. Thomas of Princeton answered the question:

The departments of literature would show how all the great writers, such as Milton and Wordsworth and Shelley, have interpreted human life in terms of its relation to something greater than itself. The departments of social science would judge all the institutions and policies they study by the standard of an ideal community ruled by the law of love. The department of history would explain the real triumphs and tragedies of humanity by reference to deeper factors than economic greeds and political ambitions. The departments of natural science would, at suitable times, point out those intimations of divine wisdom and power behind nature which have always aroused man's wonder. The practical arts and professions, finally, would be taught as opportunities to minister to human needs not for profit but for love. In short, knowledge in every department would be taught for its own sake, but also for its contribution to the spiritual life.[5]

3. Clarence P. Shedd, "The Agencies of Religion in Higher Education," *Religious Education*, p. 293.

4. John H. MacCracken, *College and Commonwealth*, p. 393.

5. George F. Thomas, *The Place of Religion in School and College*, p. 19. See also Patrick M. Malin, "Teaching Economics with a Sense of the Infinite and the Urgent," *Hazen Pamphlets*, No. 5.

At this point one can hear the howl of the anguished "scholar." If he were fair, he would say, "I admit freely that the suggestion calls for nothing sectarian, nothing intellectually unsound, and even nothing which as a result is undesirable. But as a teaching method it involves a relinquishment of academic objectivity. It makes for indoctrination and propaganda, and that way lies disaster for the educational enterprise."

We must be fair in reply. Certainly it does make for indoctrination and propaganda, but that way lies the only hope for the educational enterprise. It is high time that the college stop deceiving itself about the nature of its teaching function. Education is and always will be indoctrination of a sort, though it also is and ought to be something much more. At the present time many of those who consider themselves most loyal to "objectivity" are indoctrinating their students in antireligion. Even if the supposed ideal of "neutrality" in teaching could be achieved, there would still be present a measure of indoctrination, namely, in the mistaken idea that it is possible to be neutral about religion and its values. Impartiality among churches, creeds, and doctrines is, of course, possible, always desirable, and, except for the church-related college, even necessary; but neutrality about religion as we have used the term is nonexistent.

The choice, then, is not between indoctrination in values on the one hand and absence of it on the other. It is, rather, as to what sort of indoctrination it shall be. Nothing is gained by trying to pretend that the college espousing religion will not be engaged in propaganda, for it will, and should, and must, if it is to deal forthrightly with the perils of the secular spirit. God has stood within the shadow long enough.

"Then what becomes of the disinterested pursuit of truth?" In theory it continues as it has always been upheld, and in practice it will probably be more characteristic of teaching methods than before. The professor who combines true scholarship with a commitment to high values will present facts as facts, making special efforts to escape distortion in the process, but if his subject matter lends itself to further treatment he will not stop there. He will share with his students the conclusions and value-judgments at which others have arrived, making valiant efforts to describe their conclusions with impartiality, but he will not stop there. He will go on to give his own point of view, labeling it as his own and making supreme efforts not to dogmatize and not to force the students to agree with him. Truth is safer in the hands of such conscious indoctrination than in the clutch of an impossible "objectivity" of presentation.

Mention of the role of the professor leads to a consideration of the second positive course of action necessary for combating secularism. *The college must seek to secure for its faculty men and women who are firmly committed to high values in their personal lives and in their academic functioning.* In other words, the college must carry over into the selection of its teachers the same furtherance of its purposes that it has in mind in the ordering of its business affairs or in the development of its religious program. Over and over again studies in higher education conclude by noting the crucial importance of the character of the individual teacher. Then, as Professor Shedd has written,

Without compromising on its basic requirements of scholarly distinction and teaching gifts or its devotion to academic freedom, the college must seek to secure teachers whose philosophy of life and devotion to spiritual ends support and validate the religious purposes of the college.[6]

"But," it may be objected, "does not this mean the establishing of religious tests?" The answer is partly No. Certainly there should not be, as there sometimes unfortunately are, qualifications as to a particular denominational affiliation or doctrinal belief. Nor is there even needful, in every instance, an insistence on allegiance to any religious tradition or participation in any religious group. The quotation from Shedd continues:

While such a principle of selection would lead the college to seek out scholars of affirmative religious conviction and life, it certainly would not cause the college to exclude from its faculty scholars who, although unable to make any affirmation of religious faith, yet exemplify a religious spirit in their personal lives and their work as teachers. The faith that is found "in honest doubt" is neither alien to the spirit of the university nor to the seeking spirit of Christianity itself.[7]

In other words, there is no necessity for the kind of religious tests now employed by a host of institutions. The nominal church membership of, say, the professor of chemistry, which he undertook

6. Clarence P. Shedd, "Proposals for Religion in Postwar Higher Education," *Hazen Pamphlets*, pp. 8–9.
7. *Ibid.*, p. 9.

automatically as a child of ten, means nothing as to whether or not his teaching will possess a religious spirit.

But another part of the answer is, frankly, Yes. A college must have some assurance that its prospective employee will not aid the cause of secularism but will contribute to the support of the high values in which the institution believes. Criteria for judging this intangible quality are difficult to establish, but the college which really wants to know can find out, though not by a questionnaire which the applicant himself fills in. Even as the college seeks information from competent references as to the prospect's academic qualifications, even so it may inquire explicitly from similarly trustworthy sources as to his philosophy of life and his recognizable commitment to values in daily living. At least one organization, the National Council on Religion in Higher Education, exists for the purpose of discovering and helping to train and locate teachers of all subjects who are interested in and capable of exerting a vital religious influence among students. If the college is to defeat the secular spirit which would engulf it, it must consciously seek such people for its faculty, even though it may often fail to find them.

5. *A recognition of the needs of students.*

We now come to two underlying necessities for the religious program itself, though both have point for the total life of the college as well as for its religious activities. The first of these is the realization that the center of interest is, or should be, the individual student. The point of departure for any adequate program of religion must be the needs, problems, and aspirations of students.

Clarification may be gained by a reference to the alternatives for a college's center of interest and point of departure. Some religious programs center on religion—a body of information to be got across, a way of worshiping to be imposed, a core of belief to be transmitted. Others may have chiefly in view neither the student nor religion, but the college's dignity and well-being—a tone to enhance the institutional life, a persuasive element for winning the support of its constituency, a matter of distinction among other colleges. These may all be worthy aims, proper interests and legitimate functions, but unless they are placed in a secondary position the religious program will never be vital. Primary place should be given to a thorough knowledge of and concern for the student. In the building of the college's religious pattern, the question of first importance must be, "What are the interests, needs and problems of our students?" Only in the light of sound answers to that question can the basis for any religious program be successfully laid.

6. *Unhurried planning.*

Everything thus far said in this chapter indicates the necessity for thoughtfulness on the nature of religion, its relation to higher education, and the college's proper task. But when the broad questions of policy are decided, the need for careful deliberation is not yet fulfilled. The religious program itself must be constructed on the basis of unhurried planning.

It has already been indicated that both administrative and voluntary programs have often been at fault here. The pressure of events may sometimes seem to force immediate action not founded on thorough analysis. When military units came to many campuses, for example, innovations had to be made quickly. But most of the sudden establishment of religious provisions and enlargement of activities do not have such an excuse; and they nearly always suffer through the default of the preparation which should have been made.

A college undertaking the inauguration or expansion of its religious program should begin with its own students' needs, as suggested above. It should survey all the religious resources of the campus and community, analyzing the effectiveness of their various contributions. It should seek enlightenment from other colleges and their programs and from specialists working in the field of religion in higher education. It should enlist in its endeavors all who have suggestions to give: students, interested faculty, local pastors, regional and national church and Christian Association secretaries. Then in its announcements of the venture, the college should stress not the unproved benefits of the new program but the principles and purposes which have led to its establishment.

Planning is not finished when the program gets under way. Interests and needs of students change, local problems arise and vanish to be replaced by others, and even the emphases of religion and education vary from time to time and place to place. Planning, therefore, should be tentative, and the college should always be prepared to scrap an outmoded feature and inaugurate a new activity as they seem called for. Thorough planning, moreover, should include some means of periodic evaluation for the program. The college would do well to set up a committee of the faculty or the board, or even better, to ask a group of impartial outsiders, to observe and pass judgment upon the effectiveness of the program at stated intervals. Thus will the necessary planning become a permanent activity, and the program not only begin but continue as a vital force in the lives of the students.

B. THE PROGRAM

An adequate program will provide for all the various ways in which religion lends itself to human expression and ministers to human need. Those methods are not to be exhausted in any one brief list. Each institution will find its own special means of serving and will encourage various nonofficial agencies to make their particular contributions. In nearly every instance the total program will be composed of both administrative functions and voluntary activities, but in its details it will differ from college to college. The following list is not meant to be exhaustive, but rather indicates the core of techniques which should be sponsored on all campuses. As a minimum every program will consist of provisions for:

7. *Worship.*

The pattern will vary greatly from campus to campus. One college may sponsor a weekday chapel; another, Sunday church; still another, Sunday vespers. A "Religious Emphasis Week" will often be appropriate. Many institutions will combine these and other methods in differing ways. Moreover, no consistency should be expected in such matters as length of meeting, frequency of services, order of worship, and degree of dependence upon outside leadership. Worship will sometimes consist of appreciation, sometimes of exhortation, many times of both together. It may be small and spontaneous or large, formal, and even ceremonial.

Similarly the problem of compulsion versus voluntarism has no one final solution. Some colleges, particularly state-supported institutions, may sponsor only voluntary services; others, because of their peculiar heritage or present associations, may wish or feel impelled to impose varying requirements of attendance. Such institutions should be reminded that the very element of compulsion makes more imperative the need for careful planning and able leadership. As we have noted, strong arguments can be made for both sides of this question. The only general conclusion in this matter is: Each college, whether or not part of its services are required, should provide some experience of worship for which the students' attendance is purely voluntary. Somewhere within the college life students should be given the opportunity, without compulsion, for worshiping God.

In the midst of desirable diversity at least three other suggestions are general in their application. The second is that chapel, or whatever the worship services are called, should be dissociated from assembly. A political talk, an athletic rally, or a campus-wide town meeting, even though it begin with a hymn and close with a prayer, is not worship, however worthy it may be in itself. To drag religion in on such occasions is often to discredit religion. To pretend that in such meetings the college has discharged its obligation to provide experiences of worship is to confess to a complete ignorance as to its true nature. Chapel is one thing, assembly another, and the distinction should be preserved.

The third has to do with the quality of the program. No matter what form the service takes, it must be well prepared and well produced. Every time the chapel bell rings, religion as well as the college is on trial. A careless service makes religion appear slovenly; a boring service makes religion seem stupid; a spiritless service makes religion dead. Preparation and performance, therefore, demand able leadership. Responsibility for the services should be placed in the hands of one who is deeply interested, who is fully competent, and who has adequate time and resources at his disposal. If outside talent is called upon the college needs to exercise great care in the selection. A second-rate football team is disappointing but a second-rate chapel program is disastrous.

The final suggestion is that on every campus there should be an adequate place for worship. At some large institutions this may be a cathedral reserved solely for such use. On most campuses the chapel will be much more modest in size and design. The solution for state-supported institutions may be a building set aside for the religious activities which has within it a small, beautiful prayer chapel for the use of all communions. Even those colleges which must use their one assembly hall for all public meetings can manage to find, if they will, one room to be reserved and tastefully decorated for such use.

It is unavoidable that many colleges must hold their larger religious services in an auditorium in which at other times all sorts of other activities take place. In such instances special effort must be exerted to change the mood of the hall, lest the air of the boxing match of Saturday pervade the church service of Sunday. Some special stage design, never otherwise employed, will prove useful. A triptych, subdued lighting, flowers, ushers, an altar— these and other devices may recommend themselves. However it is done, the college must house its worship services appropriately.

8. *Study.*

Adequate provisions for the study of religion will mean, in every instance, something more than the encouragement of informal reading and discussion. We have noted the widespread conviction that religion is, among other things, a body of knowledge which the liberally educated should possess. Thus, if religion is not to appear as the stepchild among academic subjects, it must be presented in the regular curriculum.

But the varieties of its presentation may be expected to be numerous. No one could presume to draw up a list of courses which would be adequate for any college. Factors of size, background, present affiliation, composition of student body, and others make for justifiable differences among the nature and extent of curricular offerings in the field. The only general suggestion which would hold good for all types and sizes of institutions is as follows: Among the various possible approaches two are necessary. The first is the biblical and historical approach, represented by courses in the Old and New Testaments, the life of Jesus, and church history. The second is the philosophical and theological approach, represented by such courses as "The philosophy of religion," "Christian social teachings," and "Modern religious problems." Either approach without the other presents a partial picture of the way in which religion influences the mind of man and contributes to our present culture. Both are necessary for a full portrayal.

If in a small college or in a newly established program in a large institution only a few courses can be offered, then they had best fall within these two approaches. But in those situations in which the offerings can be enlarged other approaches may be found useful. The practical approach through courses in religious education has been popular and, if based upon solid work in the history and philosophy of religion, is valuable. What may be called the aesthetic approach, by means of such courses as "The Bible as literature" or "Religious art," offers interesting supplementary material. And "Comparative religions" has often been used as an entering wedge for the study of our own Hebrew-Christian tradition in those institutions which have feared to undertake more direct action. All these have their place, but the place is secondary to the two basic approaches suggested.

The need is great enough to demand the inclusion of meaty courses in the regular curriculum, but even greater to some observers appear to be the problems incident to such inclusion for state-supported institutions. So President George N. Shuster of Hunter concludes his discussion of the question: "The public college at least should offer no formal courses in religion. There is no value in watered stock." [8] But his two sentences are not complementary. To consider his second statement first, one may agree wholeheartedly that if "The Bible as literature," offered in the English department, is the only thing a college can do, then it had better do nothing, or at least not pretend that it is doing something. This is the point in stressing the historical and philosophical as the two necessary fundamental approaches, for courses of those sorts will not be watered stock.

The fault in President Shuster's remarks is the implication that negligible work is all that the public, or tax-supported, college should or can offer. In our previous discussion we have been at some pains to show that state schools may legally, and numbers of them do actually, provide curricular work in religion comparable to that in other fields. They may offer nothing sectarian, but surely no scholar in the field could hold that only the sectarian is sound and unwatered. Moreover, the basic approaches suggested above call for nothing sectarian. The teaching of such courses will always be difficult, especially in tax-supported institutions, but not impossible, as witness their presence in many state universities today. This old bugaboo of the supposed incapacity of the state institution is raised once again to underline the fact that what has been said applies to all colleges alike, irrespective of type.

8. George N. Shuster, "Common Elements in Religion and Education," in *Religion and Public Education*, p. 68. He developed the point in his "Education and Religion," *Hazen Pamphlets*, No. 10 (April, 1945).

As to the organization of courses, those institutions following a departmental scheme ought to establish religion as a department of its own. If the college is small or if for other reasons combination seems desirable, religion can most naturally be paired with philosophy, in which case the joint department should bear the names of both disciplines. The alternative to giving religion departmental status is the spreading of its courses throughout various other departments, a scheme not calculated to indicate the position of equality with other subjects which religion should occupy. The presence of a department of religion will not prevent other departments from offering courses dealing with religion which more appropriately belong under their headings. For example, the "Psychology of religion" ought usually to be given in psychology, and "Religious art" under art.

The danger in departmental status is that religion will find itself in a curricular corner, segregated from the rest by all the usual barriers set up to preserve departmental integrity. Thus, while religion is recognized as a worthy subject in its own right, inter-relationships between its and other departments should be encouraged. A divisional or group plan of organization enables religion to take its rightful place among the humanities. As colleges are more and more adopting such plans and fostering connectedness, the danger that religion or any other subject will become isolated grows less and less.

We have noted the presence in many colleges of curricular requirements in the field of religion. It is the author's personal opinion that such requirements are more defensible than compulsion in worship. You can't make a horse drink, it is true, but the educated animal ought at least to be led to know that water exists, and that others have drunk to their benefit. For colleges in which curricular work in religion is new or trivial, requirements would be a long time in coming. At some institutions requirements might always seem inadvisable, though theoretically not impossible even in those which are state-supported. A nonsectarian introductory or survey course might, in time, recommend itself as the legitimate and necessary possession of every college graduate, no matter the type of college. But the choice of material for the required course would be difficult to make. In view of the increasing emphasis on "general education," possibly the best method of guaranteeing that the students have a speaking acquaintance with religion is by way of giving religion an integral part to play in the required work in the humanities. As long as the study of religion is altogether elective, the college will not be taking seriously its desire that religious illiteracy be abolished.

Enough has been said to indicate the necessity that all instruction in religion be intellectually rigorous. Well-intentioned organizational support will be only embarrassing if the courses are "crips." Professors of religion must be as well trained and as competent as those in any other field, the work itself must be as demanding, and its results must be as dispassionately judged. Religion must not only receive but merit high status in the curriculum.

9. *Voluntary activity.*

Here, much more than in formal study, even more than in formal worship, is the point at which religion will begin to take hold of students' lives. Chapel and courses should feed into activity; they are its necessary undergirding. But the voluntary activity is, or should be, the most vital and decisive single element in the total religious program.

Because voluntary activity is vital, that is, sensitive to the interests and conditions of actual life and its changes, it defies description. No one local program is or should be the same as any other. No one pattern can be laid out. The very meaning of the word "voluntary" precludes sameness, for it refers to the unconstrained interests and actions of individuals and groups.

Yet enough similarity exists among students and among the concerns of religion to admit of one general conclusion, namely, that an adequate program will provide for both contemplative and active aspects. The contemplative will consist variously of informal worship, study, and discussion, of a nature and to a degree impossible in the chapel and classroom. Here the "sectarian" matters which have no legitimate place in formal instruction come in for thorough consideration. The emphasis will be on talk that is thoughtful. Since the bull session on religion is ever present, the effort should be to surround the natural impulse to talk with influences making for sense, not stupidity, and for faith, not frustration. The subject matter, the seriousness of its study, the amount of desirable adult guidance, these and other affairs are best left to sound appraisal of the situation and the moment. It is proper that the wind be allowed to blow as it listeth.

The active aspect subsumes those functions which most readily come to mind at the mention of "religious activities": deputations, social service work, student conferences, freshman orientation, all variety of on- and off-campus good deeds. If chapel, courses, and voluntary contemplation have done their work, students will be impelled to give evidence of their convictions in "service." Dictation as to the forms which that service should take is out of place, but efforts to insure that it will be meaningful are proper and often necessary. Whatever else develops or is consciously sponsored, the program should make sure the provision of opportunities for selfless participation in the solution of community problems. A basket to the poor at Christmastime will no more suffice than a benefit dance in the college gym, even though in each instance the cause within itself be worthy. Only that college possesses vital religious activity which nurtures on its campus an identification, in acts of mutual betterment, of the washed with the unwashed.

Contemplation and action must, of course, be related. Each nourishes the other. By a combination of the two religion gets inextricably involved in such questions as better race relations, labor, international affairs, war and peace—all of them debatable, even inflammatory. For the good of its soul the college will expect to be embarrassed on occasion. If obviously the institution, on the one hand, cannot and should not be held responsible for all thoughts and actions that are provoked by mass stretching of minds, no more on the other ought it to discourage the compulsions of the conscience short of the point where liberty becomes license. The college deeply concerned with the religious growth of its students will welcome all manifestations that religion is being taken seriously.

Thus far nothing has been said directly about the sponsorship of the voluntary religious life. In nearly every instance the major part or all of the provisions for formal worship and study will be initiated by the college administration, but religious activities may and usually do have various sponsorships. Colleges themselves sometimes support religious activity programs, but much more often the work is undertaken by Christian Associations and church foundations. These latter two are usually spoken of as "voluntary" organizations—this has been the prevailing use in previous chapters—but the activities of such groups as well as of "official" programs may or may not be truly voluntary in the sense in which the word is being used in this section. The source of the sponsorship matters very little, but the voluntary nature of the activity is critically important.

Since on most campuses the religious activity will be largely or wholly under unofficial sponsorship, it behooves the college to lend strong encouragement to the various agencies. The number of organizations will depend upon the size of the institution. Only in exceptional circumstances is the college justified in choosing among the groups those to whom its support will be given. It should help all of them. In the case of nondenominational Christian Associations, this may sometimes mean a measure of financial support. In the case of church foundations and clubs, this will always mean, except in those rare instances in which the college sponsors its own community church, both encouragement to the students to affiliate with a local church and assistance to the church itself in its effort to discover competent leadership. Christian Associations and church foundations have strong roots in the past and may be expected to continue to provide fruitful opportunities for the religious growth of students, whether or not the college is concerned. But when most or all of the activity program is unofficial in sponsorship, the obligation still rests upon the college to foster the work in every possible way. In the final analysis it is the college's responsibility to see to it that, under whatever auspices, vital opportunities for voluntary religious activity are provided.

10. *Religious counseling.*

The need is twofold. First, the college must make adequate counseling available for the students on the specific problems of religion. This means that the counselor must be thoroughly trained in religion and in pastoral psychology. It means, moreover, that the college must surround the counselor with resources conducive to his work: the counselor must not be overloaded with other duties; he must be provided with a good office where privacy can be guaranteed; his work must be recognized as a part of the college's total guidance program and integrally related with it. Whether or not students will go to him with their problems will depend primarily upon what sort of man he is, but the college must give him full chance by lending material support and spiritual encouragement.

But counseling in religion is only part of religious counseling. The second need is that the college conceive of its whole personnel program as religious in character. All the various adjustment problems of students must be approached not perfunctorily but religiously, in the sense that, whether they be vocational, financial, marital, or what-not, they involve the individual's growth in personality and in awareness of values in living. The college's concern for religious counseling will extend not merely to the work of the counselor in religion but to all the staff members and agencies responsible for the guidance of students.

11. *Professional leadership.*

Enough has already been said in other sections to indicate the critical importance of able leadership for all parts and the totality of the college religious program. But certain specific problems in providing professional leaders should be mentioned.

With all the recent growth in the practice of adding directors of religion to the regular college staffs, the majority of colleges have not yet inaugurated such positions. Secretaries and student pastors supported by extracollegiate agencies are usually found only at large institutions. For every great university which has a host of officials, variously sponsored, there are numbers of small colleges possessing no such positions at all. In such institutions the direction of the religious program is given as a collateral duty to some already overworked faculty member who, through lack of training and lack of time, cannot properly discharge the function. Particularly in church-related colleges has this been the unfortunate practice. The first need, then, is for the college to become convinced that the leadership of its religious life is no part-time, secondary job; that in the small as well as the large institution at least one full-time director of the religious program, by whatever title he may be called, is a necessary administrative officer.

But the functions of a director depend upon the local situation and local needs to such an extent that they admit of no general description. The summary at the end of Chapter XIII indicated the diversity of duties to which such a person may be subject. In the small college any or all of the functions of teaching, preparing and leading worship services, directing religious activities, and counseling students may partially or wholly devolve upon him.

Thus there is grave danger of overloading. In the establishment of such a position the college may defeat its own purposes by deluging the incumbent with so many responsibilities that he slights some phases of the work or is effective in none.

The danger in the large institution is not normally as great. Here several positions of religious leadership will be needed, and only rarely should the administration sponsor all of them. The desirable pattern may be one in which the extracollegiate organizations, such as Christian Associations and church groups, will provide part- or full-time secretaries and student pastors, in which case the primary obligation of the college will be fulfilled by inaugurating a position of over-all direction and coördination, occasionally with assistants. This chairman of the corps of religious workers may have other duties with the worship or instructional programs, but usually the scope of his functions can be more easily limited and precisely defined than those of his counterpart in the small college.

Despite the willingness of the independent organizations, the college, large or small, dare not allow all its religious leadership to be furnished by extracollegiate agencies. In some instances this may be adequate for the religious activities, but certain other aspects of the college religious life need the evidence of conscious administrative obligation, and their leaders need official status. Chapel is a campus-wide affair, and its direction should be in the hands of a regularly employed member of the staff. Instruction in religion should be provided by regular faculty members. Those state institutions which allow coördinate schools of religion, employing their own teaching personnel, to offer courses for credit, have found a workable technique for handling the old problem of whether or not to include religion. But in spite of its success in many places, it is only a compromise, for there religion has only one foot in the academic door. That religion is being taught for credit somewhere in the neighborhood of the campus is better than nothing. But the method is defensible only if the institution cannot bring the instruction of religion into the regular curriculum, by professors paid out of the regular budget—and such situations are now rare.

Yet if the college sponsors some of the leadership, its full obligation is not discharged merely by caring for its own. The independent organizations will welcome and need various kinds of help in their efforts to furnish worthy adult guidance for their work.

We have noted how many institutions provide part or even all of the salaries of Christian Association workers. Less tangible encouragement to all groups may be even more important: aid in the selection of professional workers, free access to students, use of college buildings, and the furtherance of a sense of belonging to the college community in spite of the lack of official status.

To return to the problem of overloading, solutions will of course be diverse. For the independent worker, his sponsoring organization defines his duties, and the college thus escapes the task. But brief comment is called for on the problem of the official leader. First, teaching may be the item most reasonably omitted from his functions. In nearly every college, no matter how small, the instruction of religion will be a full-time job in itself. If the college or the leader should feel that teaching is important for preserving regular contact with the rest of the faculty, then he may teach a course or two, in which case he should have assistance for other parts of the program.

Second, the temptation will arise to solve the problem by neglecting the function of counseling. Preoccupation with administrative tasks can fill a schedule to the point where no time remains for personal contacts and where students are dissuaded from "disturbing" the counselor. If, as is usual, the religious director doubles as counselor in religion, then special pains must be taken to protect the time allotted to such work, else it easily goes by default.

Though the functions applicable to all programs cannot be described, generalizations are possible with respect to the leaders themselves, their necessary abilities and traits of character. Directors of the religious programs should be trained specifically in the work of religion in higher education. They must be able to speak in public, to administer, to teach, and to counsel. If this is a large order, the only answer is that such work is a specialized ministry demanding exceptional talent. Spiritual qualifications are even more exacting; of them Professor Shedd has written:

They must be people who love students and can work in comradeship with them. They must have intellectual integrity, subjecting themselves to as severe intellectual and spiritual disciplines as any other member of the faculty. They must view their tasks as mediators of religious faith and experience and not merely as those who "give courses" or build organizations. They must know the real world and be at home in it. They must have a reasoned faith relevant to the world of today, an experience of religion that is contagious and which students know to be authentic, and a view of the Church which rises above their own denomination and many of the other barriers erected by the accidents of church history. They must be people who face with capacity and courage the divisive issues of our day and who do their work with a sense of comradeship with Christian students everywhere.[9]

By whatever name he is called, the director, and thus representative and spokesman for religion on the campus, should be as able and dynamic as any other individual connected with the institution. Finding such a person is the tremendous task the college faces when it seeks to provide adequate religious leadership.

C. ORGANIZATION OF THE PROGRAM

An adequate program will be organized so as to insure that its full strength may effectively be brought to bear upon students' lives. By implication, much has been said already about organization. It remains to state these implications openly. Many college programs, otherwise well conceived in basic philosophy and function, have faltered and even failed because of an insufficient consideration of structural needs. The college that would succeed in its sponsorship of religion would do well to pay attention to such items as:

12. *Unity within the religious program.*

It is conceivable that a college might fulfill all the requirements thus far indicated, yet the parts of the program might be as separate as marbles in a dish. But, though religion has various aspects, it is indivisible and its nurture is a total task. Thus it should be a unified task. Instruction in one corner, chapel in another, religious activities in a third, and counseling lost in the shuffle, make a harmonious whole only by accident.

Unity can be achieved in several ways. It may be found in the person of a director whose functioning touches all parts of the program. But in this case, as has already been noted, the director will almost unavoidably be overworked; and a purely personal basis for unity may prove unstable when the identity of the

9. Clarence P. Shedd, "Proposals for Religion in Postwar Higher Education," *Hazen Pamphlets*, p. 18.

incumbent changes. Unity may be attained by a faculty and administration committee on which sit representatives of all the various approaches to religion, or by a more inclusive board drawing members also from the student body, the trustees, and the church and Christian Association workers. The plan which will recommend itself to most colleges may well be a combination of the two: a widely representative committee or board, coupled with a responsible leader. No one scheme will be feasible everywhere. The necessity is not that the college adopt some one arrangement, but that unity be accomplished organically as well as informally.

13. *Relationships with other aspects of college life.*

A program can be unified and still be out of touch with the rest of campus affairs. The voice of religion raised in other concerns of the college will often prove fruitful, and religion in its turn will benefit from the advice of those not directly responsible for its promotion. This close association cannot always be gained by informal contacts. The college would do well to make provision in its organizational framework for connection between religion and, say, the personnel program or athletics or campus government or the social life. For a large and complex institution the presence of representatives of religion among the regular faculty may not be sufficient; the director or some other delegate for religion may need to sit on various governing boards and councils.

In the relationships of religion with other aspects of the college program the question of status is raised. Religion must be able to meet its fellow concerns as a peer. We have already indicated that if the curricular work is arranged in a departmental structure, religion should usually be a department of its own. The same consideration holds for other parts of the religious program, for personnel engaged in religious work, and even for the material surroundings. Chapel should have equal dignity and quality of setting with other college convocations. Religious and secular activities should receive uniform support. Professors of religion and professional workers should be given rank, salary, and tenure comparable to employees in other fields. The director of the religious program, if his position is largely administrative, should be on a level with directors of other areas of the college life. Title itself is often a point of significance in the public eye; thus such a name as "Dean of the Chapel" is often appropriate for the position of religious leadership in a large university. Since comparisons are made on superficial factors, even such matters as classroom and office location, space, and furnishings are not irrelevant. To the uninitiated this may seem a querulous quibble, but students inevitably notice which department's classrooms are in the basement and which professors' offices have carpets on the floor. Not only for its relationships with other college affairs but also for the evidence such matters give as to the degree of support it receives, religion must have high status, together with all the accompaniments which that status calls for.

14. *The preservation of student initiative.*

The last two sections have stressed the importance of bringing the various parts of the religious program into contact with one another, and religion into contact with other areas of college life. This section is to indicate the necessity of bringing the students consciously into the organizational pattern. Thus we return to a consideration of the individual student as the necessary focal point, but this time with a difference. The preservation of student initiative is a problem involving the structure of the religious program. It is not enough that students' needs and interests be given primary attention. It is not even enough that the intention exist that their initiative be preserved. The intention must be manifested and secured in the form of organization itself.

The problem involves both a clear understanding of the nature of student initiative and a firm resolve to maintain it. Student initiative means two things. It means, first of all, a large participation in both the planning and the production of the established program. "Planning" and "production" must be taken at full face value. Presence on a students' advisory council which has no power of final decision is not real planning. Ushering at chapel or furnishing refreshments for a discussion group is not real production. Students will be quick to know whether or not their opinions are, or ever can be, conclusive. They will instantly detect whether or not the actions assigned them are trivial. We have used the term "director" to describe the adult leader, yet his proper role is never direction but always guidance, for students must be free to accept or reject the counsel offered them. The religious program is the college's, but it is also, and first of all, the students'—or it is no adequate program at all.

Student initiative also means a larger freedom not to be limited to established activities or bound by established procedures. The genius of early student religious societies, the forerunners of present-day Christian Associations and similar groups, was in their completely voluntary nature. Students were at liberty to follow wherever their interests and commitments led them. If today's programs and activities, whatever their sponsorship, are to be characterized by a similar vitality and consecration, they must provide for a similar initiative. Full share in planning and production is only part of it; the other part is the chance to scrap the old and plunge off into the new, unhampered and even encouraged by professional leaders and by the college.

The encouragement of student initiative must depend to a large extent upon personal and intangible factors. The temper of the professional leadership is nearly always decisive; often the college president himself sets the tone. But the organizational pattern of the religious program can at least help, if properly framed, and that much the college must do. This means that representatives of the student body must be given a place on every board possessing the power of decision in any phase of the religious program, with the possible exception of instruction. Students should help to plan the worship services, to select the visiting speakers, to devise the various voluntary activities, and to set policies for and coördinate the parts of the total program. If they have been allowed a genuine part in the planning, their enthusiastic participation in the production will take care of itself. However it is to be done on each campus, the college must make extraordinary efforts to maintain and enlarge student initiative.

15. *Association with the religious and social service agencies in the local community.*

The reference is not to the unofficial student religious organizations, for it has already been recognized that they are in actuality an important part of the total campus program. Attention is directed rather to the churches in the town, as distinct from the denominational student clubs, and to social settlements, welfare and relief organizations, and similar activities. We noted that one of the ideals of the voluntary religious activity is that it result in the interchange of insights and benefits between students and disparate groups. The college will want to develop associations with all sorts of community agencies which can further this ideal.

With local churches the college will need to go further by distinct encouragement to the students to identify themselves with some religious body. Students should be led to see that the development of a religious consciousness ought to be accompanied by the desire to associate with those like-minded. If the college holds no Sunday church services of its own, it will need, on the one hand, to stimulate the students to consider the churches part of their total opportunity for growth, and on the other to strengthen the work of the churches themselves. The close association of the campus religious program with the local churches can be mutually beneficial. It goes without saying that the church-related college will not want to limit its association to the local congregation of its own denomination.

16. *Association with national student religious movements.*

Some of the richest experiences which a college can offer its students result from intercollegiate contacts which it encourages them to make. Some of the keenest insights which the college itself receives are from various national organizations and activities. This is no less true for religion than for any other field. The college religious program, through its several parts, should affiliate with national movements and avail itself of the strength and inspiration which can come thereby.

Nearly every denominational student agency is represented by a national body with which the local group will automatically be connected. The Christian Associations will bear a relationship to the Intercollegiate Y.M.C.A. and Y.W.C.A. and the National Intercollegiate Christian Council. Through the Christian Associations and most of the church groups, contact will be made with the recently formed United Student Christian Council and with the World Student Christian Federation. As indicated in Chapter III, other national coöperative agencies and activities exist in abundance. Many times, however, local relationships to such organizations may be purely nominal. In such cases the college can do much to encourage the vitality of the connection: by assisting students to attend national conferences, by encouraging participation in such worthy projects as the World Student Service Fund, and by inviting leaders of national and international movements to the campus.

The total college religious program has no counterpart in the national field, nor does there exist any national association of professional religious workers. But it has long been the dream of leaders in religion that someday there be established a united student Christian movement which would include almost all the religious agencies on the campuses.[10] Close approximations have come recently in the formation in 1942 of the War Emergency Council for Student Christian Work, and in 1944 of the United Student Christian Council. This is, of course, coöperation rather than unity, but it may well be the beginning of the united national program. The college which seeks to promote a total religious program for its campus and which treasures intercollegiate contacts will be in a strong position to aid in the development of the national movement-to-be.

The titles of the sections will serve as a sufficient summary. An adequate program will be based upon keen interest in and a liberal definition of religion, a conception of the essential religious nature of the educational task, a determination both to foster religious values in the total life of the institution and to combat those factors making for a secular atmosphere, a recognition of the needs of students, and unhurried planning. The program itself will provide adequately for worship, study, voluntary activity, religious counseling, and professional leadership. It will be organized so as to insure unity within the program itself, relationships with other aspects of the college life, the preservation of student initiative, and associations both with religious and social service agencies in the local community and with national student religious movements.

Will any college ever achieve this adequate program? The answer must be No. It was admitted at the beginning that "adequate" was used in a strict sense; and no college will ever convert all its students to religious values any more than it will educate all its students in liberal understandings.

But ought a college to aim at less? Similarly the answer must be No. A college's, no less than a man's, reach should exceed its

10. See Clarence P. Shedd, *The Church Follows Its Students*, pp. 293–305; and "The Movements of Religion in American Higher Education," *Journal of the American Association of Collegiate Registrars*, pp. 18–20.

grasp, or what's a philosophy of higher education for? The conclusion of the matter is simply this: Higher education must make religion its partner; and when it does, though it will always be too frail to take more than halfway measures, it must not hold halfway goals. Professor Robert L. Calhoun's statement at the University of Pennsylvania Bicentennial Conference serves as a suitable ending:

High religion, in short, and intellectual enterprise belong together. Each gains from close association with the other. The two in conjunction, but neither one by itself, can move with hope toward more effective conquest of the chaos that again and again threatens to engulf human living. That way lies whatever chance we may have for a more humane world.[11]

11. Calhoun, *op. cit.*, p. 71.

APPENDIX I

A Study of the Religious Programs of 107 Colleges, Made by the
National Intercollegiate Christian Council

In 1939 the Church-Association Relations Commission of the National
Intercollegiate Christian Council undertook a study of the nature and extent
of coöperative religious agencies and programs among a selected number of
colleges. At the request of the author the Commission inserted in its questionnaire a number of questions relating to the attitudes of college administrations toward religion and the ways in which official help was given to the
religious programs. The following information is based upon the replies to
those questions, received over a period of a year, and incorporated as Appendix A in the *Minutes* of the Commission for May 3–4, 1940.

One hundred sixty-five replies were received. Of these 58 have been omitted
from the present tabulation for various reasons: because of insufficient information; or because they were of a type not considered in the main body
of the discussion—teachers' colleges, Negro colleges, and junior colleges;
or because their elimination enabled the figures to be based upon a more
easily definable group of colleges. The remaining 107 are all on the approved
list of the Association of American Universities. According to type of institution, the totals are: independent colleges, counting New York University twice for its two divisions—45; state institutions, including the
municipal University of Akron—37; and church-related colleges—25.[1] Geo-
graphically the colleges represent 33 states, and reflect adequately, though
not entirely accurately, the regional distribution of accredited institutions.
The colleges are as follows:

1. Agnes Scott College
2. Akron, University of
3. Alabama College
4. Amherst College
5. Antioch College
6. Bates College
7. Beloit College
8. Bethany College (West Virginia)
9. Birmingham-Southern College
10. Boston University
11. Bowdoin College
12. Brown University
13. Bucknell University
14. California Institute of Technology
15. California, University of (Berkeley)
16. Carleton College

1. Classification according to type was made by reference to the "Lovejoy
College Rating Guide," in C. E. Lovejoy, *So You're Going to College.*

17. Chicago, University of
18. The Citadel
19. Colby College
20. Colorado College
21. Colorado, University of
22. Columbia University
23. Connecticut, University of
24. Converse College
25. Cornell College (Iowa)
26. Cornell University
27. Davidson College
28. Denver, University of
29. Duke University
30. Emory University
31. Florida State College for Women
32. Florida, University of
33. Franklin and Marshall College
34. Furman University
35. Gettysburg College
36. Grinnell College
37. Hamilton College
38. Harvard University
39. Haverford College
40. Illinois, University of
41. Indiana University
42. Iowa, State University of
43. Kansas State College
44. Kentucky, University of
45. Lafayette College
46. Louisiana State University
47. Maine, University of
48. Mary Baldwin College
49. Massachusetts State College
50. Miami University (Ohio)
51. Michigan State College
52. Michigan, University of
53. Millsaps College
54. Minnesota, University of
55. Missouri, University of
56. Mount Holyoke College
57. Muskingum College
58. Nebraska, University of
59. New York University, University Heights College
60. New York University, Washington Square College
61. North Carolina, University of
62. North Carolina, Woman's College of the University of
63. North Central College
64. Northwestern University
65. Oberlin College

66. Occidental College
67. Ohio State University
68. Ohio University
69. Ohio Wesleyan University
70. Oklahoma College for Women
71. Oklahoma, University of
72. Otterbein College
73. Pacific, College of the
74. Park College
75. Pennsylvania State College
76. Randolph-Macon Woman's College
77. Redlands, University of
78. Richmond, University of
79. Shorter College
80. Simmons College
81. Smith College
82. South Carolina, University of
83. South, University of the
84. Southern Methodist University
85. Swarthmore College
86. Sweet Briar College
87. Syracuse University
88. Tennessee, University of
89. Ursinus College
90. Vanderbilt University
91. Virginia, University of
92. Washington and Jefferson College
93. Washington, State College of
94. Washington University (Missouri)
95. Washington, University of
96. Wellesley College
97. Wesleyan University (Connecticut)
98. West Virginia University
99. Westminster College (Pennsylvania)
100. Wheaton College (Massachusetts)
101. Willamette University
102. William Jewell College
103. Williams College
104. Wilson College
105. Winthrop College
106. Wisconsin, University of
107. Yale University

The tabulation records the answers to the following matters about which questions were asked:

A. The provision of college rooms or of a separate college building for religious meetings or the use of religious organizations. (Indicated in the table by "Use of buildings.")

B. The presence of courses in religion in the regular college curriculum. (Indicated by "Courses.")

C. The provision of services of worship. (Indicated by "Chapel.") Subdivisions deal with whether attendance at services is "compulsory" or "voluntary," the total of these two parts equaling the figures for the division as a whole. In one or two instances to the author's knowledge the answerers denoted their services as voluntary if the compulsory element was slight.

D. The assumption of financial responsibility, in large part or complete, for providing chapel speakers or leaders at special religious convocations, such as a "Religious Emphasis Week." (Indicated by "Special religious convocations.")

E. The donation of grants to religious organizations from student activity fees or from the college treasury, in regular specified amounts. (Indicated by "Subsidization of voluntary groups.")

F. The provision of a major part or all of the salaries of workers engaged in the leadership of programs of worship or religious activities. (Indicated by "Official religious leadership.") Figures for this division include both those leaders bearing an "official" title, such as "Chaplain" or "Director of Religious Activities," and those whose title sounds unofficial, such as "Secretary of the Y.M.C.A.," as long as the latter are paid in large part or wholly by the college itself.

G. The sincere interest of the president in religion on the campus, as evidenced by his participation and public statement. (Indicated by "President's positive interest.") In order to receive an objective answer to this question, as well as to others concerned with administrative policy, the questionnaire was sent not to the presidents themselves but to religious workers, to professors, and in some cases to known student leaders of religious organizations with a mature point of view.

Obviously there is wide divergence in the degree to which each method is fulfilled in the different colleges. The endless varieties of ways in which each function is performed do not lend themselves to tabular summary. The significant facts for individual institutions are presented in the appropriate chapters in the foregoing discussion. Comparisons among the figures are drawn in Chapter XII.

For each separate method or concern the table gives the number of institutions adopting it and the percentage which that number represents of the total number of colleges in the indicated group:

Method	Total Colls. (107)		Independent (45)		State-Supptd. (37)		Church-Related (25)	
	No.	%	No.	%	No.	%	No.	%
A. Use of buildings	101	94.4	44	97.8	32	86.5	25	100
B. Courses	87	81.3	40	88.9	22 *	59.5	25	100
C. Chapel	77	72.0	40	88.9	12	32.4	25	100
1. Compulsory	46	43.0	22	48.9	3	8.1	21	84
2. Voluntary	31	29.0	18	40.0	9	24.3	4	16
D. Special religious convocations	79	73.8	35	77.8	21	56.8	23	92
E. Subsidization of voluntary groups	58	54.2	27	60.0	15	40.5	16	64
F. Official religious leadership	48	44.9	25	55.6	17	45.9	6	24
G. President's positive interest	85	79.4	33	73.3	28	75.7	24	96

* Eight state institutions, or 21.6% of the total of 37, give credit for courses in religion taught by nonofficial agencies at the side of the campus. Thus the grand total for state institutions at which religion is offered for credit, whether or not in the regular curriculum, is 30, or 81.1%.

APPENDIX II

A Study of the Religious Provisions of 263 Colleges on the Approved List of the Association of American Universities

In 1940 the Association of American Universities gave accreditation for work of the college level to 289 institutions. An intensive study of the catalogues of these leading colleges and universities was made by the author in 1941, the last full peacetime academic year. The information thus gained, supplemented in many instances by other material, is the basis of the following facts relating to the presence of departments of religion, courses in religion in other departments, provisions for worship, and college-sponsored positions of religious leadership.

Because their type fell outside the limits of this study, 26 of the institutions were omitted from the tabulations. These 26 consisted of 19 Catholic colleges, 2 teachers' colleges, 2 Federal institutions, 2 Negro universities, and 1 extraterritorial university. The remaining 263 are state, municipal, independent, and church-related (Protestant) colleges and universities, composing the group which have been the subject of discussion in the foregoing text.

A. Instruction in religion.

The presence of departments of religion in the various colleges, by type,[1] is indicated in the following table:

Type of College	Number in Type	Having a Department of Religion	
		No.	%
I. All colleges	263	178	67.7
II. Church-related colleges	56	56	100.0
III. Independent colleges of liberal arts	118	100	84.7
a. Men's colleges	23	18	78.3
b. Women's colleges	27	23	85.2
c. Coeducational colleges	68	59	86.8
IV. Independent technological schools	11	–	–
V. State institutions	70	21	30.0
a. Men's institutions	8	3	37.5
b. Women's institutions	7	6	85.7
c. Coeducational institutions	55	12	21.8
VI. Municipal institutions	8	1	12.5

1. See note on p. 299.

The figures for "V. State institutions" may be supplemented by figures for those universities at which "schools," "colleges," or "chairs" of religion are provided by private auspices, usually representing the collaboration of several of the Protestant denominations. The School of Religion at the State University of Iowa is included in the total of 21, in the table above, because it is now a regular department of the College of Liberal Arts. "Schools" of the unofficial type exist at 13 state institutions not possessing departments of their own, 12 of which allow credit for this outside work. The combined totals for state institutions read:

V. State institutions—70
   Having a department in the regular curriculum—21, or 30%
   Religion offered by unofficial "schools," etc.   —13, or 18.6%
   Total possessing departments of religion,
      whether or not officially sponsored   —34, or 48.6%

Among the total of 178 colleges possessing departments of their own a variety of titles, 43 in number, is used to describe the department. The favorites, with the number of institutions employing each, are:

Department of Religion	78
Department of Religious Education	12
Department of Philosophy and Religion	11
Department of Bible	10
Department of Bible and Religion	8
Department of Biblical Literature	7
Department of Bible and Religious Education	5

A total of 7 colleges have 2 or more departments.

The absence of a department of religion, however, does not necessarily indicate that the total curriculum is barren of all courses concerning the subject. Other departments most likely to offer courses in religion are English and philosophy, but courses are also found occasionally in the departments of history, sociology, psychology, Greek, education, and others. The following table gives total figures for departments of religion plus courses in other departments, indicating in the final column the number and percentage of institutions of each major type which offer no curricular work in religion under their own auspices:

1. Based on C. E. Lovejoy, *So You're Going to College*. Concerning a number of institutions which receive some state aid, a difficulty in classification is encountered. Of these 9 semistate colleges, 3 (New Jersey College for Women, Rutgers, and the University of Vermont) have been classified as state institutions, and 6 (Alfred, Cornell University, University of Pennsylvania, University of Pittsburgh, Syracuse, and Temple) have been classified as independent colleges.

Type and No. of Colleges	Having a Dept.		Courses in Other Depts.		Totals: Depts. Plus Courses		No Curricular Work in Religion	
	No.	%	No.	%	No.	%	No.	%
I. All colleges—263	178	67.7	58	22.0	236	89.7	27	10.3
II. Church-related colleges—56	56	100.0	–	–	56	100.0	–	–
III. Independent colleges—118	100	84.7	15	12.8	115	97.5	3	2.5
IV. Technological schools—11	–	–	3	27.3	3	27.3	8	72.7
V. State institutions—70	21	30.0	35	50.0	56	80.0	14	20.0
VI. Municipal institutions—8	1	12.5	5	62.5	6	75.0	2	25.0

But courses in other departments do not amount to much in many of the institutions. Of the colleges having no department, the number of courses in other departments is indicated, for each type of institution, in the following table:

Type of College	No. Offering Courses in Other Depts.	Number of Courses			
		One	Two	Three to five	More than five
I. All colleges	58	29	15	10	4
II. Church-related colleges	–	–	–	–	–
III. Independent colleges	15	9	2	2	2
IV. Technological schools	3	3	–	–	–
V. State institutions	35	13	12	8	2
VI. Municipal institutions	5	4	1	–	–

The small number of institutions, such as the University of Michigan and Washington and Lee, which have 5 or more courses without having a department, counterbalance the equally small number of institutions, such as Bowdoin and Vanderbilt, whose departments of religion number only 2 or 3 courses.

B. *Chapel.*

The following table indicates in four pairs of columns the practices concerning chapel services of the various colleges, by type. The first pair is the total in each instance of the second and third pair of figures; all three pairs deal with the presence of chapel, whereas the fourth pair shows the number and percentage of colleges of each type which sponsor no services at all.

It will be obvious upon examination that the percentages listed under "Compulsory" and "Voluntary" are not of the number of colleges holding chapel but of the total number of institutions of each type. As to the definition of "compulsory," many colleges require attendance at only a certain percentage of the chapel services or for only a part of the student's four-year course. The figures in the "Compulsory" column include not only those institutions at which students are required to attend all services, but also those at which there is any degree or amount of compulsion.

Type and No. of Colleges	Total Having Chapel		Compul- sory Chapel		Volun- tary Chapel		No Chapel	
	No.	%	No.	%	No.	%	No.	%
I. All colleges—263	178	67.7	127	48.3	51	19.4	85	32.3
II. Church-related col- leges—56	56	100.0	51	91.1	5	8.9	–	–
III. Independent colleges of liberal arts—118	99	83.9	66	55.9	33	28.0	19	16.1
a. Men's colleges—23	21	91.3	14	60.9	7	30.4	2	8.7
b. Women's colleges—27	22	81.5	14	51.9	8	29.6	5	18.5
c. Coeducational col- leges—68	56	82.4	38	55.9	18	26.5	12	17.6
IV. Independent technologi- cal schools—11	3	27.3	1	9.1	2	18.2	8	72.7
V. State institutions—70	19	27.1	8	11.4	11	15.7	51	72.9
a. Men's institutions—8	2	25.0	2	25.0	–	–	6	75.0
b. Women's institutions—7	4	57.1	3	42.9	1	14.2	3	42.9
c. Coeducational institu- tions—55	13	23.6	3	5.5	10	18.1	42	76.4
VI. Municipal institutions—8	1	12.5	1	12.5	–	–	7	87.5

C. *Official positions of leadership for the religious program.*

The following table indicates the number and percentage of colleges of each type which, at the beginning of World War II, sponsored positions of leadership for their religious programs as part of their regular administrative staffs. The figures do not include the sizable number of other institutions which help to pay the salaries of officers of nonofficial groups, such as secretaries of Christian Associations; in the mere listing of such "voluntary" officers college catalogues are not reliable guides as to whether or not their support comes from the regular college treasuries.

Type of College	No. in Type	Official Positions of Leadership	
		No.	%
I. All colleges	263	59	22.4
II. Church-related colleges	56	11	19.6
III. Independent colleges of liberal arts	118	39	33.1
a. Men's colleges	23	17	73.9
b. Women's colleges	27	5	18.5
c. Coeducational colleges	68	17	25.0
IV. Independent technological schools	11	–	–
V. State institutions	70	9	12.9
VI. Municipal institutions	8	–	–

The 59 colleges which provided such officers in 1941, together with the titles of the chief officer in each institution, are given in Chapter XI. At least 16 and possibly more of that group employed more than 1 official religious leader.

For many religious officers their duties concerned with the leadership of the chapel and/or activity programs are combined with other duties; the combination is usually made with the teaching of a course or two in religion. In 1941 the officers of at least 4 institutions filled concurrent positions not directly connected with religion.

Many colleges which do not sponsor positions of leadership delegate the responsibility for the direction of the religious program to regularly constituted faculty committees. The following tabulation lists the occurrence of this practice in the major types of colleges. These figures and percentages should be taken as a minimum, for not all college catalogues list the standing committees of the faculty.

Type of College	No. in Type	No. *Not* Sponsoring Positions of Leadership	Faculty Committees		
			No.	% of Total in Type	% of Second Column
I. All colleges	263	204	77	29.3	37.7
II. Church-related colleges	56	45	29	51.8	64.4
III. Independent colleges of liberal arts	118	79	31	26.3	39.2
IV. Technological schools	11	11	1	9.9	9.9
V. State institutions	70	61	16	22.9	26.2

APPENDIX III

A Tabulation of Information Relating to 702 Institutions Bearing Regional Accreditation

American Universities and Colleges, 1940 edition, edited by C. S. Marsh, furnishes information about the seven hundred and twenty-four accredited institutions in the United States. The list is composed of all colleges approved by the Association of American Universities, the American Association of Teachers Colleges, and the following regional bodies: the Middle States Association of Colleges and Secondary Schools, the North Central Association of Colleges and Secondary Schools, the Northwest Association of Secondary and Higher Schools, the Southern Association of Colleges and Secondary Schools, and (members of) the New England Association of Colleges and Secondary Schools. From the institutional exhibits supplied by Marsh are drawn the following facts concerning the presence of departments of religion, the requirements in such departments, and the existence and frequency of compulsory chapel services.

Eight of the total number have been omitted from the following calculations because they do not conform to any generally accepted pattern for colleges, or because they are extraterritorial institutions. Fourteen others have not been included because they did not furnish data on the points at question. Thus the number of institutions considered in this appendix is seven hundred and two.

A. *Departments of religion.*

The following table indicates the number and percentage of colleges, by type, which possess departments of religion in the regular curriculum. Division VI is entered in this and succeeding tables solely to serve as a summary for those types of colleges which form the subject matter for the foregoing discussion. Divisions VII, VIII, and IX, "Catholic," "Negro," and "Teachers' colleges," furnish a basis of comparison with the preceding types of institutions. In the teachers' college group are included a few which in recent years have sought to assume the functions of liberal arts colleges but whose offerings as listed by Marsh seem to denote that their major emphasis is still teacher training.

The overly curious will discover that the totals for the major types of institutions (Divisions II, III, IV, V, VII, VIII, and IX, omitting VI) aggregate 713 instead of 702. The explanation is that a few institutions falling under Divisions VII, VIII, and IX, such as Catholic teachers' colleges, Catholic Negro colleges, and Negro teachers' colleges, are listed in more than one category.

Type of College	No. in Type	Having a Department of Religion	
		No.	%
I. All institutions	702	405	57.7
II. State institutions (except Negro and teachers' colleges)	91	19	20.9
III. Municipal institutions	12	1	8.3
IV. Church-related and independent colleges of liberal arts	290	247	85.2
a. Men's colleges	39	27	69.2
b. Women's colleges	51	41	80.4
c. Coeducational colleges	200	179	89.5
V. Independent technological schools	14	–	–
VI. Totals for II, III, IV, & V	407	267	65.6
VII. Catholic colleges	115	111	96.5
VIII. Negro colleges	42	23	54.8
a. Private	26	21	80.8
b. Tax-supported	16	2	12.5
IX. Teachers' colleges	149	10	6.7
a. Private	5	4	80.0
b. Tax-supported	144	6	4.2

A word should be added at this point concerning the mistakes which unavoidably creep into any such extensive compilation of data as that of Marsh. For example, the author is aware that a number of institutions omitted from the figures above do actually possess departments: not only Princeton and the University of Oregon, which added departments immediately prior to Marsh's investigation, but also Bryn Mawr, Carleton, Harvard, Stanford and others which have had departments or their equivalents for a number of years. The table shows only 19 state institutions out of a total of 91, whereas the investigation reported in Appendix II indicates that 21 out of 70 such institutions did actually possess departments as of 1941. Moreover, the figures recorded for the Catholic colleges are probably mistaken, for all of them provide some instruction in religion, though it is barely possible that the missing four do not possess a special department, or even a "Department of Philosophy," for such instruction. The data in this table, therefore, err on the side of minimizing the presence of departments of religion; and such mistakes occur also in succeeding tables. But the intention of this appendix is to furnish comparisons that are substantially correct; and in this Marsh's information does succeed.

Among the total of 405 colleges having a department of religion, a variety of titles, 63 in number, is used to describe the department. The favorites, with the number of institutions employing each, are:

Department of Religion	161
Department of Bible	43
Department of Philosophy and Religion	35

Department of Religious Education	25
Department of Biblical Literature	19
Department of Bible and Religion	15
Department of Religion and Philosophy	12

A total of eighteen colleges have two or more departments.

B. *Requirements in departments of religion.*

The following table presents information as to the number of colleges of each type which require all prospective graduates to take one or more courses in the department of religion:

		Requirements in Religion	
		% of Those	
	No. Making	Possessing	% of Total
Type of College	Requirement	Departments	No. of Type
I. All institutions	247 *	61.0	35.2
II. State institutions	–	–	–
III. Municipal institutions	–	–	–
IV. Church-related and independent colleges of liberal arts	149	60.3	51.4
a. Men's colleges	12	44.4	30.8
b. Women's colleges	21	51.2	41.2
c. Coeducational colleges	116	64.8	58.0
V. Independent technological schools	–	–	–
VI. Totals for II, III, IV, & V	149	55.8	36.6
VII. Catholic colleges	70 †	63.1	60.9
VIII. Negro colleges	11	47.8	26.2
IX. Teachers' colleges	–	–	–

* Ten colleges which do not have a department of religion require their students to take a course in religion offered by some other department.

† Eighteen other Catholic colleges make such a requirement only for their Catholic students.

C. *Compulsory Chapel.*

The following table gives the number and percentage of colleges, by type, which provide compulsory chapel. Marsh's information does not furnish light on the worship services of those other institutions at which attendance is wholly voluntary.

Type of College	No. in Type	Providing Compulsory Chapel	
		No.	%
I. All institutions	702	367	52.3
II. State institutions (excluding Negro and teachers' colleges)	91	15	16.5
III. Municipal institutions	12	1	8.3

P. 306, line 6 from bottom, after "II & III. State and municipal institutions" add the figures
"16   11   2   —   2   3   —"

D. *Frequency of compulsory chapel.*

The following table indicates the various frequencies in holding compulsory chapel which characterize each major type of college with which this study is primarily concerned. It will be noted that in each division the total of the various frequencies plus those not furnishing information on this point is larger than the number of such institutions holding compulsory services. The explanation in every instance is that many of the colleges holding Sunday services also sponsor weekday programs of worship; thus they appear in the tabulation twice.

Type of College	No. Providing Compulsory Chapel	Frequency of Meeting					No Information
		Once a week or less	Twice a week	Three times a week	Four or more times a week	Sunday	
I. All institutions	367	63	49	51	98	42	86
II & III. State and municipal institutions	16	11	2	—	2	3	—
IV & V. Church-related and independent colleges	214	26	30	40	73	19	40
VI. Totals for II, III, IV, & V	230	37	32	40	75	22	40

Index

ACTIVITIES, student religious. *See* Christian Associations; Colleges, religious activities in; Denominations

Adler, Mortimer, 106, 253

Agnes Scott College, 293

Akron, University of, 293

Alabama College, 293

Aldrich, Donald B., 189

Alfred University, 50, 299; religious program in, 157, 159, 183, *210–212*

American Association of Teachers Colleges, 303

American Council on Education, 94, 95, 128, 179, 181

American International College, 162

American Personnel Association, 94, 179

Amherst College, 64, 68, 112, 113, 116–117, 134, 159, 262, 293

Anderson, Lauriel E., 214, 215

Angell, R. C., 46 n., 177 n.

Antioch College, 19, 101, 158, 159, 164, 293

Artman, J. M., 75 n., 135 n., 138 n., 139 n., 178

Aspinwall, Lura E., 135 n., 137 n., 138 n., 140 n.

Association of American Colleges, 44, 94, 144

Association of American Universities, 7, 136, 146, 159, 164, 174, 293, 298, 303

Athearn, W. S., 55, 145 n.

Aubrey, Edwin E., 95, 249 n.

Augustana College (Ill.), 131, 163

BAKER UNIVERSITY, 159

Ball, George H., 210

Baptists: Northern, 210, 212; Seventh Day, 211

Bard College, 162

Barnard College, 143–144, 156, 159

Barr, Stringfellow, 105 n., 106, 107 n.

Bartlett, W. W., 53–54

Bates College, 293

Beloit College, 293

Bennett, John C., 238–239

Bennington College, 19, 99, 103, 226

Bethany College (W. Va.), 131, 163, 293

Bible: interpretation of, 35–36, 42, 227, 229; study of, by colleges, 108, 142, 143, 145, 149, 229, 237, 270, 277; by public schools, 130; by Y.M.C.A., 83, 143. *See also* Instruction

Birge, Edward A., 86

Birmingham-Southern College, 60, 293

Blakeman, Edward W., 2 n., 152 n., 154, 159, 161

Board of Education v. Minor, 127

Boston University, 159, 293

Bowdoin College, 134, 137, 293, 300

Bowman, J. G., 168–169

Boyer, Edward S., 135 n., 145 n., 147 n.

Braisted, Paul J., 150 n., 252, 256, 258 n., 260

Brown, Charles R., 185

Brown, Elmer E., 81–82

Brown, Kenneth I., 213

Brown, S. W., 13 n., 124 n., 220 n.

Brown, William A., 108, 110

Brown University, 8, 38, 67, 70, 113, 134, 137, 293

Brubacher, J. S., 103

Bryn Mawr College, 137, 304

Buchanan, Scott, 106

Bucknell University, 51, 62, 63, 153, 159, 183, 293

Burton, Ernest D., 74–75, 92, 112, 114, 204 n., 246 n.

Bushnell, Horace, 37

Butler, Nicholas M., 105, 143, 156

Butler University, 55

YALE STUDIES IN RELIGIOUS EDUCATION